SUPER SEARCHERS

on COMPETITIVE INTELLIGENCE

SUPER SEARCHERS

on COMPETITIVE INTELLIGENCE

The Online and Offline
Secrets of Top CI Researchers

Margaret Metcalf Carr
Edited by Reva Basch

CyberAge Books

Information Today, Inc.
Medford, New Jersey

First Printing, 2003

Super Searchers on Competitive Intelligence: The Online and Offline Secrets of Top CI Researchers
Copyright © 2003 by Margaret Metcalf Carr

Super Searchers, Volume XII
A series edited by Reva Basch

Library of Congress Cataloging-in-Publication Data
Carr, Margaret Metcalf, 1955–
   Super searchers on competitive intelligence : the online and offline secrets of top CI researchers / Margaret Metcalf Carr ; edited by Reva Basch.
      p. cm -- (Super searchers ; v. 12)
   "First printing, 2003"--E-CIP galley.
      ISBN 0-910965-64-1 (pbk.)
      1. Business intelligence—Computer network resources. 2. Electronic information resource searching. I. Basch, Reva. II. Title. III. Series.

   HD38.7.C37 2003
   658.4'7'0285--dc21

                                                                                    2003007983
Printed and bound in the United States of America

Publisher: Thomas H. Hogan, Sr.
Editor-in-Chief: John B. Bryans
Managing Editor: Deborah R. Poulson
Copy Editor: Dorothy Pike
Graphics Department Director: M. Heide Dengler
Cover Designer: Jacqueline Walter
Book Designer: Kara Mia Jalkowski
Indexer: Sharon Hughes

Dedication

To my family
for wondrously and simultaneously
enduring, stimulating, encouraging, and supporting
my inquiring mind:
Frank and Betty Metcalf
Marty Bernardi and Barbara Walsh
Patrick, Michael, Kevin, and Karen
And—my best friend, mentor, and husband—David

About The Super Searchers Web Page

At the Information Today Web site, you will find *The Super Searchers Web Page*, featuring links to sites mentioned in this book. We periodically update the page, removing dead links and adding additional sites that may be useful to readers.

The Super Searchers Web Page is being made available as a bonus to readers of *Super Searchers on Competitive Intelligence* and other books in the Super Searchers series. To access the page, an Internet connection and Web browser are required. Go to:

http://www.infotoday.com/supersearchers

Contents

Foreword ix
   by Jan P. Herring

Acknowledgments xiii

Introduction 1

Kim Kelly 13
   CI Advocate for Winning Business

Renee Daulong 31
   Risk Analyst

Mary G. "Dottie" Moon 51
   Just-In-Time Intelligence Delivery

George Dennis 69
   Human Source Intelligence

Ann Potter 85
   On-Site Intelligence Gathering

Roberta Piccoli 99
   Client and Consumer Intelligence

Deborah Sawyer 111
   CI Services Marketing

Clifford Kalb 123
Knowledge Sponge

Wayne Rosenkrans 141
Pattern Recognition

John Shumadine 157
Team-Based Research

Bret Breeding 177
CI Artist

John Wilhelm 191
Systematic Focus

Ken Sawka and Cynthia Cheng Correia 207
Leveraging Internal Competitive Knowledge

Doug House and Anne Henrich 227
Decision-Driven Research and Comparative Analysis

John Prescott 245
CI Teacher

Appendix: Referenced Sites and Sources 263

Glossary 303

About the Author 309

About the Editor 310

Index 311

Foreword

This book provides a unique opportunity to gauge where the field of competitive intelligence (CI) stands today and to learn how you might benefit from many of its current successful programs and professional practices. Furthermore, Peggy Carr's insightful interview style has uncovered a number of professional as well as program mistakes that we can now avoid. The lessons learned from the book should be instructive for both the newcomer and the seasoned CI professional.

I have often been referred to as the CI profession's oldest student. I prefer to be thought of as one of its more serious students, having studied it for some 40 years. In reviewing the book's material before writing this foreword, I was pleasantly surprised by its breadth, covering some of the CI field's leading corporate intelligence programs and vendors as well as individual practitioners. For those just entering the field, there are personal examples of how journeyman CI practitioners go about their work and educational advice on how best to learn the trade. For experienced CI practitioners looking for new and better ways to do their jobs more proficiently, there are practical examples of how others have handled many of the problems we all face from time to time. And for those either managing a CI program or about to set one up, there is sage advice on how to approach the task as well as run it successfully.

Among the "lessons learned" from successful CI efforts is the organized and systematic approach taken by both CI program managers and practitioners alike—the professional application of what has been traditionally called the intelligence cycle, i.e., needs identification, secondary and primary research, intelligence analysis and production, and the dissemination or delivery of the finished intelligence products to the ultimate users responsible for taking appropriate actions. With differing sources, methods, and delivery styles, the CI professional and information researcher focus their total effort and intellect on meeting the expressed need of their client—otherwise the whole effort would be for naught! As I have told many senior executives and business intelligence users, unless you are able to understand it and use it, it is not intelligence, just more information.

Another very useful "lesson learned" is that contemporary users' needs for more timely and authentic CI has shifted research emphasis to human sources and primary research. Secondary sources still contribute value and utility, but this shift is causing the CI profession to enhance its primary research and interpersonal skills. This trend also highlights another very important facet of CI research, the need to access and process the constantly growing volume of secondary source intelligence information more proficiently, which in turn will require both better information technology (IT) and the professional skills necessary to use such advanced IT.

Several of the corporate CI programs described in the book appear to possess excellent intelligence analysis capabilities. Their approach to developing and using such analysis techniques and methodologies provides good examples for all CI practitioners. I found the book's attention to professional learning in general to be quite satisfying. Whether you are interested in teaching others or learning yourself, this portion of all the chapter-interviews is most instructive.

For those interested in improving their own CI management skills, there are some great lessons to learn. From the well-ordered and disciplined management of Merck's highly respected Business Intelligence (BI) program to the more pragmatic development approach taken by Compaq, the book presents some invaluable lessons in starting up and managing a successful BI/CI program. Whether you share the Compaq CI Manager's choice of a promotional model (e.g., the fight business's Don King) or prefer the more disciplined approach of Kaiser Associates' vice president, these are proven and professional models to consider.

And for those of you who are looking for a good business case or exceptional CI success story to convince your company's management that it needs a CI program, you will find both in the book. The Lockheed Martin success stories—for example, an 80 percent win rate in government proposals and participation as a member of the team that won the "fighter aircraft of the century" competition—are great. Similar success stories from Merck and other interviewees should help with your sales pitch.

As a serious student of CI, I found several of the endemic problems identified by Peggy consistent with my own experience, which in my estimation testifies to the comprehensiveness of her research. Unfortunately, there are no ready solutions, but her work helps to better define the problems for those who might solve them. Let me highlight two. The first is the difficulty that almost all those interviewed had in providing a simple definition of competitive intelligence. Until the CI profession can do this, I believe those working in it will continue to have difficulty, not only in communicating with their clients but in developing common purposes and goals among themselves, which is the hallmark of any true profession.

The second problem area the book highlights is the rather poor utilization of contemporary information technology (IT) by CI providers, often under the excuse of its additional costs. In contrast, those larger corporate CI programs seem to be making better use of IT provided by the company's internal IT department—although those interviewed seemed to view it as simply a "black box" and did not appear to be demanding much from it.

I have always considered books to be a great source of learning and enjoyment. This book is a true learning experience, particularly for those professionally interested in the world of competitive intelligence and its research and analysis work. It has much to offer to both those new to the CI field and the old pros who want to learn new things about this old profession. As one of the CI profession's oldest students, I certainly have learned some new lessons—and I believe you will too.

Enjoy and learn!

Jan P. Herring
Advisor to Intelligence Professionals
Hartford, Connecticut

Acknowledgments

First and foremost, wild applause and kudos to the awesome Super Searchers profiled in this book. It is the incredible generosity of these consummate CI professionals that has made this book possible. I have truly enjoyed each and every interview and have learned so much from them. Ann, Anne, Bret, Cliff, Cynthia, Deborah, Dottie, Doug, George, all three Johns, Ken, Kim, Renee, Roberta, and Wayne—thank you for making this book possible.

I also had the pleasure of working with Patty and Brian Shannon of The Work Station during the entire interview process. Their dedication to transcribing the interviews accurately, quickly, and with humor and ease is to be commended. Even when faced with industry jargon and obscure names, they managed to insert phonetic spellings that were easy to decipher.

Reva Basch, whom I have considered a goddess since meeting her through the Association of Independent Information Professionals in the early 1990s, has been a constant source of encouragement and support—her advice always kind, sincere, and valuable, her answers to my numerous questions calm, concise, and quick.

The staff at Information Today, and in particular, John Bryans, editor-in-chief, and Deborah Poulson, managing editor, were a pleasure to work with. John, new-found friend and fellow jazz enthusiast, was wonderful in answering numerous emails. His upbeat and enthusiastic messages were a constant source of support and encouragement. Deborah, who had to deal with all the sticky stuff, was always helpful immediately, quick to appease my fears and answer my questions, and dealt with all the digital photos and graphics with ease.

Jan Herring kindly accepted the task of writing the foreword for this book. I have always admired his vast knowledge of the evolution and history of competitive intelligence, and his engaging presentations. I consider it a great honor that he generously gave his time to read through hundreds of pages of mostly unedited transcripts, and to help me with numerous historical details in the introduction. Jan was a terrific advisor as well. Jan, thank you for all your contributions.

There were many others who willingly and generously contributed to this book, and I do hope I haven't left anyone out. Bob Bremer and Zack Russ of Lockheed Martin Corporation, whom I have had the pleasure of working with on various projects, were terrific in pointing me to competitive intelligence professionals and fact-checking tips and sources, respectively. Walter Barndt, Bob Cisek, Craig Fleisher, Bonnie Hohhof, Jerry Miller, and Kathy Shelfer were instrumental in providing numerous historical and emerging insights. Their thoughtful and timely replies to my emails and phone calls are sincerely appreciated. Vince Luchsinger, a fellow member of the Mid-Atlantic Planning Association and a professor at the Merrick School of Business, University of Baltimore, was a source of supporting material, historical insight, and encouragement. Mary Ellen Bates, Amelia Kassel, Suzanne Sabroski, and Risa Sacks, *Super Searcher* authors and friends, were marvelous in providing tips, advice, and kind words of encouragement from the very start.

On a personal note, I want to thank the scouts and scouters of Venture Crew 140. We have been on the trail together for many weekends, and their support, encouragement, and stamina—even when eleven thousand feet above sea level—were a great source of inspiration.

Introduction

Wow! I stand in awe of these CI professionals and what they are able to accomplish and impart in their daily work. A truly remarkable, intelligent, thinking, and proactive lot, these professionals are always on their toes, continuously seeking better answers, techniques, and marketing methods. A tremendous amount of activity, drive, energy, and enthusiasm is reflected in this book. I'm proud and pleased to present to you 15 CI-savvy individuals, all with terrific ideas, tips, and techniques, to aid you and your organization in performing competitive intelligence.

You will find this book somewhat different from others in the Super Searchers series. Whereas other types of research can provide *an* answer in *a* source, these CI professionals must carry out an entire *process* in order to seek out and derive "the answer."

The definitions of intelligence and competitive intelligence for the purposes of this book are those used in the *Encyclopedia Britannica* under "Intelligence and Counterintelligence" [138, see Appendix] and by the Society of Competitive Intelligence Professionals (SCIP) [258]. The *Encyclopedia Britannica* states "Intelligence means, basically, evaluated information." SCIP defines competitive intelligence as "a systematic and ethical program for gathering, analyzing, and managing external information that can affect your company's plans, decisions."

From Spooks and Spies to Domesticated Profession

Competitive intelligence sprang from the disciplined use of intelligence in the government arena. According to "Intelligence and Counterintelligence" in the *Encyclopedia Britannica*, "military intelligence is as old as warfare itself. Even in biblical times, Moses sent spies to live with Canaanites in order to learn about their ways and about their strengths and weaknesses." Numerous articles in the open source literature suggest the use of intelligence in military applications in the Far East centuries ago. European adoption is traced and recorded in *The Oxford English Dictionary* (OED) [159]. According to the OED, the first usage of "intelligence" to describe information gathering and knowledge of events, specifically information of military value, occurred in 1450. Poring through the listed sources, one finds references to "obtaining secret information," and "spies" (groan). Philip Meilinger further points out in his review of *Most Secret and Confidential* [154], "Spies have existed for millennia because governments or military commanders have always needed to know the capabilities and intentions of a potential adversary. By the end of the eighteenth century, the bureaucracy established in England for gathering this information was both extensive and credible." The OED also notes that intelligence became additionally defined as a military *technical* term, back in, but not until, the sixteenth century.

The evolution and adoption of intelligence in the private sector is still disconnected and unconnected. Even after exploring several sources and talking to a handful of academics, I got only bits and pieces. No one seems to know of any scholarly work on the subject, and most of what I did find was piecemeal. As a history major, I find it incredible that no one has tried to work out the history of CI—especially when we are such a curious lot!

Accounts point to the first potential commercial application occurring during the fifteenth and sixteenth centuries during the rise of the house of Fugger. The Fuggers were a powerful German merchant and banking family that dominated European business during this time period. They are considered instrumental in developing capitalistic economic concepts and influencing continental politics. Jakob, one of Hans Fugger's three sons, was a driving force in discovering how intelligence could be applied to advance business strategy. According to the "Fugger Family" [128], "Fugger

Newsletters" [129], "European Competitiveness and Business" [119] and "Corporate Performance Management" [110], a blend of economic, journalism, and publishing advancements, combined with the sheer tenacity and drive of Jakob Fugger, worked together to drive the need for and the adoption and dissemination of intelligence information that, in turn, kept the far-flung branches of his international trading company executives informed. The Fugger newsletters of the sixteenth century tracked local business activities, their economic results, and local economic and political trends observed and collected by correspondents. In turn, this information was published and sent to bank managers and "corporate management" so they in turn could negotiate deals, take over weak banks, influence politics, and determine other strategic moves. Due to geographic distance, this melding of intelligence collection and dissemination in print had not previously been accomplished. It demonstrated the Fuggers' understanding that negotiating in a complex business world took intelligence, a clear strategy, and a willingness to take a calculated risk.

In *Against the Gods* [90], Bernstein credits Lloyds of London and specifically Edward Lloyd with recognizing the value of customer chatter in the coffeehouses of London. The launch of Lloyd's List in 1696, "filled with information on the arrivals and departures of ships and intelligence on conditions abroad and at sea," is now credited as an initial commercial application of intelligence. It was not until nearly a century later, however, that Lloyd's List inspired the formation of the Society of Lloyd's, establishing membership, dues, a commitment to make good on their customers' losses, and a "self-regulated code of behavior." According to Schoolnet [172], Lloyd's was incorporated by Parliament for the "promotion of marine insurance and the diffusion of shipping intelligence." It had been a very slow process, from collecting chatter over coffee, to disseminating the knowledge so collected in a systematic way, to recognizing intelligence-gathering as something truly valuable to the extent that it became institutionalized and, eventually, regarded as a profession.

Another family dynasty, the Rothschilds, has also been documented as utilizing business intelligence in the growth of its European banking empire during the first half of the nineteenth century. As portrayed in *The House of Rothschild* [134] and other sources, Mayer Amschel Rothschild and his five sons worked with "commercial genius and intermarriage" establishing banks and intelligence networks and employing "agents" to build, and at times bail out, the branches of the first multinational banking houses established in London, Paris, Frankfurt, Vienna, and Naples.

In the early twentieth century, the growth of capitalism and economic pressures brought an awareness of competition. "European competitiveness and business" (noted earlier) points to Joseph Schumpeter as a major contributor in identifying competition, competitive forces, and their dynamic nature. In *Theory of Economic Development* [185], published in 1912, Schumpeter observes "a disturbance to the balance" when new products, quality methods, or methods of production are introduced, or when new markets open and new supply sources are discovered. Sound familiar?

The surge of interest in business intelligence did not occur until the 1960s, however. As observed by Ben Gilad in *The Business Intelligence System* [95], strategic planning, which came into vogue in the '60s and '70s, drove the need to approach business decisions in a different manner than looking at sheer numbers. One of the first indications of solving problems by applying research and analysis methods is Kepner and Tregoe's *The Rational Manager: A Systematic Approach to Problem Solving and Decision Making* [168], published in 1965. Additional drivers for intelligent strategic planning were identified in 1966 with the publication of Thomas J. Allen's "Performance of Information Channels in the Transfer of Technology" [160] and Richard M. Greene's *Business Intelligence and Espionage* and reinforced in 1967 with Francis Aguilar's *Scanning the Business Environment* [171].

In the 1970s, companies began to feel competitive pressure, both domestically and internationally. Interest mounted in external forces and their impact on the quality of strategic planning. Several key articles were published, including David Montgomery and Charles Weinberg's "Toward Strategic Intelligence Systems" [186]. The timeline "75 Years of Management Ideas and Practice" [89] places Michael Porter's now-famous "How Competitive Forces Shape Strategy" [163] article in 1979. In 1980, it was the publication of Porter's *Competitive Strategy: Techniques for Analyzing Industries and Competitors* [107] that solidified a strategic approach to analyzing the "competition," and driving the demand for competitive intelligence adoption in the private sector.

In response to this growing corporate need, the Society of Competitive Intelligence Professionals was formed in 1986 under the leadership of Leila

Kight [249]. Between 1988 and 2000, several articles and books—too many to list here—were published with business and competitive intelligence systems as the key idea. The marked increase in membership in the Society of Competitive Intelligence Professionals (SCIP) during 1991 and 1992 indicates that competitive intelligence had truly come of age.

The education and training of students in intelligence has evolved in parallel. Whereas intelligence education was once limited to select schools specializing in training individuals for government agency, a surge in interest in "strategic" intelligence occurred in the 1960s, and business schools in particular picked up the training ball. Promoted with "strategy," "security," and similar titles, regular courses such as that offered by Stevan Dedijer [235] of Lund University in Sweden, appeared around 1974. Competitive intelligence course electives in U.S. business schools were introduced in 1983 by John Prescott [254] at the Katz Graduate School of Business at the University of Pittsburgh and Walter Barndt [230] at the Hartford Graduate Center, Lally School of Management at Rensselaer Polytechnic Institute (RPI). In 1984, Liam Fahey [237] introduced and taught strategy intelligence courses at Northwestern University.

The teaching of CI further expanded into the library and information schools in the early 1990s, with the first known course taught by Jerry P. Miller [251] at Simmons College. Many librarians and information specialists have served as CI researchers for some time, and were integrated into CI teams around the mid-1980s. But formal training and encouragement to aspire to CI analyst and managerial positions didn't come until later, with two significant publications, "The Competitive Intelligence Opportunity" [105] and the Competitive Intelligence issue of the Special Libraries Association's (SLA) [259] *Information Outlook,* published in 2000 and 2001, respectively.

College and university CI courses now go beyond offering a course or two in how to apply CI in organizations, to nuts and bolts instruction in how to *do* competitive intelligence. Newer programs such as the Competitive Intelligence Certificate Program at Drexel's College of Information Science and Technology [236], and the degree-granting Research Intelligence Analyst Program offered through the history department at Mercyhurst College [250], reflect the increasing trend toward more CI programming at the undergraduate and graduate level. According to the CI University portion of the SCIP

Web site [258], six schools in Canada and 18 schools in the U.S. were developing or offering courses or programs in CI as of September 2002.

One disappointment, however, is that even today, enrollments still reflect a greater interest, or comfort, in applying intelligence in the government sector. Dr. Robert Cisek of the Research Intelligence Analyst Program at Mercyhurst College stated that the majority of students enrolled in their program have national security agency careers in mind. Only about 10 percent of their students enroll with an interest in the private sector, although the college is working to increase this percentage to one-third.

There Is No Magic Bullet

Just how do you perform CI? There is no single, simple answer. CI-savvy professionals have varied opinions on how to reach *the answer* that will make a difference. It is clear that intelligence is not found in a single source, or even discovered by merely combining information gathered from secondary and primary research resources. As Kathy Shelfer [256] at Drexel put it, there is no magic bullet. Intelligence is only derived after information is evaluated. That often means performing multiple functions, including gathering several disparate pieces of information from primary and secondary sources, organizing and building a picture, analyzing the whole, perhaps even taking a leap of faith, and then communicating an actionable answer. There is a process that involves multiple stages in order to connect the dots. The interviewees in this book may describe this process in terms of a cycle, a linear process, the four corners model, the scientific method, or a pyramid. They do agree, however, that you only get there by completing the *entire* process, much like assembling a jigsaw puzzle. Whether you do Step A before Step B is debatable, but if you don't cover all the bases, you can't score a homerun. Therefore, I have emblazoned on my brain, much like a slogan on a bumper sticker, Wayne Rosenkrans's warning: Don't shortchange the process.

Building the CI Sandwich

Once the process is defined, many people ask, "Where do I start and in what order do I execute the steps?" The answer from our interviewees is, it depends. The quickest and most efficient way to perform the task at hand may start with phone calls to experts in your Rolodex, or with a secondary literature search. But the group agrees, resoundingly, that from the outset one should seek and select *only* those bits and pieces that will fit into the desired or requested deliverable. As Ken Sawka states, "Don't lose sight of the ball." There is a lot of "noise" in our information society, and it is easy to get distracted. Collect, filter, and organize only the best nuggets. And ask before you start, as you would when preparing for a hiking or backpacking trip: Where am I, where am I going, and how will I get there?

Think of it as building a sandwich. You start with planning, and you finish with a deliverable. The order of the "filling" in between can vary. Whether you have to take months to frame the question, as Cliff Kalb has experienced at Merck, an hour or a few days to work with the client to develop hypotheses, as John Wilhelm at Kaiser practices, or simply time to listen to and understand your client's expectations, as advocated by George Dennis, this initial phase is extremely important. Those of us with library backgrounds tend to think of this stage as the "reference interview." Depending upon the project, the interviewees say that planning can consume as much as 40 percent of your total project time. As Jan Herring points out in his foreword, without the correct grounding in this phase of the process, all is for naught.

As to what resources and analytical techniques and models to use, opinions also vary. Again, the answer is often that it depends on the question and the deliverable desired. The interviewees suggest practical tips, techniques, and models, and I encourage you to note them all. At least 155 analytical techniques have already been identified by Craig Fleisher [238]. For sure, one size does not fit all.

Two important points are made throughout the interviews. First, recognize that research and analysis are interdependent. Information services provide analytical guidance, and analysis often drives the need for more information. Information collection isn't over until the final deliverable. Secondly, if you delay the research process until all your dots are collected and connected, you are too late. *The Art and Science of Business Intelligence Analysis* [92] underscores these observations, saying "Without up-to-date information, on a continuing basis, the analysis can be rendered irrelevant and out of date before the assessment is even completed."

And the final deliverable? Obviously, you need one. As to the format, again, it all depends. According to the interviewees, this can be anything from a phone call to a one-page executive summary, to a full-blown bound report or a quarterly newsletter. One must consider the audience and its expectations. One should also plan on "mini-deliverables"—interpersonal communications from beginning to end—starting with the definition of the ultimate desired product, then staying on track throughout the project, and then delivering the final assessment efficiently and effectively. And for heaven's sake, the interviewees warn, never deliver a total surprise. Early warning of problems or severe deviations in the assumed result should be conveyed early, and perhaps often, so that your final presentation is better received and credible to your audience.

Our Weakest Link ...

Our interviewees remarked on one weakness that has also been cited in the literature and echoed in my conversations with practicing CI professors: We still tend to overemphasize the research phase. We are criticized for spending too much time on research and not enough on analysis; we recognize that we don't devote enough time or training to the intelligence piece of competitive intelligence. We've been mired in the exponential growth of available information. Bob Cisek, mentioned earlier, also feels we were so preoccupied with learning how to *get* the information that we're only beginning to awaken to how to analyze it. Originally, the problem was getting our arms around the information and pulling it together. Now we're so enamored with what we can get our hands on—we spend the bulk of our time trying to make sure we've done a comprehensive search, tapped all the available resources—that we lose all sense of time and the analysis doesn't get done.

With regard to what analysis really is, however, we're apparently agreeing to disagree. The common denominator is that "intelligence" means you have to do something with the information you've collected in order to make it meaningful. Whether we consider analysis to be the result of examining several pieces of information and relating the parts to the whole, or of determining upon examination that a single "gold nugget" of information holds the key and reporting it as such, we are communicating the added value that turns information into intelligence. As Jan Herring observes in the foreword, all of our interviewees try to grapple with this issue. Ken Sawka goes to some length in his interview, as well as in his article "It's the Analysis, Stupid" [140], to clarify the differences between delivering research results and delivering intelligence.

And Where Is Information Technology?

Literature speaking to the development and application of information systems to support CI exists. Examples are Bonnie Hohhof's "Developing Information Systems for Competitive Intelligence Support" [116], Jerry Miller's *Millennium Intelligence* [153], and the annual "CI Software Report" [102]. In practice, however, the adoption of information technology (IT) for CI has been slow. As Jan Herring mentions in the foreword, perhaps IT isn't being leveraged as much as it could or should be. I would add that the vendors need to do a better job of marketing their products. We rarely get to see these products up close and personal, and with a few exceptions, they are not engagingly discussed or reviewed in the literature. What I do see does not encourage me to consider a trial run, much less purchase any of the available software products. Most professionals are inundated with sales literature daily, and we need to know up front what products exist, how robust they are, how they compare to other past or current products, how they're going to make a positive difference in our workflow and decision making, and how soon we can expect to see a return on our investment, given the investment of both money and time to learn the software. As Deborah Sawyer of Information Plus points out, a product's narrow application or specialization often doesn't justify the time and effort, much less the money, to invest in it. Kim Kelly of Lockheed Martin also sends the message that vendors need to check out their pricing schemes; many seem insensitive and cost-prohibitive for smaller or scaleable CI projects and budgets.

No Practitioner Is an Island

You will find that all of our interviewees' work habits include working with others. All reach out to colleagues, whether they are solo CI analysts in their organizations or one of many in a dedicated department. One does not and cannot perform CI alone. You need others to bounce ideas off, assist with your approach, brainstorm for additional sources, collect already-filtered information from internal intelligence sources, perform reality checks on your assumptions, or gain proofreading expertise on a deliverable. CI work is not performed in a vacuum. Everyone needs multiple data points and fresh pairs of eyes. The interviewees also conveyed that you cannot be all things to all people. They stress the need to specialize in some aspect of CI, be it a subject or industry area, or research vs. analysis.

The Right Stuff

So what does it take to be a CI professional? You'll find several ideas on what makes the perfect competitive intelligence practitioner. Some feel that a degree in finance, or a master's degree in business or library and information sciences is essential. Others believe a good grounding in the liberal arts with additional attributes such as Bret Breeding of Compaq's dose of passion; Roberta Piccoli's imagination, tenacity, and integrity; John Shumadine of Deloitte & Touche's treasure-hunt mentality and yearning to learn; and Cliff Kalb of Merck's "sponge" combined with a good, strong, and confident gut will go a long way. Interviewees also make practical, real-life recommendations, such as Ann Potter's suggestion to enroll in a basic reporting course in a journalism school. CI is often considered as much an art as a science; John Prescott of the University of Pittsburgh adds a terrific twist and third dimension: CI is also a craft whereby an apprenticeship helps round out the CI professional.

You've Come a Long Way, Baby?

When you consider that "competitive strategy" didn't creep into the business lexicon until the 1980s, and that competitive intelligence didn't take off until the early '90s, the pace at which CI has been adopted into the private sector is phenomenal. As you will hear throughout the interviews, customers are learning to come to the CI professionals first, get the CI unit involved earlier in the process, and include the unit "at the table" throughout the decision-making process. Has the profession arrived, then? Well, yes and no. As

Jan Herring points out in his foreword, we still struggle to come up with a simple definition of competitive intelligence that everyone can agree on.

Also, many of the interviewees agree, Rodney Dangerfield's "I get no respect" still applies. Although we can all find mentors and supporters within the institutions we support, getting a *consistent* ear, and *action*, from *senior* management remains a problem.

To some degree, the profession's roots in government intelligence work brought about a "Catch-22." Along with the disciplined structural framework and systematic approach for deriving intelligence, we also inherited (and, much to our chagrin, have kept to too great a degree) the perception and image of spies, covert operations, and underhanded detectives in trench coats—images that, correctly, are no longer tolerated in an ethics-aware society. As the interviews in this book reflect, we must move beyond the old image problem, define ourselves better and more accurately, and continue to prove our worth. Education and action will speak louder than words.

Raison d'Etre

So why do people choose to go into this profession? What energizes a CI professional even when a critical assessment is ignored or support and recognition are hard to obtain? Lots! CI professionals are inherently curious. Our raison d'etre is portrayed enthusiastically in each interview. Dell's Renee Daulong points to the thrill of the hunt, Merck's Kalb to the new adventure each phone call brings, Lockheed Martin's Kim Kelly to the drive to get the answer right the next time, and Washington Researchers' Doug House to the satisfaction of seeing the "aha!" expression on clients' faces when they see how it all fits together.

Toto, We're Not in Kansas Anymore

On the brighter side—and most encouraging to our profession—is the revelation that we have pushed the envelope in the course of our efforts to continuously improve methods, efficiency, and productivity; to improve our culling of unique, disparate, unindexed, and unpublished sources; and to deliver better analyzed answers. Our interviewees find that they too have evolved and are moving further up the value chain. We have gone beyond the traditional CI boundaries; the once-final frontier of getting the competitive strategy process down pat and "delivering the answer" is somewhere behind us. Now, our interviewees find themselves in a brave new world, invited to and participating in long-range scenario planning and war gaming, as evidenced by both Astra Zeneca Pharmaceutical's Wayne Rosencrans and United Technologies' Dottie Moon. Furthermore, CI teams are being invited to influence decisions and formulate *strategies*—as CI did centuries ago—on the basis of the research and analysis performed, rather than being relegated to merely influencing *tactical* movements of the corporation. As Deloitte Touche's John Shumadine states, the CI profession is providing "enhanced solutions." Yet another threshold has been crossed!

Onward and Upward

This book has been created for you, the reader, whether you are new to the field of CI or a war-torn vet. We have sought out a representative sampling of the best and brightest in varied industries so that all may learn and add new tips and techniques to their repertoire. The questions asked of each interviewee were designed to elicit their informed opinions on all major corners of the CI process, and to share resources, models, analytical techniques, practical tips and strategies, and seminars and literature for continuous learning, as well as pitfalls to avoid.

It has been a great pleasure to work with the 15 CI experts I interviewed for this book, many of whom I have known only by name for several years. I am particularly grateful to the interviewees for generously taking the time to convey their best practices and lessons learned. I have learned an immense amount from their insights, tips, and techniques and have truly enjoyed their candid and honest remarks. I hope you feel the same way.

Kim Kelly
CI Advocate for Winning Business

At the time of this interview, Kim Kelly was a manager of business development for International Launch Services, a joint venture between Lockheed Martin (LM) and two Russian companies. He has worked in proposal development for 20 years. He started in 1982 with IBM Federal Systems, which was later acquired by LM. Since 1991, he has been a full-time competitive intelligence professional and has provided major CI studies to proposal teams at 10 different LM locations. He is a member of the Society of Competitive Intelligence Professionals (SCIP) and was instrumental in LM's selection as one of 12 companies (and the only aerospace company) honored for their best-practice CI operations by the American Productivity and Quality Center (APQC) in 2000. Kim is now an independent competitive intelligence consultant and a partner with Knowledge Link.

KimKellyCI@aol.com

Please tell me about your background and how and when you started performing competitive intelligence.

I have an Operations Research and Industrial Engineering degree from Cornell University and an MBA in Finance from George Washington University. I've worked with Lockheed Martin for 20 years. I really spent the first 18 years in one facility and changed companies three times but never left the building! In the aerospace industry there's been a lot of consolidation. Originally, we were known as IBM Federal Systems—a little bit of an anomaly since IBM was more of a commercial computer-oriented company, while we applied computer technology to the DOD (Department of Defense) and civilian government area. We were eventually bought by Loral, and Loral was sold to Lockheed Martin. Two years ago our unit was known as LM Naval Electronics and Surveillance Systems (NESS), in Manassas, Virginia. From there I went to my current position.

I started out in an area called Cost Engineering, which is a function that estimates costs for production and development programs. "Engineering" was in that organizational name because we were involved in initial production of a new system. In other words, we weren't producing chairs or widgets, we were developing new systems. Instead of having cost tables to refer to for material and labor costs, our engineers had to calculate hardware costs—also referred to as "should costs." Should cost is a cost projection for a not-yet-manufactured or not-yet-developed product. So it was in this cost-analysis-oriented job from 1982 to 1991 that I had my first analysis apprenticeship. Much of my stint was doing software cost engineering—estimating the cost of software development—a complex process particularly since it is very labor intensive. We had a specialized department that would look at software project costs, at what the cost drivers were, and we came up with cost approaches to software development, system engineering, and documentation. This provided me with a total program cost estimation capability, leading to my competitive intelligence position in 1991. The total program cost capability was an important point, because we started CI long before most people had heard of the profession. And through the CI process, I was able to achieve a win rate of 80 percent at NESS Manassas, which was way above the industry average. The largest proposal I have worked on is the Joint Strike Fighter Program, the largest contract ever ordered by the DOD or by the U.S. government. And in 2000, when I moved to Lockheed-Martin's joint venture called International Launch Services, I helped assist in improving our win rate by 30 percent. So certainly I'm a big advocate of competitive intelligence and its impact on the business.

How would you describe your current function in a nutshell?

I'd like to split that into two pieces; tactical competitive intelligence and strategic competitive intelligence. I spend most of my time on the tactical side—day-to-day proposal bidding activities. Strategic is higher level, broad-based analysis that affects the organization over a much longer period of time. My role is to figure out the right price to bid for our proposal in order to have a competitive bid. In that process we need to forecast our competitor's bid and technical approach, our competitor's team structure, team strengths and weaknesses, and how the customer will evaluate our proposal vs. our competition's. We try to conduct this analysis months before the proposal has to be submitted so that we can have an actual effect, a real influence on how our proposal is postured, and improve our chances of winning. We'll try to influence our own team to be doing the right things by showing what our competition is doing. We'll look at our competitor's technical solution, we'll come up with a should-cost, we'll try to estimate what their win strategy will be, and go from there.

One way I like to describe our job is that we are an advocate, or a window into what our competition is doing. We have to be objective from that standpoint. I am the only person in the organization that is objectively communicating what our competition is doing. We're starting to have an influence at the executive management level of our respective companies. People know it's a valuable input and are seeking that kind of expertise, which may be why you're doing a book on it. The fact that you're doing a book about CI is a good indication that we're making a lot of progress in the business world.

With strategic CI, we conduct market analysis or look at our business strategy, and try to show how our competition or our customer may influence our assumptions and our strategies. As I perform my tactical work, over months and years, I keep an eye out for trends or issues that will affect the business at a broader scale, particularly if my customer or competitor is doing a right turn and changing something dramatically. For example, we were making a product and there was a key subsystem, like the engine of a car, and I noticed that, of the five companies that made the subsystem, two had been purchased recently by our competitors, and a third was rumored to be in the process of being acquired by a fourth. I wanted my management team to know now, as early as possible, that the five alternatives were down to three, now going down to two, and that our competition was becoming vertically integrated by buying the companies that produced the subsystems. That certainly could limit the choices that we really had in the marketplace—now what should we do about it?

You've mentioned some of the types of research that you perform now, such as SWOT analysis and market research. It also appears that you're looking at the environment and at customer trends. Can you expand any more on the kinds of research you perform?

Maybe we can divide that into primary and secondary, primary being person-to-person discussions and secondary being mostly online databases or magazines and articles, things of that nature. Both pieces are very important, and what we've found is that you've got to have the two integrated to get the best value out of both. The CI person can interweave that person-to-person discussion into the secondary research. Surprisingly, integrating these two kinds of intelligence is often overlooked.

When I'm working with organizations on a bid, I'll be working not only with our company, but I'll be getting information from our teammates. They obviously know their business better than we do, so they will know their competition in their business area. We get a lot of good intelligence from a variety of functional organizations within our own company. I'm a big promoter of internal intelligence contacts because folks who are just getting started in competitive intelligence will focus on the more obvious parts of the organization, like business development, to get an understanding of what the competition is doing. But really, there are other departments that can provide even more intelligence on what the competition is doing than business development or marketing and sales. Don't overlook program management, procurement, communications, and engineering.

Almost every organization in the company has insights on what's going on with the competition. I communicate to anyone I can get a chance to talk to about CI. One of my tricks of the trade, when I go out into organizations and promote CI, is to actually look for people that no one listens to or that no one approaches very often and asks for input. Because many times, those folks are a little bit out of the mainstream, and you need these original, out-of-the-box thinkers.

I make a point of meeting with the secondary research experts on a regular basis. If my research people know a little bit about how I do my job, how a CI process works, it makes them a lot more effective in providing information to us. The only way they can get that insight is to talk and meet regularly with the CI people, and that's what I do. It makes it into a teamwork atmosphere, which really promotes an effective and efficient process.

How do you feel CI differs from business and market research, or alternatively, how do you define CI?

I think there are two differences, and I don't want to upset the business research community in the way I'm differentiating the two. The first difference is that we're a little bit more focused in CI. From our standpoint we're not just looking at the competition. For example, we're looking at customer behavior, which actually forces us to look at the information world in terms of those constraints. The other difference is that we're an independent group;

we have to present an objective view of the competition and of our customer, so we often bring up things that are controversial.

Before, you spoke about the importance of primary research and the human intelligence aspect of the process. What other resources do you feel are essential in your CI toolkit?

We have the computer software tools, the spreadsheets. We also have a lot of industry-specific online newsletters that we review. There are also for-fee databases like DialogSelect [21, see Appendix], commercial databases of government data such as regulatory filings, contract awards, things of that nature. In my toolkit, I include people in the know in particular areas, such as technology or customers. I'll call those folks and run things by them. We also use alert emails like DialogSelect and Fed Sources FSI State & Local Headline News [127]—systems that collect your queries, retrieve related news or articles, and automatically send you email inputs on a daily basis.

The people-to-people network is very important. I founded a network of internal CI experts called the Lockheed Martin Competitive Intelligence Working Group whereby we have on tap other organizations that might be technology- or engineering-oriented that we can talk to. Every time I work on a proposal, I meet experts in a particular field that I can go back and contact—a year or two, three, four years later—because I know they'll be up to speed on the latest sensor technology or the best software language for writing commercial applications, or the best relational database that has some bells and whistles that everybody is asking for now.

When we're trying to predict the competitor's technical solution, that gets us into the engineering area, so we sometimes have to go to conferences that discuss technologies. We certainly will hook into our engineering people who are doing the same thing. They're getting Independent Research and Development (IRAD) money to study new engineering applications, and the conferences they're going to are the same conferences that the engineers at the competition are going to, so there are a lot of ways to network and find people who are doing that.

But you would be amazed at how knowledgeable folks are, particularly folks who aren't always asked for input. Certainly everybody has a really important job in your company, otherwise they wouldn't be there, and they have knowledge, and it's like uncapping something that's been waiting to burst. People get so happy that you're interested in what they know. Nothing makes me happier than to know down the line that that person's business intelligence or knowledge of the marketplace made a huge difference in our final decision making, and in connecting those dots. I really get excited about that.

You've talked about your internal network, which is very important. Do you also have an extensive Rolodex of external experts, such as industry analysts and magazine editors, whom you've hooked up with through your years of experience in going to trade shows, reading, and so on?

Not as much as you would expect. I tend to concentrate more on my internal connections, because they're so vast. That may sound way off-base, because I'm trying to project an external view of the world when I am primarily talking to internal people. Don't get me wrong; I do have external sources, but I have to be careful about contacting them. You have the unintentional opportunity to give away information that you don't want to give away. I've really cultivated my internal organizations, and I use the folks that know the external sources.

How do you weigh or balance the Internet with the for-fee database services in your workflow and research?

That's a constant challenge because the marketplace and resource capabilities are always changing. Sources are not always improving; when the dot-coms blew up, a lot of the services that were offered for free went away. There are huge differences, obviously, between the for-fee data services and the free Internet services. The Internet is cheaper but you could argue whether it is easier to use, and the data is not as reliable or accurate. Sometimes you get excited when you find something on the Internet, and it might be really misleading. But people in the CI profession are aware of getting information that is rumor or may not be accurate, and filtering it.

A very important point is that there are so many databases and sources of data out there that you really need to utilize your specialized business research or information specialist or librarian with a science degree. However your company describes that position, those folks are specialized even to the point that one might be best at accessing technical journals, another one might be really good at wading through DialogSelect, and yet another might be good at looking at LexisNexis [56]. There's really no one person that has all the answers, so the more you can identify the specialties that people have and use them, the better.

How do you cope when you are in the middle of a search and just not finding what you want or what you believe exists?

I have a couple of answers to that. One is that I expand my networking net, and pull more people into the search. Another is that I go back to the researcher and we work on our search words again. The search words may have been too broad-based, or too narrowly focused. Maybe we were a bit off the mark on what we were actually searching for. If I'm really in trouble, I will sometimes go back and reread some of the early research data to see what I might have missed.

It sounds like your secondary and primary research get quite intertwined; it's not a simple case of doing one before the other. Can you tell me a bit more about the process you go through after your research to provide the intelligence that you need to deliver?

Actually, that is an interesting point. I don't ever consider the secondary research really "done." If I had to make a process flow chart on how we do the work, certainly the secondary research would be a large activity at a certain point in the process. But then I would show that, over time, we still go back and collect more information, one obvious reason being that every day more articles are being published and made available in those databases that we want to look at.

But more importantly, the process is like a feedback loop that you keep going through over and over again. For example, you might get intel from an industry paper and then get intel from a primary person who knows something in an industry, and then see another article that by itself looks kind of bland, but there's a sentence or two in that article that, when you hook them up with the other two data points, supports a new direction that your competition is considering, that you wouldn't have gotten before. For example, let's say I'm trying to figure out what technology my competition, a software company, is going to use. If they have a teammate on board that specializes in *X*, or a teammate that always goes one way vs. the other, then that can be a piece of intelligence. If there's a new technology that no one's using yet, and you think maybe they would consider it because of their background and history, or if you find out that a commercial software company is trumpeting your competitor as being a beta test user, that's pure marketing to most people, but what it tells the intelligence guy is, oh, they're using that software, they only have so many engineers, and their engineers will be focused on the important pieces they really need.

It sounds as if you do many of the steps in the traditional Porter [163] process all by yourself. I know you have help with the research side, but it sounds like all other stages are performed in your department and not shared among others. Is that true, or do you perform a certain portion of the process and then turn it over to another department?

No, we're kind of self-sufficient. I'm the senior analyst CI individual for my location. I do depend on specialists in the company that support me in my position, such as the strategic planning guys and communications experts. You can't do everything yourself, and you need to use those sources of filtered information to perform the analysis. Their work allows me more time to take that data and formulate it into actionable information that the executive team can use. I rely on the folks that I work with on almost a weekly basis; those are the researchers, strategic planners, administrative colleagues who collect and distribute the weekly or daily industry-related articles, and all the other CI people. Then there are the other groups that are my primary research inputs, like program managers and business development folks. My experience in working with other CI folks is that they try to do too much themselves instead of depending on others who already do subsets of this type of work. There is no reason to have, and one shouldn't have, any duplication of effort.

Do you have a standard model or template that you use in order to organize your research results, or do you find that everything's pretty much custom-made?

We definitely have standard models and templates, because they give you a repeatable process that permits continual improvement. We find it also builds confidence in the organization regarding your outputs and your conclusions. The reason you have these templates, models, and things of that nature is that they feed your presentation. In order for your CI to be actionable, you have to get it in front of the executive team. That means you have a very short time to be effective. The more succinct and consistent your data formatting, the quicker the executives can absorb the results presentation and make decisions. That, then, reinforces the value of the CI professional. So it's a win-win for everybody.

What road map would you present to a researcher who is newly assigned to the CI function?

I'd suggest starting with some keywords, identifying the competitors and the companies that are on their team. We'll ask for information on business size, location, and expertise. We look at who the decision makers are, and what the management team looks like. We search press releases and statements that the decision makers have made on the strategic direction of the company. I also clue the researchers in on the specific tactical proposal. We look at the number of contracts the company has and has had with the specific customer who has requested the proposal, for example, the Air Force/SMC (Space and Missile Systems Center) or Army/STRICOM (Simulation, Training, and Instrumentation Command). If we find out that this smaller company gets 60 percent of its revenue from this particular customer, that tells me a lot. After the learning curve, it's time to go out and talk to PR, the marketing guys, strategic development, and really every single department, conducting interviews to find out what they know about the competition and the customer.

You mentioned that you use some standardized templates to help you provide predictable products and be consistent in your

presentation. Can you share the types of results you feel are essential to report, and which you make sure are contained in each report you deliver?

A typical list of section headers or key topics in our reports would include competitor's bid price, competitor's technical solution, competitor's bid strategies, competitor's discriminators/strengths/weaknesses, customer's evaluation criteria, score of LM vs. competitor using customer's evaluation criteria, competitor's business relationships with other companies or with the customer, competitor's teammates and their capabilities, recommended actions on our price, our bid strategy, our technical solution, our proposal improvements, and our teammate selection.

Keep in mind this list is not just raw data or information but reflects analysis that was based on the information collected. Be careful and do not get caught up producing competitive intelligence newsletters or competitive analysis databases that are nothing but data holders for raw information. Otherwise, you become more of an administrator, filling those databases or writing those newsletters, when you should be analyzing the data and making presentations that cause your executive teams to take action. It's easier said than done. Knowledge of company financials has little impact. What's more important are what the competitor's discriminators are, what our discriminators are, and how they compare. And if it becomes ho-hummish, you're not getting down to the nitty-gritty. I want specific examples of discriminators that they have that we don't have, and I want to be able to tell our executive team what those are. If we were a car manufacturer, every competitor could say they make a great car. What I want to know is do they have a feature I don't have—like a map system that hooks up to the Internet?

Perhaps the competitor knows the customer better than any of us. Since they've done a lot of work for them, they may have unique insights that we don't have. At SCIP conferences, people often refer to blind spots—you don't know what you don't know. When you're bidding on a proposal, it's very binary; you win or you lose. When we start to peel back the onion and look at the lessons and insights, we'll notice that we didn't understand what the customer wanted, or we weren't the only ones that listened to the customer and gave them what they asked for. It's philosophical almost, how organizations learn and improve.

Throughout the intelligence process, what percentage of your time do you allocate to the secondary research, primary research, analyzing results, and report writing and presentation?

I can be short and sweet on that. I estimate that I spend about 20 percent of my time on secondary, 30 percent on primary, and 50 percent or more is results analysis and communicating my results to the executive team. And, as I stated earlier, the more analysis, the more actionable the information is, and therefore the more valuable.

What software products have you found valuable for Web monitoring or alerts? Do you use any software packages for post-research processing or analysis?

We haven't really found any good CI software products that fit correctly into our process or that are economical. We tend to stick to general software, such as Excel [209] spreadsheets for financials. We use a simple home-grown database of very specific competitive information and process metrics to keep track of how we improve our CI process. We don't have a huge, elaborate database of CI data because there exist searchable databases like DialogSelect that put large quantities of competitive data at your fingertips. We've dabbled in Web-tracking products, but haven't found any homerun products out there. DialogSelect is one commercial headline alert service that we have found useful. However, most alert services are too expensive for multiple users; I'm still looking for an alert service that is less than $500 per person per year. We have found alert services through government agencies, proposal companies, and by digging around. Some of the ones we use are Fed Sources' FSI State & Local Headline News, Defense Systems Daily Headlines [114], and VTC Media Availability [192] from DOD. Many Fortune 500 companies have access to free email alert services from investment analysts that you can sign up for.

What was your largest coup?

I have a few, but the biggest success is the Joint Strike Fighter Program that we just recently won. It's valued at over $200 billion, and my work—including pricing strategy, working out what the avionics solution was going to be for our competition, and things like operations support costs—had significant impact. CI was really critical in helping us win there, and it was an honor just to be selected to work on that program.

I also helped win a program called CVN77, a big aircraft carrier electronics integration job, and, when I first started, back in '91, '92, a half-billion program called CCTT—close combat tactical trainer, a simulation modeling trainer for a tank. It's very satisfying to make a significant impact on winning programs, particularly those that developed into new business areas.

Have you ever had a nightmare project or a significant "lesson learned?"

Winning is great but losing is a nightmare, particularly when you first hear you lost a program. Because I'm very analytical and do self-analysis to improve the process, I immediately ask myself, why did we lose, was it something that I did, or something that I missed, something I could have done better? Even though you understand that you can't win 'em all, when you're working on a contract that means the livelihood of 500 families that work for your company, winning vs. losing is intense and stressful. Lessons learned are extremely important, and the one bright spot, the silver lining in that cloud, is that usually you learn the most when you lose. The trick is to take those lessons learned and apply them to the next bid.

How do you stay current and confident with your strategies and resources?

That's pretty easy; I think the biggest reason is that I do CI full time. As such, my sole job responsibility and focus is competitive intelligence and customer intelligence. That, almost in itself, keeps me up-to-date. It's the stuff that people don't know that's harder to find—connecting disparate pieces of information, connecting the dots. I'm always networking with my fellow competitive intelligence colleagues. This may seem like apple pie and motherhood—but I cultivate a culture within my organization so that colleagues think about me when they come up with competitive intelligence. It's really incredibly invigorating to see people start to behave and do things with intelligence in their mindset.

Another way I keep informed is through my membership in SCIP, the Society of Competitive Intelligence Professionals. I also attend industry-specific conferences, such as software products and systems, and related conferences in areas that we need to learn more about. My engineers are usually keen on going to those, but in addition to them collecting brochures and being aware of what goes on, I find it critical that a CI person attend, someone who understands the environment, competition, and technical issues. They are more focused and aware, and therefore tend to gather and absorb the necessary intelligence that their business requires internally.

What skill set and/or education do you feel an individual needs to be successful in performing competitive intelligence?

I like the words "skill set" because if I say just "education," that might scare people away. You do have to be a jack-of-all-trades to a certain extent, but the ideal background is someone who has a good financial background—who's good with numbers—and also has a technical background, capability, or understanding. You could say that, as long as someone likes to absorb information and learn, no matter what the subject is, that's a great person to have. You need someone who isn't afraid to learn things, who isn't afraid to make mistakes. Communication skills are extremely important, because if I'm really going to get intel from all organizations, then I need to relate with almost every kind of personality in the world. And one definitely needs presentation, analytical, and trend analysis skills to make the information actionable and therefore intelligence. You've got to have a thick skin, because you're going to make mistakes, get slapped around a bit, and be criticized. Buck up, accept criticism, and think of it as a self-improvement cycle, because that's what it is.

Speaking of criticism, what do you see as downsides to being a CI professional?

The worst is getting a late start, when the team gets you involved later in the process than they really should, which means you have less time to impact their decision. Once someone makes a decision, particularly at a high level, they're going to have less propensity to want to change it. This is because they've already communicated to a large organization, or to certain other key people, the decision they've made, and it's hard to change those positions.

What do you enjoy most about this profession?

Winning! If you don't win, then what keeps you going is wanting to win the next one. In my business, it's really hard as a CI professional to lose the first couple. But if you have a lower win rate at first, that's okay, because you're coming up the curve, no doubt. Another fun aspect is the complexity of the job at hand. Each one represents a great challenge that tests you every day. I am never bored.

Super Searcher Power Tips

➤ Other departments can provide even more intelligence on what the competition is doing than business development or marketing and sales. Don't overlook program management, procurement, communications, and engineering.

➤ Do not get caught up producing competitive intelligence newsletters or databases that are nothing but data holders for raw information. Otherwise, you become more of an administrator, when you should be analyzing the data and making presentations that allow your executive teams to take action.

➤ I want specific examples of discriminators that our competitor has that we don't have, and I want to be able to tell our executive team what those are. If we were a car manufacturer, what I'd want to know is do they have a feature we don't have—like a map system that hooks up to the Internet?

➤ I spend about 20 percent of my time on secondary research, 30 percent on primary, and 50 percent or more on results analysis and communicating my results to the executive team. The more analysis, the more actionable the information is, and therefore the more valuable.

➤   Integrate the analyst with the researchers. I have a weekly meeting with my researchers even when I don't need them to work with me. They just listen to current issues, which allows them to understand my job better. Later, when things get hot in a particular area, the researchers are one step ahead of me.

➤   Always ask if your work is actionable and not just nice to know. You need to have actionable data. It's the intelligence that is unique and value-added.

➤   When you see a trend that's supported by data but still fragmented, trust your instincts and draw a conclusion; be gutsy. If you wait till everything is in line, then it's too late, because everybody in the world will know it by then and it's no longer intelligence, it's just data.

Renee Daulong

Risk Analyst

Renee Daulong is the Knowledge Broker in Worldwide Procurement at Dell Computer Corporation. Previously, she was President of Information Resource Services, Inc., an Austin, Texas, research and library services firm. She has a BS degree in geophysics and an MS degree in community and regional planning from the University of Texas. Renee was the 1999–2000 President of the Association of Independent Information Professionals (AIIP) and is an active member of the Special Libraries Association (SLA). She teaches continuing education classes on proving value in libraries and competitive intelligence for nonbusiness librarians.

renee_daulong@dell.com

First of all, why don't you tell me about your background and how and when you started performing competitive intelligence?

I started doing research about 15 years ago. I owned my own business, an independent company called Information Resource Services, Inc. At the time, it was mostly technical research and a lot of manual research. I then migrated into more online research, still primarily focusing on technical. I did that for about 13 years, and for the last several years, people were increasingly requesting business information, so I started doing that as well. Then in 2000, I came to work at Dell, in a job that is primarily focused on competitive intelligence–type work. So it was really here that I was thrown into the fire and honed my competitive intelligence skills.

And what is your actual job title at Dell Computer? Do you report to a specific department?

My job title is Procurement Strategy Knowledge Broker. What that means is that I do research and analysis on a number of different levels for the Worldwide Procurement department at Dell, from economic trends to industry analyses. I'm attached to an atypical department for competitive intelligence; I don't do research on Dell's competitors per se, but on the supply base and the industries that provide components that go in computers.

How would you describe your function as Knowledge Broker at Dell? What is a typical day, if there is such a thing? Do you have routine questions or is your workday totally customer-driven?

I monitor lots of electronics industry publications on a daily basis. I try to keep up on what's going on in the computer component industries, see if any of the articles pertain to something we're working on right then, or if it looks like something might be causing risk for us or our supply chain. That's one function. I do get research requests from people within Procurement on an ad hoc basis—not a lot, although the amount is increasing. The main focus of my job relates to a methodology that we use to evaluate supply chain risks, so that's where I spend a lot of my time. Much of my research directly supports studies that are led by me or by a team member or other groups within Dell Procurement. Everything is pretty much custom-driven, and a lot of it's driven around this methodology that we use to evaluate risk. That may mean online research, reading market research reports, interviewing suppliers, performing analysis, brainstorming potential strategies, or creating a presentation. I guess that means there really isn't a typical day for me.

How do you feel competitive intelligence differs from business research?

By some definitions, what I do is probably closer to business intelligence or business research than it is to competitive intelligence, but I think the same techniques apply. I would say competitive intelligence is business research plus. We use many of the same techniques and resources that you would use for business research, but we take it a little bit further. You're not just providing raw data, you're doing some analysis. Maybe you look at industry trends or company trends over time. Maybe you do a little scenario planning. You perform analysis, turn it into a presentation, and then, hopefully, out of that you can come up with some recommendations or strategies. It's not just your old rip-and-ship research, it's taking it further, adding value.

Everybody has their favorite tools for doing "research plus." If you were stranded on a desert island, what would your essential resources be?

First of all, I would have a satellite phone. Plus some contraption like on *Gilligan's Island* to create electricity to run the computer. Seriously, I use a lot of market research reports from the big market research companies as well as the niche players. I use everyone from IDC (International Data Corporation) [48, see Appendix] and Gartner [35] down to smaller niche players, for example IC Insights [42] or Semico Research [74] in the semiconductor industry. I cross-check that with information we get from our suppliers. I also use Wall Street analyst–type reports. Because I do an awful lot of analysis on companies and industries, I don't see any point in reinventing the wheel when there are reports out there I can use. Intelligence Data's Intelliscope [47] is a good source for these analyst reports. I use some press releases and articles, but not as much as I did when I was doing technical research.

Another tool I use is 10K Wizard [2], which is a Web site that allows you to do keyword searching on companies that must submit Securities and Exchange Commission (SEC) filings. I believe their annual fee is $125 per year, and I easily get that much value in return. If I'm looking for something in particular on a company, often I can go in and do a keyword search to home in on the specific information I'm looking for. I can also search across years and across filing types, so it's a very quick way of getting information that's tucked away inside an annual or quarterly report, without having to look at every single filing. I really like that.

There are a few other key sources that I use as well, particularly for data—not interpretation of the data but the actual numbers themselves. One example is data collected and distributed by the U.S. government. Of course, its limitation is that it typically only covers the U.S. as opposed to worldwide, which is generally my preferred view. Nonetheless, you can still get some good free information from the government. One example is monthly U.S. manufacturing statistics by industry from the U.S. Census Bureau [11]. Shipments, inventories, and orders are provided for industries based on NAICS (North American Industry Classification System) [157] codes.

Another source is trade associations, some of whom publish data. That data may be free to the public, or may be available to members only, or may be available for purchase. For example, the Semiconductor Industry Association (SIA) [75] publicly releases high-level monthly semiconductor data. Additional detailed data is available only to members. You can also use contacts at those associations to get information you need or to obtain leads for further discussions. *The Encyclopedia of Associations* [118] is invaluable in identifying associations to contact. That is one reference tool I still prefer to use in paper copy rather than online. So those are the sources I would want with me on a desert island. If I could just get the satellite phone, I would be able to make those phone calls and connect to the Internet!

How much of a role does the Internet play in your research process? Would you venture a guess as to what percentage of your time you use the Internet versus the for-fee database services?

I don't think it's 50-50; it's probably less than 50 percent for the free stuff. Ideally, I want everything to be free on the Web and of high quality and available in a timely fashion, but that hardly ever happens, so I wind up turning to fee-based services. Because I use the Wall Street analyst reports so heavily, that probably skews it largely toward fee-based services. Despite the scandals involving analyst research, I still find good information in those reports because I don't look at the investment advice and I try to verify the other information using additional sources. I do use the Web to get press releases, but the thing with press releases is that they're telling you what the company wants you to know, which may not be what's really going on. In the work I do, press releases have value, but it's nominal value. I really want to see what the market research firms and analysts are saying, or maybe talk to companies in that industry and see what their take on it is, rather than just going on what's in a press release.

What do you do when you get a project and it looks like a doable thing, but soon after you get started you run into a brick wall? How do you get over "the wall"? Have you ever had to abandon a project?

I do a bunch of things when I run into stumbling blocks. Maybe I've just got a terminology issue. I'll check CMP's TechEncyclopedia [78] on the Web. We have experts within our company in most fields involving electronics, so I usually go to them and try to find other keywords or other phrases that I might be missing. I'll look at a lot of free sources on the Web, articles in trade publications and things like that, and see what terminology they use. Sometimes I'll try to find a trade association that deals in the area and use them to find out what's going on. I'll look for market research folks that I can talk to or buy reports from. There are some market research aggregators whose collections you can search for free, like Mindbranch [59] and MarketResearch.com [58]. They provide one-stop shopping for reports from large market research firms as well as some niche players. For some of the electronics component industries I'm looking at, there may be just one research firm covering that market. If I can't identify that firm through quotes in articles and such, maybe I can go to one of these content aggregators, do a keyword search and find out who's covering that area. It may simply mean picking up the phone and calling one of the quoted researchers. I try to get advice, which can be pretty hard to come by for free, or try to find out what reports they offer, or what they charge for consulting, which is usually extremely expensive.

The other thing I do is call colleagues; having a network's important, I think, in any type of research. I have a pretty good network that I've developed, especially through a couple of professional associations, one of them the Special Libraries Association [259] and another the Association of Independent Information Professionals [229]. There's almost always somebody I can call about a topic and see what they've done in the past and what's worked and what hasn't, or maybe find out that the data doesn't exist, so I know I shouldn't sit around spinning my wheels on it for the next three or four hours.

Sometimes we have had to cut bait after we've gotten some hours into the project. We deal with the bad news situation by situation. If it's something that somebody just asked for offhand, it's pretty easy to give it up, but if it's something the VP's looking for, you want to make darned sure you've exhausted your resources before you tell him that nothing's available. There's usually something on a company or an industry you can dredge up. It may not be perfectly applicable, though, so deciding when to cut it off is a philosophical question.

I often wind up creating a list of "sources checked" when I have not had much luck in finding information. I don't usually track the resources I'm using as I go along, but if I reach a point where I've gone to three, four, five sources that I consider to be core resources, and I'm not finding anything, I'll definitely start noting all the places I've checked. That helps too, if you call your colleagues for advice; you can tell them, I already looked here, here, and here.

You've talked about how, in creating intelligence, you go beyond secondary research—you phone people and interview experts to get answers. Once you've completed your book, association, market research report, and telephone research, what are your typical next steps?

I have a couple of different answers. If I'm doing ad hoc CI-type research for somebody in our department, then I usually don't take the extra steps. I just send them whatever I've got and let them incorporate it into whatever format is most appropriate for them. Maybe they just wanted some background reading, or maybe it's something for an executive review. That is the more traditional research role.

The things I do for the team I'm on, the Procurement Strategy Team, are pretty standard based on a methodology that we use. It's never a case of "here's a document, just read it and understand it." It involves pulling out particular pieces of information that fit into our methodology, and understanding what story that data is telling us. Once we understand that story, we can develop strategies to mitigate risk. We don't have a standard template where every single project presentation is going to look exactly the same and have exactly the same content. But every study I conduct does have the same methodology. There will be similar types of data for each risk factor in every study we produce. Dell

is a data-driven company, so what I'm ultimately going to produce is a lot of charts and tables and graphs I created from data I
collected. We're actually pulling the information, putting it into
something like an Excel spreadsheet, and preparing it for presentation or for massaging. Our standard output is usually a
PowerPoint presentation. I don't usually come up with reports,
per se; I'm definitely not coming up with bound print documents.

Do you ever find, when you're putting everything together, thinking you've got enough to do your PowerPoint presentation, a gap or missing data that you have to go back and fill in?

Sure, I think that happens to every researcher, no matter what
kind of research you're doing. I guess the short answer is "yes,
but ..." I do a lot of the analysis, and at least preliminary formatting and such, as I go along. That way I can get a feel for potential gaps as I go through the project. So I don't really get to the
end and say, "Oh, yikes! I don't really have everything I need
here." Actually, I've gotten to a point where I throw the information into PowerPoint as I work on a strategy project. I started out
collecting the data, then doing all the analysis in Excel, and then
creating my presentation at the end of the project. I've discovered that, for me, personally, it works better to just go ahead and
do the bare-bones PowerPoint as I'm working through the project. That way, when I get to the end of the research phase, I'm
finished, except for tidying up and tying it together and making
sure the flow's there. I also find that it keeps me focused on the
data I really need, as opposed to all the data that's out there.

Many people get caught up in what I call the high-school
research paper syndrome. When you were in high school and
you had to write a research paper, the first thing you did was go
to the school library and check out every single book on that
topic. You'd walk out with 30 books in your arms and say, "Oh,
yes, I'm going to read all these and know everything I need to
know." I try to instill in folks that that's not the way we're going to

do research. We know what our needs are, so let's go out and collect the data we need—not to the exclusion of opening ourselves up to other thoughts or analyses or interpretations, but let's really stay focused on where we're going and what we're looking at, and not just try to collect everything in the world about a really huge company, for instance. Let's just pull the research reports that are going to support the work we're doing. Let's not be those high-schoolers.

Other than that sound advice, what road map do you present when you are training someone new in-house?

I tend to point people to some Web sites and some free alerting services that seem to be pretty reliable, timely, and offer good-quality information. For example, the Web site for the trade publication EBN [117] has timely articles that are focused on electronics procurement. Cnet [12] and other Web sites have free alerts. I remind people to run a sanity check before quoting any source; that is, try to find another independent source that corroborates the information. Be careful to verify that all of the articles you find are not based on, for example, a single press release. The road map I use depends on whether the person has a research background or is new to research. Hopefully, if they're a researcher, they already have good research skills and understand the resources that are available and the importance of persistence in looking for information. I also remind them that I have access to additional resources and will be happy to help them.

Have you come up with a model for allocating your time among secondary research, primary research, and then results organization and reporting? Does budget determine your time allocation?

I don't do even a semi-formal timetable like that in my head. When I owned my own research company, I had to be concerned with billing back time and expenses, and with budgetary requirements. Those were huge issues. I really needed to make sure that I allocated my time appropriately; otherwise I wouldn't leave enough time for analysis and I would end up spending more time than I could bill.

Here, I don't have budgets per request or per project. I have an overall research budget for the year and I need to fit all my research purchases into that. I still have deadlines for completion of the projects we're working on and there are only so many hours in a day. So I don't really think in terms of "I need to spend this percent of my time doing this and that percent of my time doing that." I know when my deadline is, and I work toward that. My personal work habits are such that I tend to really dig in, hit the research hard, and then my level of effort tapers off over time. As I mentioned before, I get the data and I format and analyze as I go. Having a standard methodology with a more or less standard way to report things cuts down on a lot of effort and uncertainty because I know what my analysis should look like in the end.

The other thing is, because I tend to work on large studies that take weeks to do and involve not just me or parts of my team but also other people within Procurement who are experts in these areas, and sometimes suppliers, I don't really feel the time constraint that I felt on research projects in the past, when it was "I need this search by tomorrow." We do have deadlines that I have to meet, of course. But I have the luxury of time, to a point, in that they are usually several-week projects and I don't devote my entire day to one project. I'm usually heavily involved in two or three projects at the same time, where I'm a major participant in one study, and then I'm providing the research but not the analysis for a couple of others. I don't have the tight constraints that I did when I was independent or that other CI folks have in companies that charge back for this type of work.

You were talking about some of the types of results that are essential to report in your types of studies. How do you determine what to include in your reports or presentations?

We do mostly presentations, but they're not always accompanied by a person explaining the presentation. Our assumption when we create a presentation is that it'll be sitting on an intranet Web site or in an email and there won't be someone there to explain all the points. It has to be presented in such a way that it can stand on its own. One extreme is creating a PowerPoint with a bunch of bullets that you're just going to use as reminders or speaking points during your talk. The other extreme is a full written report with lots and lots of words. Our presentations have to find that happy middle ground where they stand alone but they're not hugely verbose, and they really cut to the point. So they're actually a hybrid of the two.

All presentations start with an executive summary that summarizes the data, our conclusions, and the strategies we developed based on the data. We make sure that the slides that follow support the story so that everything that's covered in the executive summary is contained in the slides behind it, and the analysis and data shown on the slides absolutely and totally support the conclusions that are presented on the executive summary slide. For the strategy work that our team does, I might have an executive summary and then a few slides about the industry—in other words, a market overview. After that, we turn to addressing the risk factors that we look at. We try to include only slides that answer the questions about the risk factors and not a bunch of background information or data that is not directly related to the risk analysis. Including extraneous "nice to know" information can cause the audience to go off on a tangent and lose focus. It is important to keep them focused on the story you are telling in order to achieve your desired outcome.

You mentioned earlier some electronic resources that you like to use. Do you use any specialized software for post-search processing and so on, or subscribe to any Web page monitoring or news alert services?

I was surprised when I first came to Dell that some people had subscriptions to free alerting services from investment banking or equity firms. I had no idea the public could have access to these kinds of alerts. Analysts at those firms compile and send out a standard daily alert with article titles and URLs and maybe the first few sentences of the article so you get a little bit of a description. One example is Nihowdy [156]. The Nihowdy Web site is not well developed, but they provide a weekly alerting service highlighting articles that are available on the free Web about the PC and semiconductor industries. I also receive current awareness updates from some database services and free Web sites. A lot of the free alerts from trade publications and so on are moving to the fee-based model, too, so fewer and fewer are free.

I don't know if it's a product of over-confidence, or of having owned my own business and really trying to control costs, or what, but I tend to work on a pretty bare-bones basis. I don't buy a lot of specialized software and things like that. I generally don't need to know things the minute they happen. Much of the current awareness information I get is material I'm going to take home and take a look at and say, "Hey, these are things I need to know for my own reference" or "These are articles I need to tell other people in my organization about." I don't really have a need to organize a lot of articles I find. I don't usually need things like Web page tracking software to monitor when a Web page has changed. I don't usually have to know as soon as a press release comes out.

In terms of other organizational and analysis tools, I basically use Microsoft standards—Excel [209], PowerPoint [211], and sometimes Word [212]. I haven't purchased any specialty software and I don't have any plans to do so. I'm usually looking for data or insight when searching the fee-based services, so I don't typically have the need for software to clean up search results, unlike when I did technical research. When I'm doing something in Word, I'll use a lot of their formatting functions, like the Style function to create tables of contents and standard-looking documents, or maybe create a little macro for cleanup. I find that the Microsoft Office products do the job. They have a lot of powerful functionality that I think is not evident to the casual user. When you start digging down you find that they can do a lot of what you need. For example, Excel pivot tables are an amazing feature you can use to quickly analyze data. With a few mouse clicks you can summarize data; perform calculations such as sums, counts, and percentages; and produce interactive graphs. It's a pretty spiffy high-tech tool that is easy to learn and use, and most people don't even know they have it.

Of all the research projects you've done, which one stands out as being your largest coup, or perhaps the most challenging to solve?

I was able to conduct one of our risk studies on a component that's not well covered in the literature by market researchers or analysts. It's an older component that's fairly standard and is used in almost everything electronic. It's been around forever and has one of the longest life cycles of any electronic component. Because it's so old and so common and people don't really think about it much, there was not much market research on it. We were able to put together a pretty decent risk analysis by using only a few resources, doing a lot of supplier interviews, and contacting some industry experts. For something we didn't have much information on, I'm surprised at how good the end result was.

One of the other things I do that uses CI techniques but is not directly related to the risk analysis I mentioned earlier is looking at potential suppliers. As you can imagine, a lot of companies want to get in the door with Dell. We get cold calls from people with all kinds of new and innovative things they want to supply to us. In these cases, I do a brief company and industry overview—not really in-depth like public records searching, liens, or stuff like that, but a first pass to find out if they are for real or if they're somebody with a good idea but no product, and so on. I do look at their competitors and try to understand what is going on in their industry. One company had an interesting-sounding product, and I was able to uncover that they had a lot of shareholder lawsuits and some questionable executive behavior. My research saved us time, money, and energy by enabling us to cross them off the list of people we were seriously interested in. Not a major coup, but it helped somebody out and saved company resources.

Dell is a very fast moving company; its reputation is true. One of the things I'm really pleased about is that I've been able to help people understand what information resources are out there; that helps them make data-driven decisions.

On the other side, were you ever tasked with a project that turned out to be just a total disaster?

Oh, yes. I had to do a project early in my Dell days on an area that I wasn't familiar with. I had a very difficult time understanding the appropriate data sources to use for that industry, which was not the electronics industry. I was trying not to spend a lot of money or buy a lot of subscriptions to publications for this industry that I probably wouldn't care about on an ongoing basis, at least not to the same depth. I was constrained by the research budget we had allocated for the project on that one. There weren't people in the company who were experts in that area, although we had some knowledge. The project went on way past its deadline and I wound up wasting some money by contracting out some of the research work. The work I got back from our contractor was very poor. We eventually did persevere and get enough information, after a very long learning curve, to be able to perform our analysis. But it was a challenge, and it was a very frustrating experience for many people involved. I am so very glad it's behind me.

Still, I learned some lessons: Sometimes you have to spend money to get the information you need, and spending the money up front can save you a lot of time and frustration later. There's probably some quid pro quo in that time isn't free, which people tend to forget—even those of us who used to bill for all of our time. Be very sure about the individual you're contracting work out to. I knew of this person through a professional organization and the person seemed very knowledgeable on a discussion list, but as it turned out, something didn't jibe; they couldn't perform the work I needed, or the budget wasn't appropriate. Something just went very, very wrong there. Even though I used to own an independent research company myself, it made me leery of contracting out to people whose *work* I'm not familiar with, even if I think I know *them*. For that project I probably would have been better off going to some government agencies and associations up front, rather than trying to do it all through the Web or published data sources.

Another lesson is, when you're not familiar with an industry you're trying to do research on, don't be afraid to admit that up front. Be clear about what your skills are—not necessarily to the folks you're working with, but to yourself. Don't be afraid to say, "In this case, I'm probably going to need some help." Maybe brainstorm with a colleague who has more experience in that industry. Even though my one experience with outsourcing was a bad one, I still believe that I should have called in a real expert early in the process. Instead, I wasted literally days of research time before calling in someone else. Do what you do best and outsource the rest … to a known quantity who is indeed an expert in that area.

How do you stay current and confident with the strategies and resources that you use?

This is something I have wrestled with since I came to Dell. When I had my own company, networking was a big part of what I did. I went to a lot of information professional events, primarily to market my services, but also to stay on top of things professionally. Here, I struggle with that a little, especially because I'm so isolated. I'm not part of a big library or a big competitive intelligence team. It's basically me as far as information specialists in my part of the company go, and that means I have to put a lot more effort into attending conferences and keeping up with the information industry. I just flat don't have time to do a lot of professional reading. I do stay somewhat on top of things through some discussion lists I belong to. AIIP's discussion list is pretty good and has a lot of helpful hints, especially for business research. I also rely on my colleagues, the network of professionals I mentioned earlier, that I have made contact with through the years.

On the other hand, I do find, now that I'm in a large company with a larger research budget, that trade shows are a lot more helpful than they were when I was an independent with a limited budget. I get a lot more out of the trade shows now than I used to, especially something like the Special Libraries Association conference where you have a bunch of vendors all in one room so you can quickly find out what's out there.

What skill set or education do you feel an individual needs to be successful in performing competitive intelligence?

I'm not a librarian by training; I stumbled into the field. Although I don't have a masters in library science, I've been doing research for a lot of years. So I don't think an MLS is necessarily a determining factor in whether or not you can be a good competitive intelligence professional. In fact, a lot of people in the CI business come from entirely different backgrounds, like military or government, or marketing. However, you've got to have good research skills. You've got to be able to dig down, dig deep, think creatively, think out of the box, be willing to chase leads.

Perseverance is absolutely essential, and my favorite thing—which is not really a skill but is more helpful than anything—serendipity. It's a researcher's best friend. You're looking for information on some passive component in a computer, and for some reason you get a false drop that is a perfect article about a semiconductor that you're studying. Serendipity is fortuitous luck, but I think serendipity also stems from paying attention and keeping track of things and seeing how things connect.

You also need analytical skills and logic. It is helpful to be able to look at data and see patterns in it, *before* you graph it. Another example is looking at a bunch of quotes from experts in articles and figuring out if a story emerges when you put them all together. You need to be able to say, "Does this logically make sense? Is the story plausible?" It is surprising how many people forget this last step. From a technical standpoint, if you don't have Excel skills, go get some training. All kinds of analysis and charting and graphics can be done in Excel with not much effort. It really takes the pain out of analysis, so it's definitely a skill worth having. If you don't come from a business background, at the very least learn the basic language of business. Try to learn a little about financial analysis. Listen and learn as the business folks talk.

Know the information sources, and most importantly, know what the good information sources are, who has the quality data, whom you can trust, whom you can't. Look at information with a critical eye. This is especially important in CI. Figure out if what you're reading in an article is real. What is the motivation behind it? Is it a supplier releasing information to a reporter to make you think the market is turning and prices are rising, or is the market really turning and are prices really rising? Look at what's underneath; don't just skim the surface and assume that everything is as it appears. Adopting that attitude was a big change for me in moving from technical research to CI. When performing technical research, an article about a technology is an article about a technology, and that's what it is. It's usually not propaganda. In the business world, there are different motivations for putting out information, and you need to understand what's behind that before you go off and make plans and strategies based on it. Which leads me to: Double-check data when you can, especially numbers. When information like an industry growth rate is reported, you need to be very careful and be sure you understand whether that is unit growth or revenue growth, if the data is for a particular region or if it is worldwide, and so on. You must have the ability to evaluate information and verify it.

Also, network with fellow CI and other information professionals. Your network should also include information sources external to your company like market researchers, analysts, maybe reporters. But don't forget your internal corporate network. There's so much knowledge inside the company. You want to be able to take advantage of that.

What do you enjoy most about being in this profession? You say you migrated into it, but obviously you stayed and have taken on increasingly more challenging assignments.

I love my job. I love doing research and analysis; it's what makes me happy. I like the thrill of the hunt. I like finding *the* answer. I like digging up that hard-to-find piece of information that's going to make a difference. I like putting data together in a new way that creates new insight. I like finding the best way to present the data to tell the story that needs to be told. And what I'm really fortunate with here at Dell, and fortunate in a way a lot of information people aren't, is that the work I do makes a difference in how we run our company. It makes a difference in the strategies we use in procurement, and that makes all the difference in the cost-competitive world of computers.

That leads me to some advice that I'd like to give, which is to look for CI opportunities in nontraditional settings. Don't just look on the CI team. Don't just look in the corporate library. Look at other places within the company where information and analysis happens. Those are the places you will be able to apply your skill set.

Another thing I like about CI as opposed to a lot of the work I've done in the past is the opportunity to use my analytical skills. I'm fortunate to be able to do research but also to analyze what I find; that's really super fun. Putting together crisp, insightful presentations is fun, too. It's fun to be able to create presentations that executives are going to see. That might scare other people, but I think it's pretty neat.

Is there anything you don't like?

I don't like not being able to find something when I know it's there. Nothing is more frustrating to a researcher of any ilk than not being able to find the information. That's incredibly frustrating. That's probably my big one; could you tell?

Super Searcher Power Tips

➤ Know your information sources—ones you use, ones you might want to use, ones you don't think you'll ever use. Know their strengths, weaknesses, and biases.

➤ Make sure your analytical skills are sharp. If you don't think you have analytical skills, go out and learn how to do it. Take a look at reports put out by analysts and learn how they do it. See what kind of analyses they perform and how they present the data. You'll find that much of it just isn't all that hard.

➤ Learn the hidden features of Excel, Word, and PowerPoint. With software that you've probably got on your computer already, you can do an amazing job of analyzing and formatting data.

➤ If you're trying to cull specific company information out of SEC filings, 10Kwizard.com is a great resource.

➤ Don't be afraid to pick up the phone and call. Sometimes the fastest and best answer comes through a phone call and not through searching a database or the Web.

➤ Take advantage of the work done by analysts, particularly Wall Street analysts. Ignore the investment advice and look at the rest with a critical eye, as you should with all business information.

➤ Be skeptical of free information sites on the Web. Check out the source, make sure the information has a date and can be verified elsewhere. Use the Web but make sure that you're using a credible source.

➤ Make sure always, always, always to include your source, especially when you've performed analysis, and to include the assumptions that you made in performing your analysis.

➤ Be confident in your ability but not cocky. Listen when people question your assumptions or conclusions. Always learn from feedback.

Mary G. "Dottie" Moon

Just-In-Time Intelligence Delivery

Dottie Moon has been with United Technologies Corporation since 1986. During that time she has worked at various positions within its Information Network and has been a Group Leader, Competitive Intelligence for the Research Center's Management of Technology Office. In 2001 she was named Manager, Competitive Analysis in Group Strategic Planning at Pratt & Whitney. Her goal is to share her vision of competitive intelligence and weave together the various unit efforts into a cohesive net gain for Pratt & Whitney. Dottie received her bachelor's degree in education from the State University of New York at Geneseo and her masters in library and information science from the School of Information Studies at Syracuse University. She is an active member of the Special Libraries Association (SLA) and the Society of Competitive Intelligence Professionals (SCIP), and is also a member of Competia.

mary.moon@pw.utc.com

Please tell me about your background, and how and when you started actually performing competitive intelligence.

I joined United Technologies in 1986 and fairly soon after that I had a casual conversation with a user that ended up with my developing a daily update on the aerospace industry. It became widely distributed and that helped me build relationships as well as credibility about my knowledge of the industry. I started getting invited in as a source to the competitive work that was going on. That grew to my actually being at the table, an integral part of the process. I then moved into various positions within the company, taking and making competitive intelligence a larger and larger piece of my job, until currently, in this one, I'm focused entirely on competitive analysis. It was an evolution, coming from a library science background, being invited onto the team, and then moving out of the library setting.

About seven years ago, our corporate Information Network created a new position, research analyst, in two different business units' strategic planning groups. The idea was to spend more time doing the analysis in addition to research and collecting data. That raised the bar, as far as expectations were concerned, beyond the typical information professional role of the past. From that, I was offered a job as manager of competitive intelligence. One of my main responsibilities was to take the lead on inculcating competitive intelligence into the corporation. The position was at the United Technologies Research Center in the Management of Technology Office. We had some reorganization after the Research Center hired a new director and at that time my operations were moved back into the Information Network. When I rejoined the Information Network, I took on a group of research analysts with the goal of advancing their skills and promoting competitive intelligence throughout the corporation. About six months ago I moved from that position to my current position as manager of competitive analysis with the responsibility for the competitive intelligence process at Pratt & Whitney.

How would you describe your current function in a nutshell?

One word would be "evolving." A lot of that is because we're in the process of establishing many of the baseline processes in our various units. This is challenging when there are a number of organizational changes going on in a company. My boss introduces me as the person responsible for the competitive analysis process in the company. It's not that I do it all, or have any expectation that that would ever be asked of me, but it's that I help devise the networks, electronic and human, to get it done. I keep an eye on the information flow, handle special projects, hold business simulations, and so on. Project management is key so that we can get the information to the right people at the right time. We monitor the environment, and I rely on the information professionals from our Information Services & Library to do that.

What types of research have you done and do you perform now?

In the past I did primarily secondary research, but now I do more primary, and rely on our information professionals for most of the secondary research. We have several extremely competent researchers—Suzanne Cristina, Hana Sognnaes, and Florence Wendell. The scope of our projects covers a wide range of disciplines that are important to keeping us moving forward— technical, company and business information, trade and industry, regulations, patents.

How do you define competitive intelligence?

When I first started out in a leadership position in CI back in the Management of Technology office, I tried to go throughout the corporation promulgating competitive intelligence. I had developed a definition that talked about the whole process that you go through, from collecting to analyzing to reporting it out. But now, I find that there's an emphasis on immediacy, to show value. I now think of CI as the focused and analyzed information that leads to an assessment of whatever part of the competitive landscape we're looking at. With some of my customers I refer to it as external forces analysis.

Competitive intelligence differs from business research in that you're creating unique information to make decisions; it includes your perspective on the situation. I see business research as the summation of somebody else's thoughts on the issue. CI is really your and your company's interpretation of the landscape out there and what you're going to do with it. I have mentioned technology several times; people often think of competitive intelligence strictly as competitor or industry intelligence. The need for competitive technical intelligence has been recognized and is expanding, but I don't know that everybody realizes its value.

What do you feel is essential in the CI toolkit?

Primarily it's the contacts, the people contacts and industry contacts, both inside and outside your company. Having access to the employees within your company to tap into their knowledge and content, having information professionals who can do the secondary research that is precise and comprehensive at the same time. I use the Internet constantly, and we have some internally developed CI databases that are essential to us. I'd also include in our toolkit the personal traits of having curiosity, an analytical mind, and the dogged determination to make things happen.

Newsletters are a great resource. You should know the ones for your industries. Many of them give free email updates to pull in potential subscribers. You can tap into updates for newsletters in industries related to your own. One way to monitor the borders of your own industry is to watch those that are close by. One of the more generic titles I read regularly is *Technical Insights* [183, see Appendix]. It is very good at covering technical innovations that haven't really been published anywhere else yet, so it gives you an edge at acquiring or leasing a technology that might be relevant to where you're going with your product line.

You said that you use the Internet heavily. How do you weigh it vis-à-vis the for-fee database services, and what specific kinds of sources do you use?

I do about 70 percent on the Internet and about 30 percent on premium resources because, again, I rely on our information professionals to handle the bulk of the secondary research. I use a select group of premium services when I need data ASAP. Examples include Bloomberg [9] for its real-time news as well as financials on public companies, Dialog [20] for its wide range of databases, especially the technical resources. I rely on several newspapers and trade publications—the *Financial Times* [124] has reliable coverage of the aerospace industry; *Wall Street Journal* [193] Online has several tools that are extremely useful; *Flight International* [125], Air Transport Intelligence [4], and AviationNow [7] are also great services for the aerospace industry. When covering the power industry, I use the Department of Energy sites [19], Platt's [67], *Power* [164], EPRI [Electric Power Research Institute, 27], and Current News in Nexis [63]. How do I know which one to use? By developing a knowledge of my own industry and the companies that I'm tracking, weighed against the particular data point that I am searching out. I think about how the information is made public—is a company releasing it, or is it available through secondary sources? All of that will give you a good idea of whether you're going to find it on the Web or if you're better off using a premium service.

Patents are extremely useful as an indicator of where a company has spent its R&D monies. But, because of the time lag, it's important to make sure that you're also paying attention to the patent applications that are out there and available now. Be sure when you're searching applications that you're searching on the inventors' names and not just the company. This is necessary, as the company names aren't assigned with the patent application, so you can't just go in and search on the company. Without the company name field, you need to find other ways to be comprehensive. Paying attention to the authors and the inventors is one way to broaden your retrieval.

We also use author searches for conference presentations, to get an indication of who might be working with whom. If they're on different technical projects, watching who they're collaborating with in their research might give you an indication of future efforts. Companies getting together, or companies with universities—once you know those relationships, you can check for other areas where cooperation might be a precursor to future company events.

Executive quotes are a great source for finding out what the company's strategic focus is, but searching them can be tricky. One of our researchers developed a search statement that gets pretty comprehensive results: Search the executive's name within five words of *stated* or *mentioned* or *answered* or *said* or *told* or *replied* or *quoted* or *spoke* or *noted* or *added*, plus variations of those verbs, all "or"ed together. That's been a lifesaver on many occasions when we've had to find a data point and indications of a company's strategy.

Of course we take advantage of government resources. There are so many types of valuable data you can get. For example, DTIC (Defense Technical Information Center) [17] covers research programs in progress and the dollar amounts awarded. You can look at suppliers with FedLog [31] and DefenseData [16] as well as Haystack [39] from Information Handling Services. You can seek out local records in cases where, for instance, companies must file accurate information on hazardous materials in case of fire. Those records might be an indicator of manufacturing or research efforts that are going on in that building.

A caveat: There are still some times when we have no choice; we still need paper. We focus quite a bit on engineering and technology issues, and that makes us reliant on paper for the full text of articles and other written material.

When you've been handed a project and you're just not finding what you want, what do you do to refocus or decide it's time to call it quits?

Sometimes, when you're not finding what you think you want to, it's that you really haven't framed the question properly. It might be that you're not thinking about the terminology in the way that the world at large does; you might be using jargon that's inherent within your company, and it turns out the rest of the world uses a different phrase. So I make sure that I step back and check my language and the context of the question.

Several years ago I took a class given by Jay Paap [253] at Caltech on competitive technical intelligence (CTI). It's an excellent introduction to CTI for both practitioners and management. If you have difficulty convincing your technical guys of the value of CTI, it could be useful for them to take Paap's course. He has a formula that I have used in working with employees that steps through the process from question to decision. Paap talks of developing your search strategy in terms of testing out the assumptions and unknowns, thinking about the resources that can give you insight into those unknowns. That makes me look at the question from a different point of view and more critically, to frame the unknowns and devise a path of sources that would have the information I seek.

I also like to talk to some of the people in the company who might be working in that area. If it's technical, I'll go talk to some of the engineers. If it is specifics on an industry or company, then I'll talk to the people who work that area and find out if this is something that they would expect to find out there. It may be that my expectations are out of whack.

If I'm still having difficulty, I switch tactics; if I've been looking on the Web then I'll go to a premium source. If I'm in a premium source that is my constant old reliable, say Compendex [25] vs. Inspec [46], then I'll try the other one. Sometimes when doing a business search I'll use the engineering databases, because it may be a crossover topic. For example, if it's related to how they might be spending their R&D, it could show up in a technical paper. That, again, goes back to the assumptions and unknowns, and where you think the answer might be available.

Once the initial research is done, what are your next steps?

As the secondary research is going on, we're trying to work with people in-house, picking their brains for their insight, or lining them up to do the analysis. Someone who's the expert on a company or on a particular aspect of the industry and is available to work with us is added to the project team. We try to bring everyone into the loop as soon as possible so that we're not running it as a linear process, but running things in parallel. I think of it as similar to the Fuld model [239] where you have external and internal information collection processes running simultaneously.

In reality, we're still evolving the process. Factors such as organizational changes and adapting the team to revised processes are still ongoing. I've been on the job for six months and we're looking at the whole CI process and applying our Achieving Competitive Excellence (ACE) quality program tools and techniques to it. We want to see if we can make it work more effectively, to streamline the process throughout. It's hard to drive to one generic process; there are so many variables. It can depend upon the deadlines, the requirements, or the person asking for intelligence. How it will be used and by whom determine whether the final result is going to be a white paper, an oral response, an email memo, or a formal presentation. A whole matrix of factors determines the way we respond.

To complete the analysis of the information, we make use of the skills resident here in our strategic planning group. The directors work with us to determine how many resources we're going to put toward a particular task, and I also work with our CI steering committee, which is made up of practitioners leading specific CI efforts in units throughout the company. Most tasks are done in parallel, such as the in-house interviews. We do have a more linear process for the baseline information on approximately two dozen companies that we maintain and update for use primarily by our strategic planners, who have to be able to respond rapidly to the president and the CEO on these companies. We have a quick summary on financials, management, strategy, watch points, technology, R&D, customers, and so on. This baseline of information was developed based on their track record of requests. The appendices contain the full-text documents to support the conclusions made in the summary document. The summary is a coordinated effort among our researcher, technical analyst, and financial analyst. I then take their results and merge it into a template and add my sections on strategy, etc. The resultant company folder is available in our password-protected CI database as well as in hard copy in our planning library.

Do you end up turning all your work over to one of the other analysts, or is it an "it depends" process?

It depends, in part because we're evolving a new process, and I'm the one who owns the process. In addition to a financial analyst and a technical analyst, we have quite a number of internal analysts we work with. A few other people on staff are focused on either a specific business unit or on engineering or manufacturing operations. That's a wide range of specialties that we can call on very easily, and we do.

Most of the quick-turnaround projects—36 hours and under—are completed by me with little additional analysis. Quick white papers or company profiles are the usual output and they consist of 85 percent summation of what information was available and 15 percent my analysis of the situation. Quick analyses of technical issues are directed to our point person on those issues and the same for quick financial analyses. But for a "deep dive" on a competitive issue, we are all engaged in the process. All our skills are needed.

Do you have a template or series of templates that you use for organizing the information you collect?

We do strive for some standardization. The template I mentioned earlier was developed by a team of practitioners when we had a corporate-wide CI community of practice. We wanted consistency for those who moved between companies in United Technologies. We also identified the resources to use in finding the data, and alternate resources in case there were problems locating the data. So, when you open a company folder, you see an executive summary that is similar to others, so you can very quickly go directly to the information needed. In addition, you can compare the financials because the source materials are the same and you're actually comparing apples to apples.

The use of our database and its link to our company portal is also an effort at standardizing the look and feel of our stored information. Specific fields are required for various assessments and the data used to draw the conclusion is attached for future use. One of our other really important standards is the form we use for our employees to submit information that they have gathered from conferences and trips. In addition to submitting the content, we require documentation on how the information was obtained. That goes into a queue for review by at least one CI Steering Committee as a check to ensure that it was acquired within the legal and ethical standards set by our corporation. Any questionable items are eliminated or reviewed with legal counsel. To date we have not had any problems with these systems.

What road map would you present to a researcher who's been newly assigned to a CI function?

My first thought is to make sure they understand how to frame the question or the task at hand—that they're defining the real question that needs to be answered, not just what was being stated. If they have an analyst background, I like to verify that they know what they're doing with researching. Once I've verified the quality of their research skills, then I concentrate on their learning the industry so that they understand the concepts, the hot topics, the important areas to watch, where they think outlying factors—environmental influences, new competitors, opportunities, and threats—might be coming from.

If they're coming into the CI process with an MBA or a technical background, I usually put them together with an information professional from our Information Services & Library so that they learn how to work with the researchers in framing the questions, and how to assess and improve their searching skills. We introduce them to Bloomberg and other sources we have in our department. The information pros know how to train, and they usually add to it by helping the new person develop their network of contacts. As they talk about projects, the researcher usually points out people who will help them acquire information and understand the nuances. Between us, we make sure that we round out all the capabilities that are necessary for different aspects of the CI job.

One product I used a lot in a previous position was the Fuld War Room CD [240]. I'm not training as much in my current position, so I don't use it that often, but it was a terrific resource for self-study. Users can do as much as they want at their own pace, so that it augments what they are getting from other on-the-job experiences. The quizzes are useful as a check to see how they are doing.

The other thing we do right up front is make sure that they know the company legal and ethics policy on competitive intelligence and compliance. We have a Web site as well as booklets that supplement in-person training. The booklets help them understand the process and guide them if they receive something questionable. Together with our legal department and our CI Steering Committee, I work with people in each business unit to clear the information and ensure that standards are in place, worldwide.

Lastly, I encourage people to get a mentor. I've had a number of useful mentors including a peer-to-peer mentor relationship that was invaluable—a trusted colleague with whom I could be as smart and as dumb as I needed to be, and she with me. It shortened the learning curve and taught me much that I would never have gotten on my own.

How much time do you allocate to the planning, secondary research, primary research, and then the presentation? If the CEO calls you up and needs an answer today, obviously you don't have much think time.

Right, and we do respond to stuff that may not be strictly competitive intelligence as well. Papers are put together that talk about competitive positioning but aren't necessarily competitive intelligence products. It really can vary, and a lot of it depends on primary research and then analysis. That aside, if I had to give an average, I'd say it works out to 60 percent secondary research, 10 percent primary, 15 percent analysis, and 15 percent organizing and reporting. Over time I'd like to see the primary research as well as the analysis percentages increase.

What types of results do you feel are essential to report?

Again it depends on the question and its purpose. For our baseline company information, we have the overview, financial highlights, strategic focus, products, recent developments, hot spots to pay attention to, M&A, partnerships, risk-sharing, joint ventures, a technology assessment that includes R&D and intellectual property, and a key management executive bio section. I also feel some kind of conclusion or recommendation for action is essential. That is where we put our unique perspective into the report, which differentiates it from a business summation of the issue.

Do you have any special software products that you use for news monitoring, or for Web page tracking or analysis?

We do have a home-grown database that has been cloned for our various lines of business. It is based on the Lotus Notes/Domino platform [206/205] and is designed to aid in collection, alerting people to new items that fit their profiles, organizing projects around key intelligence topics, and completing assessments. The database also helps us with reporting our conclusions and maintaining the documentation so that when the issue is revisited we understand how they reached the conclusion they did. Getting that system out to the various businesses has been my focus, as far as software is concerned, since coming on board here.

The database is Web-based, so our users do not have to know anything about Lotus Notes to use it. That makes sharing the info so much easier. A cool feature that was built into the system and is maintained by the CI administrator is a matrix of permissions. That matrix, running in the background, controls the who and what for all the content. The CI team and senior executives can see all the assessments, but some users only have access to the public domain articles. We are also linked into the company's portal software and have developed a "submit" button so that any employee can send in information that they have heard. We designed it with a series of controls so that we have documentation to show that it was obtained legally and ethically, as well as controls on getting the data into one of the databases. I look forward to adding sensitivity analysis tools and data visualization and war gaming software to our toolbox in the future.

Of all the projects where you've had to add the competitive intelligence component, what would you say was the largest coup, or some wonderful discovery you made?

In my previous position in the company, we were looking at where a particular company might be going with its product offerings, and I predicted where they would be expanding in two areas. It was so cool when, about two years later, it proved to be true. It was gratifying to see that prediction come true especially because I had worked with another, more senior, analyst who had come up with a different prediction. To have scored against that particular analyst was a big win for me.

From a value-delivered-to-the-company perspective, again in a prior position, I was given the green light to a pitch I had made proposing that a CI function be set up for one of the business units. From sharing in the interview process to coaching the business analyst to take on the CI role, and establishing the processes, I had the opportunity to put it in place. I shared my vision of how to run the function and ways to be effective, how to set up a CI board, and how to think about the information flow. I also shared my experiences on how to work with the CI board to establish the priorities and how to report out results.

How about your worst nightmare or lesson learned?

Actually, my worst nightmare was when the director of the research center shut down the Information Network last year. The proposed replacement was a few electronic resources, but the people were let go. This nightmare lessened a bit for me as Pratt & Whitney quickly stepped in and hired the people that had been assigned to this business. They recognized their value. However, we lost the connections that we had to our analyst in Europe. That was quite a loss to our guys in the field, as she had been monitoring the industry and customers for them. My fear was that my new focus was going to devolve into being an information service, that the percentage of time spent on analysis would be drastically altered from what my expectations had been, coming into the job. I truly felt that they would pass on the CI to ensure the flow of information. Fortunately, I didn't have to face that.

As you say, you and the process are still evolving. What resources do you find are the best for staying current and confident with your strategies, resources, and process?

I have the advantage of being part of our strategic planning group, so that means we're aligned with the strategies of our business units. The group serves as a quasi-competitive intelligence board, which sets the focus. It's great to have it right here in the group so that we can bounce ideas around as we determine the direction and focus of the CI efforts. We are also placed on teams dealing with strategic, competitive issues so that we are integrated into ongoing processes. Another component of our operations is the synergy with the unit CI leaders, via our CI Steering Committee. Its primary focus is to deal with all the logistics— skills training, upgrading the databases, knowing who's working what, and so on. It also aids us in dealing with information flow; it is my primary conduit to the field representatives, as I am their primary conduit to the senior executives.

As for staying current, our company has a strong belief in continual employee development. We each have a development plan, and I use it as I think about my strategies and resources going forward. For example, the use of mentors and associations such as SLA [259] and SCIP [258], as well as training opportunities from Drexel [236] or Fuld. I build those into my plans for skills development or enhancement. I also find association publications and some Web sites, such as SCIP, SLA, Competia.com [233], Fuld, and Washington Researchers [261], very useful and a quality check for myself.

With regard to resources, there are always constraints. This is a constant dialogue that I have with my boss and strategic planning. I look for synergies, such as sharing products with the Information Services & Library group, finance, or one of the CI units. It takes a good business plan to make it happen.

You mentioned that people in your organization have come into the analysis business with a lot of different backgrounds. What skill set or education do you feel that an individual needs to be successful in performing CI?

I think of it in two distinct buckets. I steal this idea from SLA's competencies document for special librarians [103]— which by the way, is a great starting point for thinking about the competencies of members for your CI team. First are the professional competencies that I look for: searching skills, which involve knowing how to manipulate the various resources and having a knowledge of those information products, particularly for your own industry; understanding the way your industry works and how it could change; and various analytical techniques, be it SWOT (Strengths, Weaknesses, Opportunities, Threats), conjoint analysis, scenario planning, or one of myriad other techniques. Second are the personal competencies you want them to come with, such as curiosity, perseverance, ability to work with all types of people, good communication skills—both oral and written—and a knack for being able to put together divergent information. These personal competencies are necessary for various aspects of CI but aren't necessarily trainable kinds of skills.

What do you enjoy most about this profession?

The variety. The chance to work with a whole range of people from different disciplines and experiences. Being able to partner with them to assess needs, devise a method to get what's needed, and use it. I'm a big-picture thinker, so it is energizing to work with the decision makers and know that you are helping to set the future direction of the company. It is fast-paced, never boring and, if done well, very visible in the company. There are also so many cool tools, from databases to SWOT analysis to scenario planning and war gaming.

And what do you like least?

The clever people who always want to take your picture with you wearing the Sherlock Holmes hat and peering into a magnifying glass. I've never done it, but I've had many requests! The point is, there is still a perception of CI being cloak and dagger, that if you are doing it in a company, you shouldn't let on that you are doing it. We still need to better inculcate it into our organizations. One or two executive champions can really help raise awareness as well as dedicate resources to the effort.

I mention resources, as I also believe the lack of time allotted for CI is a problem. It's so important for us to get the people in the field, in engineering, and all the different departments to give their assessment as data points appear. They know it's significant, they have a sense of why, but it's difficult for them to take time to pass it on.

Any last bits of advice we haven't covered?

I can think of three things. One is a bit of very practical advice: As you develop spreadsheets, white papers, or whatever, make sure you cite the sources so you can get back to them easily. This is particularly important if you're citing information from Web pages. If it's really great data, grab it while you can as it might not be there tomorrow.

Second, build relationships with everyone, from the field reps to senior executives, so that you're recognized as a credible source. Share appropriate information in all directions so that you are not viewed as always taking information. Know how to speak the jargon, but keep your reports from being filled with it. Be succinct and targeted.

And finally, continue to learn. Sources change, requirements change, and we need to change as well. What was great research and packaging a year ago may not meet the demands of your customers. Raise the bar and have more fun as your job stays interesting and fresh.

Super Searcher Power Tips

➤ I think about how the information is made public—is a company releasing it, or is it available through secondary sources? All of that will give you a good idea of whether you're going to find it on the Web or if you're better off using a premium service.

➤ When you're not finding what you think you want to, it may be that you haven't framed the question properly. You might be using jargon that's inherent within your company, and it turns out the rest of the world uses a different phrase. I make sure to step back and check my language and the context of the question.

➤ Sometimes when doing a business search I'll use the engineering databases, because it may be a crossover topic. For example, if it's related to how they're spending their R&D, it could show up in a technical paper.

➤ I encourage people to get a mentor. I've had a number of useful mentors including a peer-to-peer mentor relationship that was invaluable—a trusted colleague with whom I could be as smart and as dumb as I needed to be, and she with me. It shortened the learning curve and taught me much that I would never have gotten on my own.

➤ Make sure you're spending your resources on the key issues. Confirm that you have negotiated the question completely so that you're focused on the real question, because your time is expensive and you can only use it once.

George Dennis
Human Source Intelligence

George Dennis is a nationally recognized practitioner and leader of corporate intelligence organizations. He has more than 15 years' experience searching out key facts that shape events, first as a trade publication journalist, then as a specialist in corporate intelligence. Most recently he implemented and directed the intelligence operations for Telcordia Technologies, a billion-dollar provider of telecommunications software and professional services. His firm, George Dennis Associates, specializes in training and supporting clients in undertaking intelligence gathering and analysis for themselves, as well as providing support in trade show operations, psychological and management-style profiling of opposition executives, and custom intelligence gathering. He is a frequent speaker and writer on business intelligence subjects and holds an MBA from the University of Colorado.

www.geodennisassociates.com

Tell me about your background and how and when you started performing competitive intelligence.

For most of my working life I've been involved in marketing some form of technology, wireless usually. In broad strokes, the transition was from being a salesperson for a wireless equipment company to working for one of the industry's trade magazines that just happened to be located in the city I live in. It was a monthly magazine for business wireless communications, two-way radio, paging, and very early cellular. I think there were only two cities with cellular service at the time. Because we were a monthly publication, we had to have information that was deeper and longer-lasting than our nine competitors. Some of those competitors came out every week, some every two weeks, and some were monthlies also. Our editorial goal was that whatever else the reader read, they would read us, too.

I always knew I would get back into the industry as a participant rather than just an observer, so after five years of building up a terrific Rolodex of contacts as an editor, I became sort of an in-house reporter for a couple of companies. Basically I kept my contacts current and put them at the disposal of my current employer when they needed some unpublished information about subject *X*, or the Federal Communications Commission, or other vendors, or big customers. I was still a reporter but my audience was perhaps four or five—the executive committee of these companies. The publisher I worked for also owned about seven major trade shows, two in the wireless industry. In my role as the designer of the panel discussions and recruiter of speakers, I got to see firsthand all the inside workings of trade shows.

Eventually I wound up at Bellcore, the software and consulting arm of Bell Labs. At the breakup of AT&T, Bellcore still had control of all the software and standards that ran the U.S. telephone system. But they were about to be cut loose from the seven Baby Bells. Each wanted to become competitive in its own right, and sharing an R&D lab, even one as comprehensive as Bellcore with its 6,000 engineers and software architects, wouldn't help that. Bellcore was about to come out of a very sheltered existence and fend for themselves in a very competitive marketplace, except that they knew nothing about their competitors, and for a while wouldn't even accept the notion that they had any competition.

I was there to assist with marketing their wireless network management systems, and in the meantime I joined SCIP (Society of Competitive Intelligence Professionals) [258, see Appendix] and took some seminars from various folks who worked for the government. When Bellcore, now called Telcordia Technologies after the spin-off, decided they needed to know something about competitors, my name came up. I was invited to head the department—but there would be no new budget or

organization or headcount. The organization I built was modeled after the French intelligence system, which is a very small
bureaucracy but has a huge cadre of what they call "correspondents," people in business, industry, academe, and the arts who
can be called upon to use their connections, specialties, and so
on for the good of the country. It was the right model for a global,
multiproduct, multidivisional company. Unfortunately, the senior management didn't want to hear what we were finding out,
because there were disaster warnings all over the place but they
had 26 years of seniority to protect. A lot of what we did didn't
necessarily get acted on, but it did come to pass, so we knew
down the road we were right. So I picked myself up and went
back home to Colorado.

When we first met you were working for BRW LeGrand, and part of your function there was performing competitive intelligence through a human resources angle. Can you describe those tasks and some of the information modes you use?

My experience at Telcordia, being surrounded by 6,000 people
much brighter than myself, proved to me that intelligence has
nothing whatever to do with being smart, and everything to do
with getting smart people to help you. In the corporate world,
that means there are departments and individuals within large
organizations who know a tremendous amount, and furthermore, they have additional contacts that the people who deal
with day-to-day competitive issues don't. The trick is to harness
what and who those people know, and induce them to share it
with you when the need arises.

For example, there was what we called an intelligence correspondent in human resources, and that correspondent had a
very simple task: she was fed a hot list of companies that we were
most interested in competitively. If she saw any resumes from
people at those companies, we got them. We wanted to know

who was about to quit, what level they were, and why they wanted to quit. Very often, people within our company would know the guy, because in telecom, like any other industry, people are very well acquainted with one another. So the HR people would keep an eye out for interesting resumes. They would also tell us what the recruiters were hearing. A headhunter might call our HR department and say, "I've got three Java coders that are leaving company XYZ." Rather than say, "Oh, we really need three coders; send them on over here," our intelligence correspondent would say, "Well, that's really strange, I thought XYZ was growing. Has their project been discontinued?" It was amazing what XYZ's outsource company knew and was willing to share. But rarely is HR asked to play an intelligence role, or to support a company's market strategy other than by providing bodies.

HR was not the only department that had useful information. We used to take financial data to our financial department. One guy there was a really quant-jock—a person who lives and dies by spreadsheets—the kind of guy who uses Excel for everything from financials to shopping lists. This person loved spreadsheets and putting into words what seemed to be happening on the financials. So we made him an official intelligence correspondent. He was very pleased that someone had recognized he had more to offer than just being a bean counter.

Our trade show department was certainly very active, both in gathering and in counter-intelligence, keeping visitors from getting too much information out of our people at the exhibits.

Customer service departments are really helpful. We had a whole telephone service group of software troubleshooters. Instead of saying, "Well, thanks for calling us, have a nice day," we taught them to ask the customer, "Well, I'm glad we could fix your problem. What do you wish we could fix that we can't?" That triggers the customer's desire to complain, and they would name companies and products and people, most of which we had to interface with. Every week our correspondent in the customer service group would send a couple of pages via email of the week's take in hints, rumors, and first-hand observations of competitor products and personnel. That was another very helpful information source that came in on a steady, routine basis.

Sometimes we could pull everyone together on a major operation at a trade show. Human resources would supply a list of the employees who'd left recently that we'd love to have back. Because we had placed our trade show guy on the exhibit committees of some of the largest telecom shows, he was able to legitimately get the pre-registered attendee list. One of our tech correspondents would merge the two lists and find out that 60 or 70 people who had left us in the past 18 months, going to work for someone else, were going to be at the trade show. The intelligence department would invite them to an "alumni party," which was actually our sales department's hospitality suite. The alumni got a very special invitation—please come to this party, meet your old friends and get your special alumni gift; I think it was some little key chain or something. While they were getting their alumni gift and turning in their official invitation, the person at the door was pinning their special alumni badge on, which flagged them to seven of my interviewers working the party. We only had two questions: One, did you want to come back, because that's what legitimized the whole operation. If we could hire them we absolutely wanted them, there was a job for them, it was legit. But if they didn't want to come back, the second question was why not? What was so exciting over there? And we got a good 20 or 25 pages of incredibly high-quality intelligence. Little things helped, like making sure the alum's best friend from our company was also at the party; things like that just made it very smooth. It was a good operation.

If a company is big enough to have its own travel department, they can be helpful too. I would be thumbing through a magazine and see this little technical conference off someplace, and call our correspondent in travel services to kick me out a list of all the people who ordered tickets for this town and this time-frame. Turned out that four or five people were going, and management at our level had no idea. We would call them up and say, "Hey, as long as you're going to this little conference here, there's a guest speaker from a company we're interested in. We'd be very interested in hearing what they've got to say. So you go ahead and spread your resume around, which is probably why you're sneaking off to this place, but you're going to do this for us in the meantime. And your secret is safe."

How do you define competitive intelligence, and how do you feel it differs from business research?

Competitive intelligence to me means information that helps you comprehend, anticipate, and eventually control events. If you're brand new at it, you're just watching whatever it is the salespeople come in scared to death about. That's being reactive, but that's comprehending events. Then you get to the point of asking what is it about this company that might indicate they're going to do something; how might they act if we launch a new product, cut a price, or launch a new service; and what will we do when they eventually react. CI involves thinking a step ahead. So I would say it's gathering information specifically, not to predict the future, but to come up with several alternatives as to how that future might unfold.

CI takes you into being able to extrapolate into some trends or future scenarios. When I'm explaining research vs. intelligence to people, I tell them to think of intersecting circles: one is competitive intelligence, one is market research. Competitive intelligence, your job is looking out the window; market research, your job is looking down the hall.

The sources for market research are usually very willing. They're prescreened so they have what you want, and they are probably compensated—sit down and take this survey, be in this focus group, whatever—they usually get paid something for their contribution. Competitive intelligence sources can be anywhere from cooperative to downright hostile. They may or may not know who you are, what information specifically you want or why you want it, and they're definitely not compensated; that's just not ethical. You can't pay someone for their future marketing plan. But what you can do is stand in line behind them in a trade show and gripe about business travel, it was bad before September, now it's impossible, and you lay out three cities you have to go to after this trade show. The target is going to get macho and say "I have it tougher than you, I've got five cities after the show," and he'll name them. You win, your schedule is tougher than mine. Then we email the sales people to watch out, the competitor is headed your way right after the show; be sure to tune up your customers on counter-competitor company arguments. Two weeks later, the guy can't figure out why his life suddenly got more difficult. That's the big difference between market research looking at what has happened and how did the customer like it and how could it be improved, to CI thinking what might they do if we do this? There isn't anybody you can really ask without tipping your hand, so you have to be very careful.

If you were marooned on a desert island tomorrow, what would you need to have with you in order to perform your CI functions? What would be in your toolkit?

A laptop and a satellite phone would pretty much cover it. And a couple of solar panels to power it all. Again, it's knowing smart people instead of trying to be smart about everything yourself. If I need research about a company, I'll call my researcher and have her put a few hours into the Net to dig up whatever facts are commonly known. You have to assume whatever's on the Net or whatever's been published is known by all. But more importantly she'll look for people's names and their attachment to the target company or the target event, because we'll want to contact them and do some telephone interviewing to get more than whatever came out on the document. I would personally go over to a target's Web site and just for fun poke a wildcard and a spreadsheet extender like *.xls in their search window, or *.doc for Word and *.ppt for PowerPoint. Sometimes you get some amazing documents to fall out that way. But generally, as far as the Net as a tool is concerned, there are people who do it much better than I do, so I prefer to pay them to do it.

Once you've compiled your information, do you continue to handle it through the analysis process to delivering the report, or do you interface with other folks further in the process?

Most of our clients want to do their own analysis, but they need just a few more facts to be sure. Or they need a broad-brush portrait so they can come back with a second project later. We almost always give an opinion, because when you're doing human source research, you get a whole bunch of good stuff, maybe little snippets that don't mean anything to this project, but we put them in the report anyway, because they might indicate something else of interest to the client.

For instance, perhaps we'll see a bunch of people leaving the ship; then we might think there's something going on. The Monster [60] Web site is great; one can sign up to view the resumes just like a potential employer. Headhunter.net [40] and 6FigureJobs.com [1] have proved useful, too. Our researchers put in the target company's name and come up with resumes for 30 or 40 people who still work there and are looking for jobs. Or they get employees of customers of the target company who list the target's products or technologies as a skill set. The target is Cisco and the individual works for Verizon but lists Cisco servers as an expertise, or something like that. That gives us a pool of people we can call or email. Because it's a resume, there's probably going to be a personal email address on it. Do a search on the email address and you can learn if the person contributes to Usenet [189] newsgroups or similar chats. The source might be interested in winemaking, rock climbing, and telecom software. We might decide to approach him through the winemaking list because, people being what they are, the conversation almost always turns to work. In one of the technology newsgroups there was an individual who would answer anything that anybody asked; he was Mr. Answer Man. If he didn't know the answer, he'd make it up. We watched him for a few weeks, and he was very knowledgeable, so we did a search on his email address. He was a member of only one other discussion group on the Internet, and that was the Arizona Singles. So we knew that he was technically adept and wanted to meet girls, and so we provided him with a business unit manager who was part of my distributed organization but decidedly female, and engaged him in conversation in the Arizona Singles. He was very appreciative of anybody who expressed even the slightest admiration for his expertise. We worked him for almost 18 months, and it was very helpful. Our experience was that email was effective when in-person was not. When the phone calls weren't being returned, or if we weren't reaching the right people, we found that sending a quick "can you help" and "this is why I'm asking you" email often produced a useful response.

It sounds as if you've also trained others in your various roles. When you're showing somebody the ropes on collecting disparate pieces of information, do you have a standard 5- or 10-step training program?

Almost half of our business is in training. I give a seminar called "CI in a Box," which outlines in one day how you can start up a department that will be effective the next day. Unlike my professional colleagues, I have yet to find any hocus-pocus to this business, so anybody can do it. To define steps, I think about the presentation. The first is to know what you don't know. That's hard, because it means you have to go around your entire organization and build a network with three-by-five cards or a database or something. Sharon Jones has an MSEE (Master of Science in Electrical Engineering) and she used to work at this company, and she is particularly good with fiber optics. You need to do that, so when the question comes down from on high, you have people that you can go to. And then you need to really define what the questions are. Then you look at the gaps and ask, can this be fulfilled by telephone research? Can this be fulfilled by a human source, or do we have to actually go see the product? I like intelligence to be an ongoing, flowing process rather than a start-and-stop project-based thing. And that's what I teach companies to do.

How do you budget your time to put the data together and turn it into a report to the client?

Ten to 15 percent at both ends of the project—first the gathering-up of information, secondary research, framing the questions, and defining a strategy for getting the answers, then 70 to 80 percent for the actual gathering, and then another 10 to 15 percent to put them in a form that the client likes. Some of them prefer a personal presentation, and some of them like text, some want just PowerPoint, some say just give me a voice mail and tell me are they going to do this, yes or no. You have to present to the client in the way that they want to absorb the information. You could deliver a 4-inch-thick binder and their personality might just be to read the executive summary and ignore the rest.

Time is money, and you may have a lot of nice-to-knows that the client's not paying for, but it costs you to go get. You have to get out of the mindset of, "I have to deliver an inch-thick report for $2,000 and a two-inch-thick report for $5,000 and a binder for $10,000," and instead get a sense of what value the client is placing on the answers. In other words, are they going to build a factory based on what you find out, or are they going to change a couple of lines of copy in a brochure? That tells you what the value of the information is, and I think we're here to deliver value to our clients.

Are there certain types of results that clients always want to see, such as an overview of the

industry or financial positioning? Or is it always "just answer this one question"?

If I had to point out one thing that really floats the client's boat, it's verbatim quotes from the interview sources. They like seeing it right from the horse's mouth, even if we don't identify who the source is—which we don't, maybe just their title or something. Your client may have distinct ideas about why the situation he's trying to fix exists, and when the person causing that situation tells him, without editorializing or charts or graphs or any other stuff, it's very attractive to the client. When a source says, "We tried the competition's product and after four months it falls apart. We've seen that a few times, so their product stinks," that's it.

Of all the projects you've done, George, what would you say was the largest coup?

I had an office mate who was not part of the CI organization; he was a CPA, actually a business manager for a product unit. But he was relentlessly aware of what I did because I was his office mate. Now, he was always getting mailers about continuing education for CPAs. He had to take so many hours a year to keep his license current. One of the refresher courses happened to list the CFO of an archrival as the instructor. My roomie thought how great it would be to have a chance to play the intelligence game. The instructor might say something useful during a break, or he could try some of those interview skills that I'd been training everybody else on. My office mate came back the next Monday morning in a state of shock. The rival CFO had used his coming year's financial plan as his course material—80 PowerPoint frames of expected investment, expected rates of return, countries to be opened and closed, products launched and discontinued; it just went on and on. Not only that, there weren't any "confidential" markings on it. I asked him, can this stuff be true? He said, "Do you think he's going to fool a room of 40 CPAs?" We gave him a plaque at the end of the year for capturing this company's coming financial plan.

This haul of valuable data cost us $43 and he got three continuing education credits to boot. What was most gratifying was that somebody was aware that we do this work, and that the information was very important to the company.

And of course we try to recognize the people who take the trouble to bring information to us. Recognition is the scarcest commodity in any large organization. It doesn't cost anything to give, but people will jump through their own eyeballs to get some. We had a successful worldwide network of people contributing information consistently because we recognized them for their effort. The intelligence department put out a weekly newsletter, so when someone sent us an email saying they heard this at a breakfast meeting where these three guys were sitting at the table and they didn't ask who I was, they were just yakking away and here's what we got—we recognized and applauded them for it in front of the whole company. I would re-edit what they told us as an article, give the sales guy or whoever it was out in the field the byline, and suddenly he was recognized all over the company. That's all it takes, really. People will continue to bring you stuff to get company-wide recognition.

How about your worst nightmare or your most serious lesson learned?

I haven't had any true nightmares. I've walked away from some really great gifts of information. Once, a competitor's proposal wound up on my desk in a plain brown wrapper because some idiot inside the customer's organization thought he was doing us a favor. What do we do with this; can we even peek? Things like that.

I think my worst fear is either missing a great information opportunity that completely changes what we think the outcome of the issue's going to be, or inadvertently getting ourselves or one of our sources into real trouble. We had a legal–ethical behavior procedure, so anything in question, like that proposal, we sent to legal. The lawyer called and said that we had a nondisclosure (NDA) with this company; maybe we could try to twist that so we could read this thing. They tried for three days to interpret the NDA in all different ways and realized that they couldn't, so without having looked at the proposal, they called a courier service with the locked briefcase and the whole bit, and sent him off to the headquarters of the competitor with a note that said some well-meaning dope sent us this, we haven't read it, you just have to take it on faith that we haven't and, as a measure of good faith, here is your proposal back. That's about the best you can do.

How do you stay current and confident with your strategies and resources? You mentioned that your CPA friend had no choice but to go and earn three credits a year. How do you augment your experience in order to keep up with strategies and information sources?

I certainly keep up my Rolodex. I spend a great deal of time making sure that the addresses and email addresses are current. If something bounces back, we go find the person if they've been useful in the past. That contact list is not just information sources but also people who know a lot about industries and people who know a lot about the Internet, who know a lot about searching, who know a lot about the law, all kinds of things. You have to be a people person to do this kind of work.

I read a lot of history, particularly how the intelligence agencies of all the major countries have evolved and how they operate. What I told you earlier about the alumni party at the trade show was actually modeled on something called *The Sword and the Shield* [182]. Right after the Russian Revolution, Felix Dzerzinsky, the head of Lenin's secret service, actually set up an *anti*-Bolshevik organization. All of the Czarists joined up; the United States even sent it money. That way they had a good list and a close look at all the people who might possibly try to overthrow the Reds. That was the model for the alumni party. And there are other ways you can apply how governments have worked to the CI environment.

What skill set or formal education do you feel an individual needs in order to be successful in performing competitive intelligence?

You have to understand how business works, and a general business education would probably be the minimum. My specialty is actually the trade show, and organizing field operations and training. I didn't come through school as a trainer; I have an undergraduate degree as a marketer. But you need a very broad general knowledge so that you can address some of the really odd things that you come across. And then you find the smart people to flesh it out for you.

You need a lot of curiosity. You should also be a little bit skeptical. No one goes to war on one data point, but you can get one great piece of information and have it color your whole analysis; without some confirmation, you're really on thin ice. But I had that skepticism from my press background; we really tried to make sure that what we said was so, *was* so. "I don't know" has to be a fair answer as well. If you are going to attempt human source collection you have to be a people person.

What do you enjoy most about the profession?

When I was in sales I sold two-way radios, like you'd find in a plumber's truck or a garbage truck, and what I found most interesting was learning about how the other person's business worked. What were the key drivers and the key liabilities and the big risks and all the ins and outs of running a concrete company, for example. It is always more complex than meets the eye. CI compels me to learn about an industry or about a product or about an issue—or about people, because we do psychological profiling as well. But I don't have to live with any particular one. I have a short attention span; I like new situations to come along. So this is a good business to be in. I can do a project and learn something. Each project, of course, teaches you a better way of doing projects, or a snappier way to do the deliverable. I both love it and hate it when the client is so pleased they say "you really could have charged a lot more for this."

What do you like the least?

The fact that CI is not as understood or as demanded as it should be. Also the fact that sometimes you do your best work and then find out that management really didn't want to know. That was very frustrating in my corporate life. We would make recommendations and set up operations and write reports, but it didn't seem to go anywhere, didn't seem to have a great deal of influence. You have to be comfortable with the fact that you did a great job, you did it by the rules, you got the answers or you have good indicators of what we think the answers are. We made a pretty good educated guess, let's call it a day right there.

If you want to be a mover and shaker, you will not and cannot be in this business, because you're a necessary evil in a lot of the boardrooms. It doesn't matter if you have good news or bad news. Either way, you're going to go the CEO and say, this is what the situation is. He's going to have to do something, either real-locate resources or change his strategy or do something other than what he'd planned on, either to avoid a threat or to capture an opportunity, or he's going to look like an idiot. And boy, they don't like having their boats rocked. That's why you try to look as far in the future as possible, so that you have lots of time to make changes and reallocate your energies while there is still time to apply what's been learned.

Super Searcher Power Tips

➤ Make sure you familiarize yourself with all the available sources of information: print, personal, online. Understand the limitations of each. Become very good at one of them.

➤   If you do human source collection, then get very good at interviewing people, knowing that, on the downside, they could be lying. You have to find someone else to corroborate what you've heard.

➤   Understand what your information is going to be used for. Something may come along out of the context of your project that might really be important, but you don't know that unless you know where the project is going.

➤   Leave the Net searching to people who are real bulldogs and have blinders on.

➤   When summarizing results for delivery to the client, whether it's a presentation, magazine article, or report, pretend it's Western Union and you're paying for every word. You can probably take 15 percent of the words out of a report and not lose one iota of meaning, but it will be easier to read.

Ann Potter
On-Site Intelligence Gathering

Ann Potter is President of Ann Potter and Associates, a Minneapolis-based consulting firm specializing in customized research for strategic planning and product/market development. Her background includes work in corporate and governmental environments, and on a wide variety of industries and products. The goal of her business is to help clients make smarter decisions by providing them with a clearer view of the competitive scene through intelligence gathering, analysis, and recommendations.

ap@annpotter.net

Tell me a bit about your background, and how and when you started performing competitive intelligence.

I have an undergrad degree in international relations and political science, and I also took several English courses. I have an MBA in market research, and I've also taken a lot of journalism classes. I had a four-year stint in the corporate world, in two different jobs—strategic planning for a heavy equipment manufacturer and a physical vapor deposition process development start-up—then a two-year stint in state government, where I worked in Minnesota's World Trade Office on agriculture trade issues and economic development. So I've been my own boss for 16 years now, and I love it. Starting around 1992–93, I really got into competitive intelligence when clients started to ask me to do it more and more often. I realized I had a knack for it, and I loved the challenge and creativity, so I just expanded my repertoire to meet my clients' needs.

How would you describe your function in a nutshell? How would you describe a typical project?

Our function is to make clients thrilled, in terms of the information and insights we can bring them. But I try not to define myself too tightly. I go against what all the business plan models say about specializing in an industry. I really am a true business research generalist. And I use both primary and secondary research skill sets, so I can act as my client's de facto research department.

We can subcontract out parts of a job, keep it all inside, or whatever seems to fit. So my role really varies; sometimes I'm an active team player with the client from the very start, sometimes I'm sent off to put together my own team, and sometimes I'm the lonely hunter and gatherer. It all depends on the client, and of course for every job we wear a different combination of hats: the librarian hat, the detective hat, the investigative reporter hat.

For some projects, competitive intelligence is 20 to 25 percent of what I do, but other jobs are 100 percent CI, and some have hardly any aspect of CI in them. I've done work in several industries: financial services, construction—I'm doing a lot in construction right now—and energy, as well as food and medical devices. The mix has tended to reflect the economy of the upper Midwest. But then again, I get a fair amount of global work: Japan, Australia, Denmark, Nepal, and so on.

And that's part of the appeal of this business for me; I love the variety. I took some journalism classes because at one time I wanted to be an investigative reporter. Those skills have come in very handy—having to learn an industry quickly, having to learn the vocabulary, the players. It's also a form of anthropology, being plunged into a new culture. So the idea of focusing on one specific industry for my entire life makes me a little nervous. Not that I haven't built up a strong expertise in certain industries that I like; I have! But I like the challenge of applying skills and insights learned from one industry to another.

I've read that not only do you gather information from secondary and primary research sources, you actually go on location to gather specialized information. Can you give me an example of a project that involved that kind of work?

We were asked to work on assessing value-added opportunities for specialty pears. The up-front work included literature searching and source identification. I then traveled to orchards, packing houses, processing plants, equipment suppliers, and retail outlets, really learning about each stage of pear processing. Our prime objective was to educate the client about the nature of the industry, so we could go on to the next step. That step was finding successful value-added "model" products made from other specialty produce, learning how these products were made and marketed, and checking with pear processing experts as to how feasible these models—freeze dried, individually quick frozen (IQF), fresh-cut product, new preservatives, etc.—would be for pears.

It was exciting and challenging to be asked to "find out how this industry works, and locate the opportunities for us." While the original research objectives did not specify any competitor-specific intelligence, we *did* uncover great information on specific equipment, processes, and forthcoming innovations from a couple of key industry competitors, all of which thrilled the client.

How would you define competitive intelligence vs. just doing research or business research?

It's about context, a way of thinking, a certain mindset while you are conducting the research that goes beyond fact-finding or number-crunching or cut-and-paste. You have to know enough about the client and his situation to be fully conscious of the market, the industry, and the drivers behind the need for your information. It's an ongoing sense of the impact of what you could uncover, the ramifications of what even the smallest piece could mean for the client.

It's also about seeing the process in an ongoing competitive context. Like it or not, the competitive environment "parade" keeps marching by, every day, with environmental regulatory changes, patent expiration dates, changing consumer tastes, supply chain kinks, not to mention pure innovation. The toughest part comes when the client doesn't have this same way of thinking about CI's ongoing nature, when the client sees CI as a one-shot deal.

What do you feel is essential in your CI toolkit?

Ah, the desert island question. First off, a phone and access to the Internet. I would add the AIIP (Association of Independent Information Professionals) [229, see Appendix] and SCIP (Society of Competitive Intelligence Professionals) [258] directories, and I'd also throw in the *Encyclopedia of Associations* [118], *Ulrich's Periodicals Directory* [187], and *Fulltext Sources Online* [131]. I'd also put in a very good road atlas and world atlas, and other maps. I'm really a visual person, so I like to know what the terrain looks like, where the roads are. It's critical when you're dealing with plant sites and traffic patterns. I'd add a good, relevant industry directory, whatever the industry happens to be. I would want my local library in my toolkit. We're lucky enough in St. Paul to have the James J. Hill Business Reference Library [51], which is just wonderful. I would also include some contact management software. And I'd include a big white board; I like to draw patterns of distribution channels, organization charts, and other notes, and it's helpful to be able to just look up at what's on the wall while I'm on the phone with someone. Finally I'd throw in a telephone headset and a good camera—with fresh batteries.

How do you weigh Internet and for-fee database services in your workflow and research methods?

In the first phase of a CI job, it's critical to lay a solid secondary foundation. I rely on both Internet and fee-based services to learn an industry and identify possible contacts. On a typical job, I would say it's a 70-30 split—70 percent fee-based database services and 30 percent Internet—but it really depends on the job. It might be 60-40, or even 20-80. But in later phases of the job—contact development, phoning, field work, and so on—the Net becomes more of a quick-reference tool to follow up on new leads, new competitors, new contacts, or trends that float to the surface in the course of the job.

How do you cope when you've made some headway on a search, turned up a few leads, and then you reach a bunch of dead ends? What do you do?

I take a shower. I don't know why, but there's something about water that helps me think up new avenues, new people to call, new rocks to turn over. It's just a cleansing thing for my brain, and it usually works. It's always critical to manage client expectations, and to know when to warn the client that we may not find as much as we'd thought. But you can't just stop. It's like being in a bullfight. Sometimes I think of myself as the picador; if I throw enough spears at this bull from different angles, something dramatic will happen. I have to trust that it will. And it does.

Once you've done your background and secondary research to come up with primary contact information and flesh out the leads,

what are your next steps? Do you have a particular order in which you systematically deal with information as you go down the road?

I do subconsciously go through a series of phases. After the secondary phase, there's usually what I call a digestive pause. You just stop, review everything—and make sure you've got all the stuff from the client that they were supposed to send over—and then you start to strategize: What have we got? Where are we weak? What do we need to find out more about? Do we need to add to the methodology, do more internal interviews, and so on. Then comes what I call the hit list compilation stage: Finding the appropriate gurus, association people, brokers, former employees, editor types, mutual competitors, and so on. You start to put a list together, compiling relevant background information on these people as you strategize about how to approach them.

The next phase is making actual contact, working the list. It's critical to prioritize that stage. I agree with Michael Sandman from Fuld [239], who talks about working from the outside in, in terms of concentric rings of increasing proximity to the competitor. So the first calls are most likely to those people farthest from the competitor, and then you work your way in. I call this the "churning" stage. You're contacting people, digging up new leads, reviewing new search results, ordering new avenues of investigation—including secondary research—and sharing preliminary notes with other team members. And your brain is constantly switching thought processes, back and forth, from tactical to strategic, from nearsighted to farsighted and back. It's a focused, all-encompassing effort. And then the final step covers summarization and analysis, with scenarios and implications for the client.

CI has been called a parade that never stops marching past you. But I also have an image of a pyramid. You keep building this pyramid, but the pyramid keeps moving ahead, like it's on wheels. A lot of what's out there in print on CI makes the whole process sound scientific, formulaic, almost plug-and-play. But it's an organic process as well, and you have to make room for the serendipitous event to happen. You have to keep the chimney open for that elusive gift to fall through. And unless you make some space and *allow* such an event to happen, it may not happen.

How often do you end up analyzing the information yourself and presenting a finished product to your client, vs. handing over projects to senior analysts in a company to massage with their internal information?

I have a pretty solid report when I'm finished, but how it gets incorporated into the bigger picture at the corporate level varies. Often I hand over my finished report to the CI individual who combines it with their own internal research, but not always. I've done lots of presentations to rooms of senior execs, too. So it really varies, depending on a lot of factors—internal capabilities, breadth or scope of the project, research objectives. It might also depend on the client's own level of sophistication or insecurity. With some clients, you're left wondering whether the information will have an effect. Will it ever be listened to? That's when I have to go home and wallpaper the hallway, or something else that makes a big dramatic impact.

Do you have a standard model or template to organize your research results? Or is everything customized, varying from finding trends that support a rumor to "give me everything about this current entrant into the market place"?

I don't have any standard templates. I customize my efforts to the individual client, and it's rare that I ever have similar types of CI projects. Some clients will provide a grid or laundry list or outline to work from. But I mostly use Microsoft Word [212] with a lot of tables, PowerPoint [211], and Excel [209] files.

These days my clients are asking us for the tougher stuff, about production capacity, margins, likely behavior, distribution strategies, sales force structures, customer trends. They're not too picky about what form it comes back in, as long as results are solid and presented in a manner that they can quickly assimilate. Visuals are always important to get the message across. My clients seem to really love grids these days.

When you're budgeting your project time, what percentage do you allocate to performing the secondary and primary research, the results organization, and articulating the findings to the client?

This is one of those "depends on the job" answers. A given job can run from two days to two weeks to six months. You might make a couple phone calls to an industry you already know a lot about, or you might need more time to get to know a whole industry, which could take a number of weeks or months, especially if you're coordinating global efforts. Fuld estimates that 10 percent of CI effort goes to secondary and 90 percent of it to primary. But for me, a lot of the primary includes some secondary sprinkled in here and there, so it's tough to measure. Regarding results organization, if I'm doing it right, I should be compiling results as I'm going along. After all, to construct a good pyramid you need to find the information gaps and fill 'em as you're going up the slope.

Do your clients expect certain types of results, like an executive summary, that are essential to report consistently?

It's a balancing act. It's important to provide a context for your findings: Why are the results the way they are? What are the implications for the client? Yet you never want to spend your client's budget on what they already know. So it's important to have a good reference interview up front with the client, to gain a sense of what the client knows and doesn't know, and what pieces could provide additional value. You not only start from a higher foundation, but you prepare your sixth sense to recognize the "a-ha!" factors you'll run across later on.

Are there software products that you have found particularly helpful in your research and analysis processes, perhaps for tracking Web pages or monitoring news?

Not too many. MS Word, Excel, and PowerPoint, as I mentioned, and I use Office Accelerator [216] by Baseline Data Systems, Inc. for my contact management software. I'm not sure why; over the years I've just gotten used to it. I've also been using Infominder [202] for tracking changes in Web pages. It seems to work well, notifying me via email based on my time window, the number of changes, and so on.

You spoke about the a-ha! factor. What would you say was your largest coup out of all the projects that you've done in the last 14 to 16 years?

We did the legwork and were able to inform our client that their number-one customer, worth tens of millions in annual sales, had formed a joint venture with our client's number-one competitor, and that they were planning to jointly develop and operate a new facility right under our client's nose. Our client totally refused to believe our findings, saying, "no, no, this customer is wonderful, it's been a great relationship." But later, when he called up his best customer and learned the truth of our findings, he was impressed, and grateful. That was a pretty satisfying job.

Another client was planning to invest a huge amount of second-round capital extending an R&D effort on a specific production process. Our extensive fieldwork uncovered the fact that the client's proposed process was much less cost-effective than other processes used by the rest of the industry. We also uncovered production data that told how the industry was already awash in excess capacity. So basically we told them to stop work and forget it, and they did.

How about on the other side; what project became your worst nightmare or largest lesson learned?

I don't know if it's a nightmare, but it sure was aggravating. Once, while we were working on a new product CI job, our client hired a young, naïve marketing type who decided to brag to the industry about the new product they were thinking of launching. Our team still managed to get the information the client wanted, but he made it a lot tougher.

Lessons learned? I have this memory of being at a technical conference as a tall American female, trying to strike up a casual conversation with four introverted Japanese scientists. It didn't work very well. I needed to be a small male scientist. Lesson: It's important to recognize one's limits.

How do you stay current and competent with your strategies and your resources?

It's tough. There's a lot of ink out there on competitive intelligence, a lot being published. But I find that there's not much actually being said, especially about tactics. And most of it seems to be aimed at the corporate level, rather than at independent, project-oriented vendors. I end up reading a lot of trade journals in my clients' industries to keep up on what trends are happening, regulatory changes, and the mindsets of decision makers. I look at general information industry sources too, such as *Searcher* [174], *Information Today* [136], and *Online* [158].

What skill set or education do you feel an individual needs to be successful in performing competitive intelligence? Has your MBA held you in good stead?

The MBA has helped, but probably the most valuable classes I took were in journalism—basic reporting, specifically. We were forced to get on the phone, track down strangers, put them at ease, and get them to tell us what we wanted to know. So the skill set list would include developing phone skills—feeling comfortable talking to strangers, sometimes hostile strangers—and other skills of persuasion, persistence, and bravery. A new CI would also need analytical, writing, communication, and presentation skills, which are critical to provide the client with findings and implications of real value, along with some concise, bottom-line recommendations.

One also needs to possess many of the same skills that are needed for general business research—that love of investigating, hunting and gathering, creative thinking about possible sources, assimilating disparate items, and parallel tracking—the ability to run down different avenues in your brain at the same time. But then, there's that little extra something: If you're not the kind of person who's haunted by rocks not yet turned over, people not yet called, or connections not yet made, then I don't think CI is the right job for you.

What do you enjoy most about being in the profession?

The learning. I love the variety. Where else do you get paid to learn about third-party administrators, fresh produce, trust funds, and insulin pumps? It's great! I especially enjoy identifying trends and patterns across industries, in distribution, production, common marketing tricks, and so on. And I love the creativity, not only in selecting secondary sources but also in choosing and locating primary sources and selecting the right methodologies for each approach. It's also extraordinary to select and manage a customized team of CI specialists. And finally, there's the absolute thrill of finding the unfindable. It is tremendously satisfying to have the chance to amaze our clients by giving them detailed answers they never dreamed were possible to find.

And what do you like least?

It can be stressful. There's a lot of pressure in getting to a key contact and making the most of the interview. You've got to be very cool about things. Especially while you are trying to manage an impatient client who unexpectedly says, "Just stop halfway and give me everything you have." You can't just slice up results like French bread. You are building a pyramid, and being halfway through it doesn't mean you have half the results. So it can be a balancing act, managing expectations and educating the client about the CI process itself. And then there is the constant challenge of educating internal CI managers to become the internal hero, stress the value of CI to top management, and gain CI support and budgets.

Super Searcher Power Tips

➤ Develop great phone skills. Learn to sound earnest and convincing. Be respectful, yet persuasive. Consider taking some reporting classes. Learn to ask questions of strangers.

➤ Understand your targeted industries. Learn the language, trends, players, and customers, so you can predict the next question your client will have.

➤ Select some contact management software and learn it. Start building your own phone books of experts you can contact by industry.

➤ Work closely with your client to gain their trust and educate them about the value of sharing as much information as possible with you up front, and then work together on analysis. If the outside CI person hasn't been let in early on a lot of inner workings, he or she can only go so far.

➤ Get to know your local business reference librarians. "Take a librarian to lunch." They're all smart, fun people who can help you with elusive resources, or just brainstorming.

➤ Get a monthly massage, more often if you can afford it. CI is a pressure-packed line of work. Your body will thank you.

Roberta Piccoli

Client and Consumer Intelligence

After beginning her career at the *Chicago Tribune* analyzing consumer and retail trends in the Chicago market, Roberta Piccoli spent 21 years at J. Walter Thompson where she analyzed national competitors and consumer trends in more than 60 industries. More recently at FutureBrand in New York, Roberta led a team to create and implement a global intranet. Leveraging her advertising, marketing, and consumer intelligence experience, she founded her own business, Search Source, which enables its clients to build sound strategic planning decisions through research and analysis of competitors, industries, and consumer trends. As a consultant, Roberta also designs and implements strategies to maximize the benefit of internal and external information to an organization's bottom line. She is currently based in New York.

rapiccoli@yahoo.com

Note: This interview was conducted via email.

Tell me about your background and how and when you started performing competitive intelligence.

After earning a BA in history and English and a master's degree in Library and Information Science from Dominican University, I began doing competitive intelligence without knowing it, on my first job in the *Chicago Tribune*'s marketing research department. We were often asked to quantify consumer buying habits and to update demographic information. But early on, I needed to conduct primary research to create a published quarterly report on new retailers and shopping center developments in the eight-county Chicago metropolitan area. In preparing that report, I contacted competitors throughout the building and development industries, so I consider that my earliest competitive intelligence project.

Next, at J. Walter Thompson's Information Center, I learned from a crack team how to find competitive intelligence in over 60 industries, as we identified our clients' current niche after comparisons with their competitors. We did analysis to pinpoint challenges and opportunities for our clients. For strategic planning, we also needed to study past consumer behavior, charting past practices to gauge trends. From our research and analysis, the ad agency would plan the unique and most advantageous positioning. Determining the prime consumer target groups and building an integrated communication plan to effectively reach these groups were also critical elements. Our research intersected with professionals throughout the agency to grow our client's reputation and business. In the last three years, we launched and marketed a global intranet to improve access and communication throughout the firm. I also designed and implemented a dedicated competitive intelligence unit to conduct more in-depth research and analysis, and to brief client and new business teams on our findings.

After 21 years at J. Walter Thompson, creating and launching a global intranet for the brand consulting firm FutureBrand in New York proved to be an irresistible and satisfying challenge. We created an online vehicle to showcase case studies, product design images, training modules, and capabilities pieces. Understanding the competitive landscape proved a real advantage as we built the framework and chose, then edited, the case studies.

How would you describe your current function in a nutshell?

In my own business, I partner with all types of organizations to offer customized competitive intelligence, specifically research and analysis that contributes to solving business problems. I've developed a talent for homing in on company background on my clients and their competitors, and combining product knowledge with the prediction of consumer behavior, based on studying lifestyle and purchase trends. Consulting gives me the opportunity to listen, then to design a process, which may include new technology tools and services, to most fully leverage information to benefit an organization's bottom line.

What types of research have you done, and do you perform now?

At J. Walter Thompson we provided focused business research on 60 clients and industries in seven U.S. offices. During my 21 years there, our research was always "filleted" to highlight the key company and industry trends. By "filleted," I mean that only focused articles, which featured highlighted passages of pertinent data, were given to our internal clients. Our opportunities to do more robust analysis were limited because of the large number of client requests. Our average project turnaround was 24 hours. Realizing that leaner agency-wide staffing and the increasing demands of our clients called for a new approach, I designed and implemented a dedicated Competitive Intelligence unit. We turned focused research into analysis that pinpointed client and industry challenges and opportunities. We delivered trends reports with an oral briefing. From there, the account, planning, and creative teams could move more quickly and efficiently to build effective client strategies and win new business. Industries we explored included health insurance, computer services, and consumer packaged goods.

As Director of Knowledge Management at McCann-Erickson's brand consulting arm, FutureBrand, in New York, I led a team to successfully design and launch a global intranet. Its purpose was to make the firm's "best thinking" more accessible. It was used for training, compiling capabilities presentations, and building innovative solutions to client issues.

Over the last 20 years, my individual competitive intelligence projects have included marketing encyclopedias in electronic formats, women's health, deregulation trends for electric utilities, and programs to stimulate consumer and employee loyalty. I have delivered fact books, reports, spreadsheets, presentations, and briefings.

How do you feel CI differs from business research? How do you define CI?

Competitive intelligence begins with business research and supplements it with primary research and interviews as needed to analyze markets, products, industries, and consumer behavior. Competitive intelligence identifies the challenges and opportunities ahead to enable better business decisions. At its best, its practitioners keep abreast of the mission of their parent organization so that they continually focus their competitive intelligence efforts on the key issues facing their firm.

What is essential in your CI toolkit?

Besides a telephone, computer, and Internet access, I consider the following resources to be invaluable: *The Encyclopedia of Associations* [118, see Appendix] gives me a quick survey of specialized trade and not-for-profit organizations with contact phone numbers if I need to check for specialized research and experts in a given field. The *Standard Rate & Data Service (SRDS) Directory of Business Publications* [177] allows a quick survey of those trade publications devoted to a given industry, along with their representatives, who are knowledgeable in their industry. The *Statistical Abstract of the United States* [178] provides the latest statistics, from demographics to food consumption, along with the government or private source for these figures.

How do you weigh Internet and for-fee database services in your workflow and research methods?

First, I use the Internet to experiment with terms and to identify initial trends and key organizations. Secondly, I use the for-fee database services to create tighter searches over a broad array of sources in one step. For example, using the "reduce duplication" feature in Dialog [20], I can conduct a search in a customized set of sources chosen from a wide range of commercial sources. Once I have read and digested this research, I turn back to the Internet to see if I can plug any gaps in the research before conducting interviews.

What do you do when you are in the middle of a search and just not finding what you want or what you believe exists?

I take a 10-minute break to stand up, drink a glass of water, walk around the room and stretch. Then I rethink my original strategy and review the terms I have used in my search to see if I can find another way to approach the topic. If I'm satisfied with the search strategy, then I call the trade association and/or major trade publications serving the industry, and double-check to be sure there are no strategies or sources that I have overlooked. I read and highlight the research to mine everything that secondary sources can supply. Then I conduct phone interviews to fill in any gaps that remain. Next, I prepare the analysis with the agreed-upon objectives of the project clearly in mind.

How and when do you interface with the process folks? Do you ever turn your work over to a senior analyst or CI individual who combines your external research with internal information? What happens once you're done with the research?

In my early years at J. Walter Thompson, my "filleted" business research would go to a planner who would determine if primary research was needed and, if so, execute it. That might be a large-scale survey or focus groups or an Internet-based survey. Later at JWT, we analyzed the business research and delivered a report and oral briefing that identified challenges and opportunities facing our clients. Now, in my own business, I conduct the business research and interviews, present the analysis, then recommend and partner with a specialist in large-scale primary research if it proves to be necessary.

Do you use a standard model or template to organize your research results? Why or why not?

In the new business development work at J. Walter Thompson, we did use a template. We filled in many of the same categories when we looked at a prospective client. Besides exploring its industry's challenges overall, we pulled the client's or its parent company's financials. We researched, then analyzed the client's marketing history, then highlighted the latest marketing trends. Top executives' biographies gave us insight into our potential marketing partners. Past ad agency and advertising, including media vehicles used, were important indicators of client strategy. Then we identified and studied our clients' competitors before comparing our client's products to the competitors' products. We also included Web site URLs for our client and their top competitors, along with analyses of each one's positioning.

Today, each of my Search Source projects is so different that in each case the client and I agree on the objectives, the decision to be made, and the most useful final format for the project.

What road map would you present to a researcher newly assigned to a CI function?

Learn all you can about the internal or external client's business and listen carefully to their goals. Before you start, be sure that you understand what decision they will make based on the competitive intelligence project that you provide. Get a clear agreement in writing from your internal or external client that details this objective, what you will deliver, its format, and when it will be completed.

How much time do you allocate to the secondary research, primary research, and results organization?

I allocate approximately 30 percent to the secondary research, 15 percent to the primary research, and 55 percent to the organization and analysis, although it can vary. More primary research may be necessary if I find little in publicly available sources.

What types of results are essential to report—such as overview, financial position, risks?

Since most of my client projects focus on advertising and marketing objectives, financial trending is less important. My projects will always include an industry overview, profiles of the major players, their products, their market positioning, and the challenges and opportunities ahead.

What software products do you use for applications like post-search processing or Web page tracking?

Actually, none. I rely on Microsoft Office [210] for all my needs such as word processing, spreadsheet, and presentations. Adobe Acrobat [195] is also essential. I am reviewing products that lead to more relevant Internet search results.

What was your largest coup?

When I identified and profiled top candidates for director of a not-for-profit organization at the request of the Ford CEO, it proved that I could use mostly primary research to succeed in an area that I normally did not research.

And your worst nightmare?

Trying to find the top advertising agency mission statements for the previous five years. First, very few ad agency marketing campaigns were detailed in the press. Although I tried Web sites, they were not as advanced as the ones we see now, and they may only show the most current mission statement anyway. When I turned to primary research, few agency information professionals could even name a well-defined current mission statement, much less the progression of mission statements over the last five years.

How do you stay current and confident with your strategies and resources?

I roam the exhibit areas of professional conferences and listen to pitches that, at the time, may seem unrelated to my core business, then fully digest the vendors' literature and demos when I get home. I listen to colleagues at professional conferences discussing their challenges and techniques, as well as reading professional literature. Society of Competitive Intelligence Professionals (SCIP) [258] publications, AIIP (Association of Independent Information Professionals) [229] list messages, and Special Libraries Association [259] publications are all important sources for the latest techniques and technology.

Knowledge management sources also keep me abreast of the latest trends, and their Web sites permit topic searches. Some of the ones I use are Brint.com [10], *KMWorld* [145], the Knowledge Management Resource [54], the Knowledge Management Server at the University of Texas at Austin [55], *Knowledge Management News* [146], and *CIO Magazine*'s Knowledge Management Research Center [53].

Fast Company magazine [121] and my local *Crain's New York Business* [111] are both essential. The *Wall Street Journal* [193] and its online *CareerJournal* [100] site are also staples. I browse, then choose to read some of the latest business strategy books that I see in airports and bookstores. In looking back, I still value my copies of *Working Knowledge: How Organizations Manage What They Know* [194] by Thomas H. Davenport and Laurence Prusak and *Intellectual Capital: The New Wealth of*

Organizations [137] by Thomas A. Stewart. Both have influenced and inspired my career.

What skill set/education does an individual need to be successful in performing CI?

My college double major in history and English has served me well, and the master's degree in library and information science has proven invaluable for knowing how to strategize and approach a project. But I think the main attributes of a successful competitive intelligence professional would be imagination, tenacity, integrity, and a passion for stepping into the client's shoes.

What do you enjoy most about this profession?

I thrive on the variety of client challenges. It's like working through a new maze every day. I can't imagine a more satisfying profession than taking raw information, then analyzing and focusing it to solve a business problem.

And what do you like least?

Finding that the role of business researchers is all too often regarded as a second-class contribution to the competitive intelligence product. The quality, thoroughness, and efficiency of their research are critical to the power of the final CI analysis.

Is there anything else you think I should know?

If, in the course of your business research and interviews, you discover anything unfavorable to the client, it is critical that you deliver that insight to the client. Competitive intelligence should provide the earliest possible warning system to a client. Once competitive intelligence has proven to be invaluable, it will be a critical component of the decision-making process from there on out.

Super Searcher Power Tips

➤ Obtain a clear agreement with your client of the objectives, the decision to be made, and the expected deliverables of the project. Make sure that any mutually agreed upon changes that will affect either the costs or the content of the project are documented in at least an email acknowledgement.

➤ Whenever possible, research existing and public sources first, then scan the output to identify gaps before interviewing industry sources and experts. In fact, the articles you find may identify industry experts to call. By immersing yourself in the industry first, you can make better use of the interview subject's time to probe for unique insights.

➤ When you initiate a call, have a script ready that briefly tells who you are and why you are calling, as well as how long you estimate your questions will take. Have an outline of the questions you would like answered, but be ready to capture unexpected insights they may offer that you never thought to ask about.

➤ When working from a home office, it helps to stand when you initiate a call. Smile and show that you find the challenges of that industry fascinating as you ask each question. Be sure that the interview participant feels you appreciate their expertise and contribution to their industry. Clarify your notes from each interview and briefly process what you have learned before turning to your next, improved interview.

➤   Trade shows can be extremely valuable for discovering a great deal about an industry in a short time.

➤   If the client does not specify a desired format, choose the one that best showcases the key information needed for decision making so that it can be assimilated quickly.

Deborah Sawyer

CI Services Marketing

Deborah Sawyer is President of the Information Plus group of companies, with research and consulting service offices in both the United States and Canada. In addition to working for Fortune 500 corporations, her own experience in operating research companies, a business writing seminar firm, and a health consultancy has given her an inside track on what it's like to compete in services and how difficult it can be to learn about the competition. She is the author of four books about information and has published numerous articles, including a regular column for *Competitive Intelligence Magazine*.

www.sawyerbooks.com

Can you tell me about your background, and how and when you started performing competitive intelligence?

I have a degree in Library Science. When I first started Information Plus I was actually doing indexing, which has nothing to do with research. But over the years, people asked me and my staff to perform information retrieval tasks, and that evolved into research. Then, out of that, came the specific application of research for competitive intelligence. We started performing competitive intelligence in the early '80s, and we did competitive intelligence work through to the mid to late '90s. At this point in time, we have two or three clients we still perform it for.

How would you describe your function in a nutshell?

My function within the company is to meet with clients. I do nearly all the client contact work and then act as research director for the projects. Part of my responsibility is finding out exactly what the client is looking for, and that involves going to the client meetings, usually sitting down and having some in-depth discussion of their objectives and the problems they're trying to solve.

What types of research have you performed over the years?

It runs the gamut. We did customer/client, lost account, and prospect research for companies involved in business-to-business markets. We researched and built customized, qualitative databases for business-to-business direct marketing. We did market and industry research. We researched products and people. We supported merger and acquisition decisions, new product launches, sales campaigns, litigation, and more. And we did this successfully in more than a dozen industries.

How do you feel CI differs from business research, and how do you define CI?

It differs in how the information is used. In terms of the actual methodologies used or sources that you tap, there probably isn't a lot of difference. It's a question of how the outcome is interpreted and how it's used that differs.

What sources do you feel are essential in your CI toolkit?

As far as primary research goes, it's not really any particular source, like a database or library-type material. Being able to ask good questions is the most essential tool in our toolkit. It's also a good idea to keep an eye open for eclectic sources; you never know when an association of dowsers or a collector of industrial weights and measures may be able to assist you. It's not a given that the sources you need will be designated "business" sources. Sometimes "realia"—or artifacts if you prefer that term—can come in handy. Over the years, we did a lot of work in the area of smoking cessation and we purchased a whole variety of patches, gums, pellules, and so on to assist in our work. There's also what might be termed the experiential source, where you actually experience a service or product in order to gather information. One time, we were looking at the home energy audit industry, so our researchers all volunteered their homes to experience what the different companies offered. However, you have to know when to say no; we drew the line at volunteering our eyes while researching intraocular lenses.

How do you weigh the Internet and the for-fee database services in your work flow, and in terms of the research methods used to collect CI information?

We wouldn't rely on any of the secondary information, whether it's databases or Web sites or library materials, for more than about 10 percent of any project. We would use that material to look for sources and for angles, in preparation for doing the interviews. It's not something we'd rely on heavily; we've actually done projects where we didn't use online or secondary stuff at all. We just knew that, because it was so new a product that the client was bringing out, that no one had written anything about it, and there wouldn't be any point in looking for it. In Canada, there's often nothing anyway, so we're very used to working without any kind of secondary sources; whether it's Internet or for-fee database services, there isn't as much material available.

What would you do when you're in the middle of a search and just not finding what you

wanted or what you thought you could get to? How would you re-gear?

We'd never rely 100 percent on, say, online; we would always use libraries and print sources as backup. That might mean ads or promotional literature or some sort of material that is not indexed, either online or in print. For example, when we worked in the financial services industry, we would send our researchers out to the bank branches if we were targeting a particular company, do onsite visits and gather up what they were giving out in the branches, to see if they were promoting themselves a certain way and what was going on. That's very much a grass-roots approach. If we did get into an online search and didn't find anything, it didn't really stump us because we had all these other options we would turn to as a matter of course.

You've stated that sometimes you can't start with secondary research, because it's just not something that would lend itself to that process. Can you tell me how you determined when you would hop onto the primary research first, and your process from there on?

We would have a 1-2-3-step approach that we used if we were targeting a particular company. We would not go directly to that company with the primary research. Once we'd done the secondary or preliminary kinds of searching and had some background to go on, we would look at third-party sources, which might be associations, industry groups, regulators, some organizations very much on the periphery, who might have some insight into the broader issues. When we'd done that, we would move on to second-party sources, which might be customers, suppliers, trade unions, and other parties or groups that deal directly with the target. Then and only then would we proceed to actually making direct contact with the target company.

Once you accumulated that information, did you package it in any particular way?

We always handed in a complete report with charts of the findings, the verbatims of the interviews we'd done, and any background material we felt was pertinent. We used a general framework that included "Notes to the Research" as a starting point. We would report our research process, and if there were any particular obstacles or issues that we had encountered and wanted the client to know about, we reported those as well. We always included an executive summary and, in some cases, additional section summaries with concise presentations of the findings. We also included interview results, and a listing of background materials and sources consulted. Beyond that general template, we would customize quite heavily with each particular research project, allowing the results themselves to dictate the structure.

What road map would you present to a researcher newly assigned to a competitive intelligence function?

My answer would vary depending upon whether you're talking about someone who's working in a client company as opposed to a supplier such as ourselves. There are also variations from industry to industry, in terms of where to go for a secondary search, and how they would need to proceed. So I don't think there's any one road map. I do know that people come into the work with unrealistic expectations of what they can find; they need to have realistic expectations when they start out. If they are working at a client company, they need to learn to tap their own people internally first, because that old saying is often true—80 percent of the intelligence you need is found within your four walls.

How much time would you allocate to the secondary research, primary research, and results organization? Out of 100 percent, how would you allocate percentages across the entire CI process?

Each project would have its own allocation, but if we were doing a typical secondary-primary and then writing a report, I'd estimate 5 to 10 percent on the secondary research, at least 75 percent on doing interviews, and the balance on preparing the report. But of course there's some sliding between those categories, depending on the topic. The interviews always took the lion's share of the time available.

What types of results do you feel are essential to report to the client?

It's question dependent. We would always look at what the particular client wanted to know and what they were planning to do with the information, and we would also let that dictate how we would present things. We would highlight what facts we might put into a chart versus facts we'd leave out of a chart, that sort of thing—because, again, it's how they're going to use it and what they're going to do with it that's the ultimate decision maker in the process.

Did you find any software products that were especially helpful in either performing a search, doing post-search work, monitoring of any sort such as Web page tracking, or managing your bookmarks?

With our reliance on primary research over secondary, it wasn't really necessary for us to keep that much on top of things. When we did monitoring work for clients, again, it was very grassroots, field oriented. We would do a lot of interviews rather than, say, seeing what a competitor had been publishing or releasing on their Web site. In terms of software products to help us analyze the information or anything like that, I've always believed that the human brain is vastly superior to any software. I have a strong anti-technology bias, and I don't think that's a secret. I actually find it alarming that so many companies do rely so heavily on software, which is supposed to be a tool, but not a dictator. Sometimes people put themselves in a position of allowing the software to tell them what to do. I feel that's a bad direction to take.

What about presentations? Have you found that the standard office suites of software pretty much answer all those needs, or have you needed any specialized programs?

No, because most of what we put together was still heavily text based. We weren't doing the kind of work where we needed to do pie charts or bar charts or anything like that. We would often take qualitative information, even nuances and innuendoes, and summarize it for the client. That kind of information doesn't really lend itself to tools that have a more quantitative slant to them. We did look at purchasing software that lets you do a certain amount of charting or prettying things up. But it was a question of whether it was worth buying and then learning to use it, because we might not use it very much. In all cases, we decided not to make the purchase because we would not receive adequate return on our investment.

Can you think of a project that you would consider your largest coup?

It would be very hard, after 23 years, to single something out. I do recall that we once did a project on what they call person-weighers, which is a fancy word for the scales that they used to have in places like Woolworth's, where you put your money in and you got your weight and sometimes a little card telling you what your weight was. They used to be on every street corner, and it was an industry that had sort of existed, vanished, and was making a comeback in the context of the fitness industry. We were trying to find out why it had vanished, and I remember finding this guy who was 89 years old, and he had all the information. It wasn't recorded anywhere; this was an industry for which there was very little in writing. But this man was still at a desk at the age of 89, somewhere where I could reach him—he has probably long since passed on—who knows, a year later he might not have been available for an interview. I always feel that finding someone like that—it was a very circuitous path to get to him—and being able to interview him, is a real coup. Times like that, when you find someone who's a mine of information, are really a fluke. Some of it's science, in terms of how you go about finding information, but there's a strong element of luck involved, too.

How did you stay current and competent with your strategies and resources?

That was always driven by the work we were doing, in that clients would come to us with things that were new, sometimes leading edge. Staying current was driven by the need and capability to go out there constantly and invent a new strategy or find new resources in order to achieve an objective.

What skill set and/or education do you feel an individual needs to be successful in performing competitive intelligence work?

I think the two most important skills are persistence and patience. I don't think it's necessarily driven by formal education, though that helps. Having a fairly encyclopedic knowledge of a lot of things is helpful, but you really have to have the determination to stick with it, and persistence and patience in reaching people and getting the information. A lot of people don't have that; if they phone and the person they want to interview isn't there, they get fed up and they give up—and that's not the way it goes. You have to be the one to put the hours into tracking people down and chasing them and telephone-tagging and all those things. It does take a certain type of person to do that.

What did you enjoy most about the profession?

The creativity and the inventiveness. Also, "back in the old days," it was just plain fun! Getting the information was like playing a game. Even the clients only took things seriously up to a certain point; they kept their sense of humor. There was a lot of verbal fencing during the interview stage of research, but no one was hurt by the experience. As one of my researchers put it, what we were doing wasn't malevolent. It was helping raise standards. If our client improved and became better than their competition on account of our work, well, sooner or later the competitors had to improve; so we were really just fostering this continual upward spiral in which customers were the real winners.

And what do you like least about the profession?

What I came to dislike, and one of the reasons I am no longer doing CI, is that over the years I felt that a great many clients became totally unreasonable in their expectations of outcomes, unreasonable in terms of what they were entitled to. Clients felt that because they had formulated the questions they were enti-tled to the information. There's no law that says that just because you want to know about a competitor, they're obligated to give out the information. So there was this horrendous imbalance that came into the profession in terms of client expectations.

They also became unreasonable in terms of not being willing to invest in the process. They wanted a certain fact, and they thought we should be able to go out and just pluck it out of thin air, not realizing that the way you get good information is to start further back and work toward your goal. If you do it the right way, you can get good information, but in terms of the time and dollars they were willing to invest, too many developed unreasonable expectations.

I just felt that the whole industry had sort of gone down a few notches. There's also been an influx of people who are less than ethical as practitioners, particularly from certain areas of government. Some underhanded practices have been introduced, and while clients might talk a good talk on the ethics side of things, I think that at the end of the day, if you don't deliver the information, they probably won't want to pay your bill. As a result, people are being forced to use more and more underhand tactics to get at the information they need. I decided that I simply did not want to be associated with that anymore. Print that if you dare!

Super Searcher Power Tips

➤ Recognize how many sources there are other than online. You can go into bank branches and pick up promotional literature, which is perfectly above board; I mean, the stuff's there for the taking. You need to look at the full range of places you can go and sources you can tap. We've gone into supermarkets and read labels to find information. There are so many ways you can get tidbits of information that go to make up the whole that you're trying to put together. Cast a wide net and keep a very open mind about what constitutes a source and where you can find one.

➤ Be persistent and patient. I often used to get to people by phoning every five minutes, all day if necessary, until I reached my target. I wouldn't just settle for voice mail. If you leave a message, you are giving up control over the situation, and then you can't keep phoning. It's better to retain the initiative and be the one to place the call.

➤ If you just want to do 9-to-5, that's not going to work. Be prepared to get up early in the morning, because a lot of executives are there at 7 and 7:30; you will get more interviews if you're willing to do that. I've had staff literally phoning at midnight when they're trying to get people in Singapore and Malaysia. I myself have gone home at 6 or 7 at night and phoned Australia because it's 9 or 10 in the morning there.

Clifford Kalb

Knowledge Sponge

Clifford Kalb is senior director of strategic business analysis with Merck & Co., Inc. where he directs a staff that conducts intelligence, economic, and pricing analyses. Clifford has nearly 30 years of experience in the pharmaceutical industry, including employment with Marion, Pfizer, Roche, and a small biotechnology firm affiliated with Johnson & Johnson. A past president of the Society of Competitive Intelligence Professionals, he is widely published and speaks frequently on CI and business analysis. Clifford holds a bachelor's degree in biology and psychology from Rutgers University and an MBA in pharmaceutical marketing and economics from Fairleigh Dickinson University.

clifford_kalb@merck.com

Tell me a little bit about your background, and how and when you started performing competitive intelligence.

I began as a *consumer* of intelligence before becoming a *producer* of intelligence. I spent 15 years in a variety of roles in the pharmaceutical industry, including line management, marketing, and business development positions. In those capacities, I was a consumer of intelligence, and staff groups provided advice and recommendations to me on the business decisions we made. When I joined Merck, I switched to the other side and became a producer of intelligence. The majority of my clients have been more senior in the organization than I was as a consumer of intelligence; as a result, the business decisions we analyze have greater financial implications than the decisions I made in previous positions. Having worked as a consumer, I was able to "walk a mile in the customer's shoes." That has given me an orientation to how intelligence is best used, and how it fits into the decision-making process. This kind of background is a bit unusual for people in this field.

How would you describe your function in a nutshell?

The function has evolved over the years. The Merck team began as a provider of basic data, which I would call first-order CI, and then matured into a group that did analytical work, first on the environment, then on specific competitors. Over the years, its responsibilities have broadened, and now it is a global group with experts in particular regions of the world, specific competitors around the world, and also individuals focused on different fields of business—known as *therapeutic areas* in the pharmaceutical industry—in which we compete. For instance, we might have an expert in the antibiotic or antihypertensive field, or someone with vast firsthand experience in Latin America. We also have a responsibility for business analysis in general, so we support deal-making, pricing policy, and economic analysis of options to determine how Merck should optimize its business around the world.

During a talk you delivered to the SCIP Washington, DC chapter, you spoke about how you embrace the Five Forces Model from the Harvard Business School. How does that model affect the types of research you perform at Merck? Do you conduct company and industry research, or do you also look at the economic/political issues?

We do both. We look at the environments in which companies compete, as well as the nature of the competitive landscape. For instance, we might be asked to look at whether Merck should expand its business into a certain region or country. That kind of analysis requires an understanding of the local political, economic, demographic, and, of course, competitive situation. The competitive part is certainly an important element of this type of analysis, but the ultimate recommendation on whether or not the business should grow in that direction is made on the basis of all of those factors.

I should also stress that we do not work alone. Often, we work on cross-functional teams, where each member of the team offers greater functional knowledge in areas such as finance, marketing, drug development, or regulatory affairs. As a result, the expertise captured in our analysis is derived from people who have a depth of understanding greater than those in our group. Our group serves to synthesize the knowledge. We are responsible for knowing who knows, and tapping the expertise that exists in the company, to bring the best minds together in order to make the best recommendations.

How do you define competitive intelligence, and how do you differentiate that from traditional business research?

Competitive intelligence primarily focuses on the two sets of competitors that are most important to any business. One is today's competitors, and the second is tomorrow's competitors. Of the two, our general focus is tomorrow's competitors. We are pretty familiar with today's competitors and have very detailed profiles built up over the years. Forecasting who tomorrow's competitors will be—and whether they come from industries that one would not necessarily expect—is where we try to provide our management the greatest competitive advantage. Sometimes a firm is blindsided by a new technology from an entirely different company or industry that was not anticipated to be a direct competitor. Alternatives to the current products or services may be offered by this unexpected competitor, ultimately displacing current products because of a technological change.

When comparing CI to the scope of traditional business analysis, the latter is typically broader. Elements of business analysis may include financial analysis, economic analysis, or analysis of a business partnership, for example, from a cultural compatibility perspective. In general, the business analysis skillset includes competitive intelligence activity, but is broader and requires a background in a variety of business disciplines.

What do you feel is essential in your CI toolkit? I'm referring to resources, equipment ...

We are not as dependent on computers as one might think, although the ability to rapidly access electronic published literature is assumed. We use a system at Merck called WISE, which is an acronym for Worldwide Information Sharing Enterprise. It involves a continuous feed of several hundred different external publications and databases that comes into Merck headquarters through a satellite. These feeds are widely available and updated in real-time. Each person can customize the monitoring of these databases based on their particular assignment. This tool is then replicated for those in other parts of the world, and they have customized screens as well. In terms of secondary literature, we select the individual outside publications, trade press, and other sources that are most valuable to our work. These sources always become the basis of research when we begin a project. For general business and marketing intelligence we start with the FDC *Pink Sheet* [122, see Appendix], *Scrip* [173], *Medical Marketing & Media* [150], *Pharmaceutical Executive* [161], and *Medical Advertising News* [149]. For financial intelligence we use company and product Web sites, Wall Street analyst reports [86] such as those from Lehman Brothers and Goldman Sachs, EvaluatePharma [29], country studies like those from EIU [26], Stat-USA [77], and the World Drug Market Manual [45], as well as Espicom Company Profiles [28]. For R&D and scientific intelligence, Pharmaprojects [66], *R&D Focus* [167], IdDB database [43], Adis Insight [3], Genesis/POV reports [36], and *Physician's*

Desk Reference [162]. For disease, burden of illness, and epidemiology intelligence, we look at publications by Decision Resources [15] and Datamonitor [14], among others; Timely Data Resources Epidemiology Database [82]; *ICD-10 (International Classification of Diseases)* [135]; the *Merck Manual* [152]; and the *Merck Index* [151]. For sales, purchases, advertising, and consumption intelligence, IMS Health Market Reports [44] such as their purchase, prescription, and standard unit audits; CAM Promotional Audits [99]; Nielsen [64] and IRI [49] Studies; and Scott-Levin Audits [70].

The second phase usually involves primary research, if necessary, to confirm a hypothesis we have developed from the literature. We call on a contact network that exists both inside and outside the company. At Merck, the members of our team have accumulated names of key contacts who are industry professionals with many years of experience, and this network has proved invaluable as a source of "knowing who knows."

Finally, and probably most important, is the knowledge and ability to synthesize this kind of information. It is not just the tools that come from outside the company; it is what is in people's heads. Of the sources we use most, it is this human resource and its collective knowledge that is most valuable. Our headquarters group has approximately 35 people. Collectively, we have 426 years of pharmaceutical industry experience, have worked in 52 drug companies, lived in 105 countries, and speak 27 languages. Thus, as a team, the resource that we find the most valuable is our own staff. I believe a deep understanding of our industry is critical for success in this area of decision support.

How do you cope when you're in the middle of a search and just not able to find the information you feel should exist in some form?

We rely on our human network when secondary sources do not provide the information we are seeking. Often, it is a brainstorming opportunity. One of the benefits of having a large central group, which is the way Merck is structured, is that we are able to consult with each other easily due to our close proximity. Having direct access to our clients or other human resources is a tremendous benefit. When we are working with a client on a project, we never start the project, work independently, and then only come back at the end with the result. We work with the client throughout the project, in the form of drafts and ongoing interaction. Often, when we reach a point where we feel we have either reached a dead end or not achieved our mutual objective, we go back to the client before the project is finished and ask, "Are there any other leads you can give us that you think might be helpful?" This makes for a unique, iterative process, where we have direct interaction with the customer. This type of interaction fosters a richer understanding of the issue and allows for the relationship with the client to develop into a true partnership.

Do you generally tackle the secondary research first and then go on to primary, or have you found another methodology that you use consistently?

We always begin with secondary research first, and then go to primary. It is important to emphasize, however, that before starting the secondary research, a far more important step is the proper definition of the question. I would rather spend four weeks with a client refining the question, refining the analytical method, and agreeing on a deliverable, whether we do secondary or primary research, or both. Often, the open and productive dialogue between an intelligence consumer and an intelligence provider, prior to initiating a study, narrows and focuses the analysis. This allows the work to be targeted at an objective that is actionable and immediate. It improves the benefit to the company, from both a competitive and a financial perspective. Many times, we stop with research in the public domain, and never do primary research at all. Sometimes, with a little bit of speculation and what we like to call "seasoned executive judgment," we can get close enough to the answer that confirmation through primary research is not necessary—especially when primary is a more expensive method.

From what you've described thus far, it appears that your team performs all the steps in the intelligence process, from planning to results presentation. Is that generally true, or do your folks sometimes provide a few links in the chain and then pass it along to another department?

We are generally responsible for the entire process. Definition of the question is the essential first step; I think this is one of our greatest skills. The group leadership is very good at helping clients clarify and resolve the business issue in a way that makes the project relevant and actionable. On the other hand, roughly 50 percent of the questions we get are diverted elsewhere if the real question is one where we know that someone in another division of Merck has better expertise. For example, if the issue is strictly financial, we generally refer the question to the finance department. We know where our expertise lies, and where other expertise exists in the company, so we serve two functions. One is to take traditional business intelligence projects where we are the experts right from the beginning to the end. The other is to redirect projects to different resources in the company when we know expertise exists elsewhere. In this regard, defining the question is one of the single most important skills that we can offer. We are generally able to get the client directly in contact with the person with the knowledge that will lead to the best solution.

Do you use standard templates to organize your research results? For example, do you have a consistent set of bullet points you use for an

"environmental situation" report, or do you find that every project that goes out the door is tailor-made?

It is not an all-or-nothing phenomenon. Certain projects we take on proactively, as a routine part of our responsibility. These projects may follow a type of template. For instance, we issue, periodically, an overview of our global competitive position relative to other companies in our industry. Our clients are the senior management of Merck, in the functional areas as well as the geographic heads. They are used to seeing a standardized approach to this overview, which allows them to compare performance in the prior period with performance in the current period; it is trendable. We have designed templates for this that are updated routinely, and they are widely expected as standard outputs of our department.

However, the ad hoc assignments, which form the bulk of our project work, have no pattern with regard to the format of deliverables. We do not have much success with sending out lengthy text-filled documents. A traditional format for us is a one- or two-page executive summary of findings and recommendations, with in-depth backup. This might be a PowerPoint presentation, or a presentation that has notes in bullet-point format, with slides that can be linked to the text by an oral presenter. Slide presentations, where we orally brief the client, is actually the most common way to deliver our results. At times, those are 30-to-40 slide presentations with a summary at the beginning. In other cases, it is two or three slides with an interactive Q&A in place of a formal presentation.

The best way to learn how to develop the deliverables in a format acceptable to the client is to understand the client's decision-making style. If they need a lot of depth to support a recommendation, then that is part of the deliverable. If the client just wants the top line, the support for the top line is available as backup, which allows for delivery in a shorter format. The communication style varies based on individual client need, and the better the intelligence provider knows the client, the greater the working rapport.

In your SCIP DC presentation, one of your slides portrayed a process most of us were exposed to back in our school days. It employed a systematic approach that many of us had long forgotten, and you have resurrected it at Merck. Can you comment on that?

This is a series of 10 steps (see Figure 8.1), collectively called the analytical process, sometimes referred to as the intelligence cycle. The analytical process is often disguised as the scientific method.

Step	Time Range to Complete
1. Define Question	Variable: 1 phone call to 4 months debate
2. Develop Hypothesis	Variable: 1 phone call to 4 months debate
3. Gather Data	Up to 15 days
4. Filter & Organize Data	Up to 10 days
5. Analyze Appropriate Data	Up to 10 days
6. Prepare Findings and Select Best Recommendation	Up to 5 days
7. Prepare Draft Report	Up to 5 days
8. Review & Approve	Up to 14 days
9. Issue Report & Deliver Presentation	Up to 3 days
10. Seek Feedback from Client	Up to 7 days

Figure 8.1

But, quite simply, that is how we conduct CI work. The analytical steps and timeframe were developed after studying patterns of more than a thousand projects conducted by the department. The reason for the 10-step table is to communicate to potential clients that this work is not easy. There is extensive digging, thinking, connecting the dots, filling in pieces of a jig-saw puzzle, particularly pieces that do not appear in the public domain and have to be added through primary work. Ultimately, a key competency is the weaving of the pieces into a fabric and a coherent story. Business intelligence is not the kind of work where an analyst gets a phone call and the client says, "I need a forecast of the future of the pharmaceutical industry in Europe for the next five years and I need it by two o'clock." These types of assignments are not reasonable because we recognize how long it takes to study these issues properly and complete them with professionalism and accuracy.

Have you found any software products that are particularly useful, either for searching, post-processing results, Web page tracking, Web monitoring, analysis—anything along that line?

We are offered many software tools by many different ven-dors. We have found that those that are proprietary to our com-pany and designed internally by our information technology department are the best. IT staff support our group to meet our information needs, and we meet annually to discuss the kinds of databases and other analytical tools we would like to have devel-oped. As we use the tools, if we find features we would like to add, we have a regular support service that makes adjustments in order to make the tools even more useful. It is a luxury to have these information services available. At our firm, when given the choice between buy or build, we generally build our own tools and systems.

You have performed thousands of projects. What would you consider your largest coup?

It is a case in which we preempted a competitor in the mar-keting area. The pharmaceutical business has very long cycles and lead times. From the point where a product is a twinkle in a scientist's eye to the point where it becomes a marketable prescription drug is generally between eight and 10 years. As competitors in this industry develop their compounds, they reveal pieces of what they are doing in their studies that appear in the public domain. This particular case was one where paying close attention to a competitor's clinical trial plan for a product, before it was introduced to the market, allowed us to construct a hypothetical positioning strategy for that competitor. Our product was already in the market. If that competitor launched with a particular positioning strategy, they could potentially steal our market share. Based on that hypothesis, we repositioned our product into the space where we anticipated they were planning to go. Our revised strategy in the marketplace preempted their plan to displace a portion of our business. This required the competitor to supplement their application to the government for approval so that they could move out of that proposed competitive position into a different one. That process delayed their market introduction by two years. That two-year gap, in turn, allowed Merck to continue to actively market its product. The benefit of that project was in the range of $150 to $200 million dollars in revenue.

This is a good example of where anticipating and preempting a competitor's plan results in financial benefit that is measurable. In some ways, justifying its legitimacy is one of the weaknesses of the CI profession. Often it is very difficult to determine how an activity undertaken by a CI group impacts the top or bottom line. In this case, we were able to measure the impact, which was a big coup because we actually kept the competitor out of the marketplace for two years, enabling us to continue to market our medication and grow its market share.

Looking at the other end of the spectrum, how about a worst nightmare or a serious "lessons learned" experience?

In 1994, we were a much smaller group than we are now, with much less experience. Often, we were asked to create hypothetical merger analyses. Our industry was, and still is, going through a lot of consolidation. As a result, companies that were merging would create new competitors. We saw a couple of hints in the public literature on a Friday that competitor *A* and competitor *B* were considering merging. We decided to take a chance and create a profile of what the merged company would look like, and what threats it would present to our firm if the merger occurred. We prepared the analysis rather quickly, and sent it to the senior management team.

Coincidentally, this happened to be in the summer, and I was traveling that same day to go on vacation. The following Monday morning, when I awoke in my hotel in Arizona, I saw the news report that said that two companies did merge. One of them was company *A*, but the other was a completely different company. We had just issued a report predicting that companies *A* and *B* were going to merge, yet it turned out that *A* and *C* merged. I turned to my wife and said, "It's going to be a long vacation. When I get back, I may not have a job, because I gave the wrong intelligence to my management."

When I returned from vacation, I walked into the building and got onto the elevator. As the elevator door was closing, a hand popped through the doors, and someone else got on the elevator. By chance, on this day, it was the CEO. It was just he and I on the elevator together. I looked at him and said, "I'm sorry." And he looked at me and said, "Why?" By this point we were at my floor, which is obviously several floors below his floor. I was about to step out and he pushed the hold button, looked at me and said, "You warned me prior to this merger that company *A* was a takeover candidate. If I intended to take action as a result of that, I had been advised. If it turned out that they merged with company *C* instead of company *B*, that really didn't matter. What mattered was that I had the option to act, and you provided me the intelligence to do that. Thank you."

When the elevator door closed, I felt like a million dollars. I had originally thought that my career was over, but this case actually gave me the incentive to pursue greater risk taking in my projections of the future. I learned that my management encouraged risk taking; even if we did not have the specifics right, as long as we came close, it gave them the sense of the competitive landscape they needed if they intended to take action. What turned out to be a terrible forecast in terms of accuracy became a success because my management saw the glass as half full rather than half empty.

Now that you're a risk taker and have the guts to follow through, how do you stay current and confident with your strategies and resources?

The resource that I consider the absolute best is a group I participate in and used to chair, called the Conference Board Council on Competitor Analysis [234]. This is a group of 25 to 30 people who are the highest-ranking officials in their companies in the intelligence field. They have to work for multinationals; they have to be managers of groups; and they have to have a significant amount of experience in the field. It is a global group, cosponsored by the Conference Board and SCIP. We meet quarterly, usually at a company's site. We all represent different industries, so there are no direct competitors in the room. That allows free discussion of individual cases that might be current in one's industry. Having no competitors in the room permits one to ask the group for advice on how they might approach the problem.

Over the years of my membership in this group, the advice and counsel that I have received from my colleagues involved in CI work in other industries has been a superb source of knowledge. It is like getting free consulting, and from people who are real practitioners. Not people who are selling books or ideas on how it should be done, but people who live it. I have been a member for about nine years now. Pragmatic learning from my peers is my best way of staying current.

What skill set or education or combination do you feel an individual needs to be successful in performing competitive intelligence?

One of my goals when I was president of SCIP was to establish the intelligence field as a recognized and legitimate major or area of specialization in an MBA program at a leading university. I believe this is important because a new business discipline earns legitimacy once it gains recognition at the academic level. SCIP has sponsored academic conferences where curricula have been developed to create such programs. The first several programs are now underway at universities in the U.S., Canada, and Sweden. The core competencies that are taught in those programs involve some disciplines that are cross-functional, and do not follow traditional MBA patterns. The first CI program to be developed was at Drexel University [236]. There, the program was cosponsored by the business school and the IT school, so the deans of both colleges have worked together to build a curriculum around IT skills, as well as those skills necessary in traditional business disciplines.

An additional skill that I find useful is often best illustrated by those who are more senior in the function—an ability to effectively manage a project. This involves preparing a time line and then executing and managing the work according to the schedule. This is crucial because the timeliness of the output is often linked to the success of the recommendations. Project management skills are very important. I also think that certain skills that have to do with forecasting, statistics, quantitative methods, and both oral and written communications are critical to intelligence work. If I were asked to identify the single most important overriding skill in the profession, I would say communication. This relates to writing, listening, and also speaking in a way in which respect is generated between the intelligence provider and the intelligence consumer.

I do not think the "intelligence skill set" involves anything really special beyond what I have just described, other than a general broad business education. A successful person in this field might be called a knowledge sponge—someone who absolutely loves to capture, hover around, and absorb everything there is to know about the industry in which they work, in a way that the knowledge can be selectively used and applied to problems that the company may be facing.

What do you enjoy most about this profession?

When the phone rings, the next adventure begins. What has kept me in this profession for 15 years is the lack of repetition, the diversity of assignments and the breadth and depth of exposure to aspects of the business that I never thought would surface as CI project material. The problems that are thrown our way to solve are unique and different each day. Some of them are small and simple, while some are large and complex. If I ever reach the point where I am asked to do the same thing twice, then I will probably want to leave the profession. As long as the work continues to be stimulating, different, and offers new challenges every day, the group will enjoy their work. I characterize myself as a perpetual student of my industry, and I will always be learning.

Any pitfalls? Downsides?

What I enjoy least about the job is that I am not the decision maker. If I conduct an analysis that is thorough, analytical, has evidence to support my reasoning, and offers logic on which to base the recommendations, ultimately, I am an advisor. The decision maker has the right to reject the recommendation, without necessarily providing a reason. There may be reasons that intelligence consumers are not able to share, or they may have had contradictory advice from other groups. Often, it is frustrating when one has tremendous conviction regarding the recommendations of a study and considers it the best course of action for the company to take, yet the client rejects it without a clear explanation of the rationale for choosing a different course. The end point of my work as a senior staff advisor is a recommendation, not an action.

Is there anything else you would like to share that we haven't touched on?

Yes, the issue of ethics as it relates to CI. Of the aspects of this profession that receive publicity, it is often the ethics that become public, and part of the reason for that is the use of the word *intelligence*. That word, in and of itself, sometimes implies spying. Thus, it is the obligation of every intelligence professional working in business to either create, if it does not already exist, or abide by, a corporate ethics policy. SCIP can provide ethics guidelines if a company does not have such a policy. An ethics policy is the single most important guideline for the way CI work is conducted. A company that does not have an ethics code, or a company that is not following a code, or that is asking for work that may be on the borderline, runs the risk of painting the entire profession with the same brush. This is especially true if an incident occurs that turns out negative, particularly in the minds of the press.

Guidelines or ethical principles should be established in every organization where CI professionals exist and should be followed to the letter. At any point in any project, particularly during the collection phase, an individual who feels uncomfortable about what they have been asked to do should consult with their management, legal department, or ethics department before proceeding. It is also important to take guidance from professionals in the field who have been involved in CI work for many years. The profession will continue to grow as long as sound ethical principles are followed. Impeccable ethics is something I stress with my group, and I make sure that, as I communicate on behalf of the SCIP organization or of other professionals in the field, it remains the number one priority of people engaged in this kind of work.

Super Searcher Power Tips

➤ We rely on our human network when secondary sources do not provide the information we are seeking. Often, it is a brainstorming opportunity.

➤ The best way to learn how to develop the deliverables in an acceptable format is to understand the decision-making style of the individual customer. If the client needs a lot of depth to support a recommendation, then this is part of the deliverable. If the client just wants the top line, the support is available as backup, allowing for delivery in a shorter format.

➤ My absolute best resource has been the Conference Board Council on Competitor Analysis. It is like getting free consulting from people who are real practitioners.

➤ A successful CI practitioner might be called a knowledge sponge. Someone who absolutely loves to capture, hover around, and absorb everything there is to know about the industry in which they work, in a way that the knowledge can be selectively used and applied to problems that the company may be facing.

➤ It is the obligation of every intelligence professional working in business to either create, if it does not already exist, or abide by a corporate ethics policy. If the company does not have one, SCIP can provide ethics guidelines.

Wayne Rosenkrans

Pattern Recognition

Dr. Wayne Rosenkrans is Global Intelligence Director at AstraZeneca Pharmaceuticals. In that role he has responsibility for all CI in support of Global Commercial, Clinical, and R&D Operations. He is a recipient of the Society of Competitive Intelligence Professionals Fellows Award, and a former President of SCIP. Previous positions include Director—U.S. Intelligence at AstraZeneca, Competitive Technical Intelligence Group Leader and Research Planning Analyst at Zeneca Pharmaceuticals, Director of Strategic Intelligence Systems for Windhover Information, Director of Drug Intelligence Systems Sales and Marketing for Adis International, and Associate Director and Head of Strategic Intelligence for SmithKline Beecham Pharmaceuticals R&D. He has presented at various forums on aspects of CI, knowledge management as an intelligence tool, strategic intelligence, benchmarking, and the use of information technology in support of strategy. He holds an S.B. in Biology from MIT, a Ph.D. in Cell and Molecular Biology from Boston University, and received postdoctoral training in Cancer and Radiation Biology at the University of Rochester.

wayne.rosenkrans@astrazeneca.com

Can you please tell me about your background and how and when you started performing competitive intelligence?

My background is scientific and technical. I have a Ph.D. in cell and molecular biology, and did postdoctoral work in cancer and radiation biology. I taught for a number of years on the faculty at the cancer center of the University of Rochester, and went from there to SmithKline and French, working in licensing for a number of years. I went through the merger with Beecham, and at that time, about 1988 to 1989, was moved over to what was then called computing and information sciences, to put together a competitive intelligence function. That function grew from two people to 12, servicing primarily R&D but also global business development and what was called strategic product development. I left in '95, went to a small publishing firm called Adis International and ran their sales and marketing operation for their electronic database products for a couple of years, as well as doing new product development there. I left Adis in about '97 and spent a little less than a year doing the same kinds of things with a company called Windhover Information, another small publisher doing high-level strategic commentary on the pharmaceutical industry.

I found myself kind of lonesome for the industry, though, and went to Zeneca, running a technical intelligence and resource planning function in the R&D division. In a true sense of déjà vu, I then went through the merger with Astra and was moved into running a combined commercial and technical intelligence unit for the U.S. business and the U.S.-based R&D functions. Most recently, I have some coordination responsibility for emerging intelligence activities in the global therapy areas and some of the country-marketing units in addition to the U.S.

Your current function is that of global intelligence director and you have oversight of a few units, including therapeutic. Would you say you concentrate on therapeutic research?

Well, we have a highly matrixed organization here, which is corporate code for "it's hard to describe." I have direct oversight for a team here in the United States, which is working with our U.S.-based R&D and commercial teams, with U.S. strategic planning, and with several of our emerging mega-brand teams, the big blockbuster launches. I also help coordinate some of the global resources. That includes resources in our global cardio-vascular area, our global respiratory area, our global pain and infection area, and our global gastrointestinal area. In addition, there are dedicated CI resources in some of our country marketing units, most specifically a couple of folks in our Canadian office, a couple in our Australian office with responsibility for Australia and New Zealand, and an individual in our Shanghai office who's responsible for China. We're very geographically dispersed.

The unit in the U.S. in particular is responsible for a wider net than just our historical focus on the therapy areas. What we've been doing lately is pushing up a notch, looking at big environmental and industry issues that cross across the therapy areas, a lot of which is coming out of some long-range scenario and strategic planning work that we've been involved with. It's looking at things like the role of government, the role of the consumer in decision making, things of that nature, that are more broad-brush than just specific therapy area work.

How do you feel CI differs from business research, and how do you define CI?

We use the fairly classic definition here, which was taken from the National Security Agency [62, see Appendix] and Ben Gilad [242], which states that, at its base, intelligence is predictive; it is a means of anticipating and understanding the competitive environment and competitive reaction to that environment. It makes use of all available resources, which includes all of the usual secondary resources as well as primary resources within the company and external to the company. So it's broken into a collection phase, for which we rely on our field sales staff and field medical people and our scientists to help collect primary information, and an analysis phase in which we combine primary with secondary information, then look for patterns within that information. We cover a wide environmental swath, to ultimately draw some conclusions and make recommendations to management at various levels, ranging from product directors up to divisional presidents. So CI is that entire process of needs assessment, planning, collection, research, analysis, and ultimately communication of the intelligence to the customer group. It is always based on future orientation; it's proactive and predictive, inasmuch as it can be.

Where CI differs from business research depends on your definition of business research. I think there are large gray areas that overlap. As I look at my colleagues in market research and so on, where we differ is the long-term focus on being predictive and proactive. The market research folks are trying to gauge customer reaction and show where the market is evolving in terms of trends. I like to say that the market researcher's job is to never be wrong. They will set up studies to collect as much data as possible, and create a meaningful story with a quantified confidence level around it. An intelligence person's job is to never be surprised. They don't have the amount of detail or data that a business analyst does, but they have to be able to string a story together out of a few bits and pieces that hang together and make sense logically, creating an early warning signal for their company management.

What resources are essential in your CI toolkit?

They break into two main components. There's the collection side and the analysis side. The collection side is a mixture of typical information management skills that involve being able to access our secondary information services as facilely as possible. However, it also includes being able to talk to somebody on the phone or in person and elicit answers to questions in an ethical and legal way. So there are phone skills, there are interpersonal interviewing skills, and the ability to follow up on a story. It's a lot of the same skills that an investigative reporter has.

There are also some broad coordination skills. We run programs that we call quarterbacking sessions prior to our major conferences, where we marshal large numbers of resources from our field medical staff, our sales force, headquarters people, and so on, to help in a collection effort. A number of companies do this. Part of that process is also sensitizing our people to what they shouldn't be talking about; that's the other side of the coin, which is called competitive assurance—protecting our own internal assets from other companies that are trying to find out what we're up to.

The other side is the analysis toolkit. We have a bevy of things here that we can dip into, from classic business school Strength-Weaknesses-Opportunities-Threats (SWOT) analyses, to more sophisticated value-chain analysis, blind spots analysis, sciento-metric analysis—I think we're one of the few pharma firms that actually work with scientometric models. We run strategic war games, where we'll get a large team of 60 to 70 people together to game out potential strategies. We also do a fair amount of strategic long-range scenario planning and using that as an analysis tool for predicting where the environment's going to evolve.

And then, of course, you've got your essential pre-game and end-game skills—the ability to sit down with a client and figure out what it is they really want to know, why they want to know it, and what decision will be effected; and being able to present effectively to an individual or small team, stick to your guns and be able to defend what you're saying, sometimes in the face of fairly entrenched opposition from someone who may be a senior manager. So, I like to say, the people who do this need fairly thick skins as well.

How do you weigh the Internet against the for-fee database services in the research process?

They're both tools. We include the Internet in virtually everything we do, often to generate leads for primary research. However, realizing full well the limitations of the Internet, we avail ourselves of the full spectrum of for-fee databases made available within the company.

How do you cope when you're in the middle of a search and you're just not finding what you want or what you believe must exist out there?

First of all, we don't do much searching. We interact heavily with our information science and knowledge management teams who do a lot of searching. We're more of a customer for the folks who are doing searches for us. It's the nature of intelligence questions that there will not be adequate—or even any—information found in a search; that's when a primary collection activity comes into play. We'll use search results, not so much for the actual content, but for names, people to call and start to build a network around the solution. Who is working in the area, what are they working on, what does that tell us, where is it pointing us, etc., etc. We will take a couple of nuggets out of a search, and we'll use those to point us in various directions where we'll get additional nuggets; ultimately, we'll get a string of nuggets, and with a good dose of analysis, we'll build a pretty good story around an answer to the question.

Do you have team members who perform the secondary and primary research or do you get research results from your knowledge management team and then carry the information through the rest of the intelligence process you described earlier?

It's pretty much the latter. We are functionally split up around customer groups, so we have a group that works with our strategic planning function, a group that works with our government affairs function, a group that works with our discovery function, and a group that works with product teams. They are generalists, coordinating the overall process in terms of getting a question identified, figuring out how best to obtain an answer, marshaling resources to get an answer, looking at all the material that's been brought back and going through the analysis. They really do follow the entire cycle. We're not split into specialists who have collection vs. analytical responsibilities; people follow the entire cycle for a particular customer.

Do you have a standard model or template that you use to organize certain types of research results? You did mention earlier that you sometimes employ the SWOT analysis, and sometimes you utilize other business models. Do you use standard templates to plug in your data, or do you find that everything is completely customer-driven and tailor-made for each user?

It's largely customized. What we frequently address as part of the planning stage is not only where you are going to go to answer the question, but how are you going to analyze it when you get the data back. Hence, we give thought to "will this question lend itself to a value chain analysis," or "will this lend itself to a war game, in which case we need these kinds of bits." Of course, sometimes you can't find those bits, but you can find other bits, in which case a change of analytical paradigm may be indicated.

I would say folks usually have some sort of virtual template in mind when they're thinking about an analytical tool they're going to use, but we don't do anything codified in terms of something that can be pulled out of a Word document or whatever. We *have* gone to a templated output for things that are going to be analyzed by multiple small teams as input to a larger analysis. For our strategic early warning, we utilize small teams of fairly senior people to monitor certain driving elements, and a core strategy team further analyzes their output. In cases like that there has to be some consistency to what the output looks like, how the evaluation's been done, and what kind of information or data supports the evaluation.

What road map would you present to a researcher newly assigned to the CI function?

Our classic guidance, and what we reinforce with people, is not to shortchange the process at any step, because you'll miss something. The starting point is a customer with a question or a set of questions. We will first arrange what we call a KIT-KIQ meeting—key intelligence topic, key intelligence question— where we sit down with the team and run them through a process to help them identify their true question. This basically involves a bit of free-think at the beginning, and then what we call the five whys: Ask "why" five times. It's amazing how, after you do that, what started off as one set of questions looks entirely different when you get to the end. What you end up with will be a fairly cogent set of three to five real, genuine needs that the team has to answer in order to make its decisions.

Once those are in place, and their subsidiary questions identified—specific elements that will help answer a particular question—then you move into a planning phase: How are we going to get the answers? That includes developing some sense of how we are going to collect the data and what analytical tool will be used to analyze the data later. That process always begins with the secondary information search done by the knowledge management or information science groups, basically doing our homework. Then we may run a conference quarterback operation, or do a series of external interviews, or decide whether we are going to post the question to the sales force, or all of the above, or none of the above. Basically we determine how we're going to generate the information, and how we're going to analyze it.

Then the plan is put into motion: Go into the collection phase of pulling material in and constantly evaluating it. Here you may need some cross-corroboration and come up with some new questions. Ultimately you end up with a reasonably sufficient amount of information to start some kind of an analysis and come up with an answer. We have weekly meetings where projects are reviewed and questions are brought up within the team: How are you going to do this? What do you think? The answer seems to be looking like this … There are interactions not only with the intelligence team but with the client team as frequently as possible to assess progress, examine the analysis, and test answers.

Finally, there's some kind of a final output, which we usually try to make either a face-to-face meeting or a small group meeting with the client team so that we can get some meaningful interaction around the findings, as opposed to just sending them a report. Quite often that final report itself is a slide deck from the one-on-one or from the small group presentation, which inevitably yields more questions. And so you start over again.

Have you come up with a formula for how you allocate your time for the planning, data gathering, synthesis, and analysis, and then producing your output and communicating results?

That varies so much depending on the type of project. My advice usually is to spend whatever time is necessary on that KIT-KIQ process at the very beginning. That is *so* important, and if you get off on the wrong foot, or on a wild goose chase, you'll have wasted all kinds of time. Spend the time to work with the client up front, and really understand, and check that they understand also, what the question really is that you're going to be working on. Like I said, often it isn't what they initially think; it frequently morphs during the course of that process you go through. The planning phase means spending the time that's necessary. The collection phase, you can never predict. Sometimes you get really lucky and it all sort of falls into your lap, in which case it can take a minimal amount of time. Other times, it can be extremely protracted, with little bits and pieces trickling in, sometimes conflicting, for which you need confirmation, or you just can't find the people with the answers. It can be a lot of luck, pure dumb luck. If you keep at it long enough, luck starts to work in your favor. That's why data collection is really hard to predict.

The analysis phase can't be shortchanged either. Go back and check your logic, look at the methodology used, double- and triple-check everything you're going through, check it with other people. The final presentation itself is often anticlimactic, really, because the client has been pretty well involved in the process all along. So that part usually ends up being relatively brief. So, I'd say 20 percent on the KIT-KIQ and the planning, maybe 40 percent on collection, 30 percent on analysis, and 10 percent on the presentation.

You mentioned that you have several models you use. Can you identify any specific results that are essential to include in every report?

Yes; it's all about predicting competitors—either competitor behavior or competitive environment behavior. So if you're doing a product-related project, the issue becomes how can we expect this competitor to behave when we launch our product, or when somebody else launches their product, or when the FDA works in a certain way? That becomes the key finding in the report; e.g., this is how we expect Pfizer to behave when such and such happens. That always includes some sense of how that will impact us and maybe what we should do about it. For example, if we are predicting that Pfizer is going to reconfigure their sales force in response to some environmental change, that may have an effect on our own field force allocation. We won't go so far as to make actual tactical recommendations, but we will always point up areas that need to be actively considered in terms of a company response, the "so whats." What comes back again and again is a predictive index—what's going to happen, and what we should be doing about it.

Have you found any software products that are useful for post-search formatting, say, or Web page monitoring, or analysis?

We have a highly customized version of Knowledge Works from Cipher Systems [203] that is our core process tool. The tendrils from this tool reach into the field organization, R&D, and field medical, as well as HQ for collection, and it provides some rudimentary analytical capability. Its primary utility, however, is in organizing the process and the outputs. We have experimented with some textual pattern recognition tools as well. I know it's a plug for Cipher, but I'm not aware of anything else that does what this tool does.

What was your largest coup? Perhaps you could speak about the project that was included in the "Spies Like Us" article [176]?

That's the Taxol one. It's funny, that's almost become part of the intelligence lore. It's a very old story, actually; it goes back to the early nineties. It's really just a classic story of stringing nuggets together. We found out initially that Bristol-Myers Squibb was going to be giving congressional testimony on the Pacific Yew Act, and that tipped us off to something unusual going on. Taxol is a semi-synthetic product that's made from the bark of the Pacific yew tree. We sent somebody to listen to the hearing, and found out BMS was asking the government for a special-use permit to increase their harvest of Pacific yew tree bark about 200-fold, which was an incredibly politically incorrect thing to do at the time. So we started looking a little deeper and found out that they were massively increasing their recruitment of both patients and investigators in the clinical trial programs. They were really pushing hard to get patients recruited into trials, so they needed more investigators, so they needed more drug; it all linked back to this congressional testimony. We concluded that they must be moving up their FDA filing date. The team we were working with, which was for a competing drug, took all that on board, and developed a set of contingency plans for implementation if it could be shown definitively that Bristol was doing this. Several months later Bristol announced that they had moved up their New Drug Application filing date for Taxol by 18 months, due to more rapid patient recruitment. So the product team that we were working with was able to rapidly implement their contingency plans, and more or less keep their window of opportunity open.

We had another instance involving a major deal between the pharma company and a large biotech. The deal-making process was not going very well; some huge egos were clashing. We were asked to do some personality profiling on the principals involved, to figure out some way to break the deadlock. We were able to show our management team working on the deal that there were certain "social" things they were simply going to have to do. They did, and the deal got done, becoming one of the largest deals of that type ever done.

More recently we had a question about sales force allocation at a competitor that nobody had been able to answer. Through a combination of working with the sales force, some directed interviewing, and conference intelligence work, we were able to get not only an answer but a thoroughly complete answer to that question. This led to some reorientation in what we were doing, which saved a considerable amount of resources. That's a very tactical example; it worked out pretty well.

How about on the other side; do you have a worst nightmare story?

Well, there are always nightmares. In my experience, it usually involves having to be the bearer of bad news, where something you've turned up doesn't jibe with the party line. Depending on the client group, that can be an instructive situation for everybody. In one recent case, we were coming up with information from two channels that was contradictory to what this team was hearing from another channel. The team refused to believe what we were hearing, which generated an uncomfortable situation. I kept trying to indicate that nobody was wrong, that the fact that it didn't all add up was telling us something, and that we needed to understand what that was, not just simply conclude that one of these channels was wrong. We never really succeeded in getting them into that mode.

We used to publish kind of a quick alert to certain events that were happening in the environment, with some analysis and recommendations, that went to a very senior management list. In one instance we made an evaluation and a recommendation on an event and thoroughly ticked off the senior vice president of business development. She thought it was ridiculous, the whole analysis was flawed etc., etc., etc., and she called and read me the riot act. I was able to turn it around and say it really wasn't important if she agreed with it or not—that set her off again—but wasn't it better that she thought about it now rather than two months from now when she was sitting in the senior management team meeting? She finally agreed, and she actually became one of our staunchest supporters, but for an hour and a half there on the phone my ear was ringing pretty well.

How do you stay current and competent with your strategies and resources?

I attend and present at conferences a lot. I rely heavily on my network and on one-on-one interactions with people, supplemented by the reading I do, such as *Technology Review* [184], *In Vivo: Business & Medicine Report* [139], *Harvard Business Review* [132], and so on. I also make certain I talk to people who aren't in the pharmaceutical industry. I spend a lot of time talking to people at Rolls-Royce, Shell, Boeing, or Ford and finding out how they do things. You get an enormous amount of cross-fertilization that way.

What skill set and/or education does an individual need to be successful in performing competitive intelligence?

If you go to the SCIP Web site [258], you'll find a presentation called "Developing a CI Resume" [115], which I presented at this year's convention. An advanced degree is usually useful, whether it's an MBA or a Ph.D. or whatever. But, beyond a certain level of general familiarity with science, industry, and commercial concepts, the successful CI person has something else. It's a combination of a thirst for the big picture and skill in recognizing patterns in small data. Successful CI practitioners tend to be good at working with people, particularly one on one. Their Myers-Briggs personality type [61] tends to be either ENT or INT, either an introverted or extroverted intuitive thinker—"the architect." In fact, some studies done with both SCIP and the National Security Agency show a high self-selection ratio for ENTP-INTP in intelligence work. This type of individual is relatively rare in the population at large, between 1 and 6 percent.

Conversely there are folks that aren't very good at CI; they tend to be the SJ, the sensor judgmentalist—the "builder." They aren't as inquisitive, aren't as investigative, and prefer the detail rather than the big picture. We run a two-day basic intelligence program here at AstraZeneca, and have both an advanced analysis and an advanced collection course. I try to go to those whenever I can, so I can look at people—you know, this person's really getting this, this guy's really good, I need to watch him—or, this person doesn't have a clue. That's how I find personnel.

What do you enjoy most about this profession?

I think it's that big picture. I really enjoy being able to take pieces and generate a story that'll hang together, and if it's surprising and unusual and makes people's mouths drop open, all the better.

And what do you like least?

The constant selling. This is not taught in B school. Constantly having to sell intelligence as a process to new managers gets to be tiresome. You've got to do it, and we've always got our marketing hats on, but there are things I'd rather do.

Super Searcher Power Tips

➤ At its base, intelligence is predictive; it is a means of anticipating and understanding the competitive environment and competitive reaction to that environment.

➤ We break the process into a collection phase, for which we rely on our field staff and our scientists to help collect primary information, and an analysis phase in which we combine primary with secondary information, then look for patterns within that information.

➤ Our analysis toolkit includes everything from classic business school Strength-Weaknesses-Opportunities-Threats (SWOT) analyses, to more sophisticated value-chain analysis, blind spots analysis, scientometric analysis, strategic war games, and long-range scenario planning.

➤ We use a technique called the five whys: Ask "why" five times. It's amazing how, after you do that, what started off as one set of questions looks entirely different when you get to the end.

➤ You have to be a passionate analyst—someone who is very analytical in their thinking but gets passionate about the analysis. If you're interested in CI, you're probably already analytical in nature; nurture that and grow it. You will probably crave the big picture, cultivate that as a positive trait.

➤ Industry knowledge is probably a good thing but not absolutely essential. I've hired people that had very little knowledge of the pharmaceutical industry but came out of military intelligence, and picked it up very quickly. A broad base of experiences is very useful.

John Shumadine

Team-Based Research

At the time of this interview John Shumadine was a senior manager leading a regional research and analysis team at Deloitte & Touche. Previously he was a senior consultant for PricewaterhouseCoopers LLP, a senior economist with the Central Intelligence Agency, and a research specialist for the U.S. Army Intelligence and Threat Analysis Center. In addition to his years of qualitative and quantitative analysis, he holds a BA in International Studies, an MA in International Transactions, and an MBA in Finance. Some of John's more notable experiences include being awarded the highest intelligence medal for Operation Desert Storm, briefing two Presidents, testifying many times before Congressional and Senate intelligence panels about issues of U.S. national security, and negotiating a multilateral investment and trade accord with 18 other countries. John is now Director of Competitive Intelligence for Deloitte & Touche.

jshumadine@deloitte.com

Tell me about your background and how and when you started performing competitive intelligence.

It started when I joined Army intelligence. I was trained in military intelligence and supported operations during the Gulf War. I went on to continue my education in economics and began doing economic intelligence at the CIA. I eventually left after 10 years to work in forensic accounting, investigating corporate fraud and embezzlement at major corporations. About three years ago I took an opportunity to lead a Research and Analysis team at Deloitte & Touche. I've really enjoyed the experience, because it's helped me broaden the different types of intelligence analysis that I've been doing.

How would you describe your present function in a nutshell?

I'm a senior manager of research and analysis. In a nutshell, this team helps the firm's leadership make decisions about the marketplace. That's about as nutshell as I can get. It really comes down to understanding the marketplace, knowing what's going on, and assisting our partners with strategic and tactical decisions.

I understand that Deloitte & Touche has a team model they have refined over the years for research and analysis projects. At one time, research and analysis for a project was performed by the same individual. However, I believe that has changed and team members are now dedicated to either research or analysis, not a mix. Can you describe how that change has gone and what you've found works best for you?

I think that separation is critical to intelligence. I have to admit, while it may be unusual in many corporate environments, it's fundamentally the way the CIA practices intelligence; it separates the researchers from the analysts but keeps them working closely together. This separation is essential because the researchers have to adopt an attitude of optimism that they will find the critical intelligence that will be most valuable to the decision makers. But the analysts need to be very critical, almost pessimistic, about looking for source bias and for information that may contradict the currently accepted beliefs. By keeping the two separate, you can have the researchers finding information and passing it on to the analysts who filter it down to just what is most essential and critical for the decision maker.

If you had the same person doing both jobs, you would tend to get large volumes of information and the key stuff really wouldn't surface, because researchers get too tied to the information that they come up with and try to find a way to incorporate it into the final product. But analysts don't have that bias, because they don't realize how·hard a researcher may have worked for that one piece of information, and therefore they don't have a problem eliminating it. So I think it's critical to have that separation, but still keep them working together. It allows the analyst to focus on understanding and analyzing the information, and the researcher to understand what search tools are available and what information resources are out there. Both can become specialized in what they do.

Do you have a training mode where each team member has to wear each other's moccasins for a certain period of time, so that the analysts spend some time in research to see what they have to live through before they're an analyst, or vice versa? Or do you bring people on for just one job or the other?

They pretty much stick to one job, but the groups aren't separate; they sit side by side. So there is an understanding, to some extent, of what the other person's going through, and quite a bit of communication occurs. The researcher can observe what the analyst is most interested in learning more about and what the analyst might be having issues or troubles with, so the researcher can proactively assist. If the researcher hears that the analyst is concerned about a particular area, and is out surfing the Net or exploring some other resource and finds something pertinent, they know to pass it back to the analyst. Having them sit in close proximity is very helpful. However, the talents that are required, as well as the training that the two groups get, are different enough that they never really switch places. It does require a different skill set.

How do you feel competitive intelligence differs from business research, and how do you define competitive intelligence?

They really can't be separated; they're so close that you really can't, and maybe you shouldn't try to separate them. Some projects emphasize one more than the other. But you have to understand the business environment in order to provide good analysis. So, while the competitor is one component, it's also important to understand the marketplace within your region, the firm, how the firm's doing, and what its core competencies are, as well as your firm's core competencies within a specific region. Once you have your firm's core competencies, your region's core competencies, the marketplace and its opportunities and people out there, and then you throw competitors into the mix, that's where you really develop some good strategy.

So, would you say that the difference is that intelligence includes outlining a strategy rather than just delivering, saying, "This is what we found?"

We almost never say, "This is what we found." We always take it to the next level of value added. The partners rarely have time to read through a volume of information and come up with assessments, so we provide analysis that enables them to take action based on the alternative scenarios we came up with, or our key findings. That helps the decision makers make the best strategic and tactical decisions.

What resources do you find are essential in your CI toolkit?

It's hard to generalize, because it really depends on the project. We're definitely an all-source research and analysis unit. We do so many different things that it's essential for us to change from project to project. The only core components are the members of the team. We try to survey what resources and what tools are available before we tackle big projects. If we need to get a new resource for a particular project, then we'll do that. But for the most part, we stick with broad, familiar resources. For business intelligence we may use commercial databases such as D&B (Dun & Bradstreet) [24, see Appendix], along with the Internet, company Web sites, press releases, and those sorts of resources to pull information together. For CI, we tend to focus more on primary source information.

One of the most valuable resources you can have for competitive intelligence is a Rolodex. Spending a lot of time building that Rolodex is really key to a successful CI effort. That's what makes CI one of the most challenging things to develop in a corporation—so often they want immediate return on investment. But it sometimes takes years to develop a Rolodex within your own industry, a repository of information and a collection of individuals that you can network with. There's not an immediate payback. I think that's why many corporations limit their focus to business intelligence, because with business intelligence you can concentrate strictly on analyst reports, investor reports, and things like that—secondary information that can be pulled together into a quick deliverable and handed over. The problem is that those aren't always the most valuable sources you can find, and they don't give you the whole picture.

How do you weigh the Internet and the for-fee database services in your workflow and in your research and data collection?

As I mentioned before, we are an all-source intelligence unit, and we like supporting evidence for our analysis to come from as many sources as possible. The Internet's loaded with useful information as well as inaccurate information that should never be taken at face value. It often generates great leads or provides supporting evidence through other sources. Message boards and related sources of information are never the types of resources you want to base your analysis on. However, sometimes the information on a message board can lead you to deduce or induce the reasons for a firm's actions, and when you put it all together, you can obtain a clearer picture. So, while we're always evaluating sources for bias, and the Internet can be one of the most biased resources, it can also provide a lot of unique information that can't be found elsewhere.

We rely heavily on fee-based services for numerous analyst reports. We read what Wall Street puts out on public companies. Dialog [20] and LexisNexis [56] have been useful in some areas. *ValueLine* [190] is good for some unbiased financial analysis. But all of that's just one component of our research; you have to pull in a lot of other areas. We'll often find that a piece of information gained from a primary source can be the cornerstone, kind of the "golden nugget" of the report, and we use a lot of secondary and fee-based databases, such as Dow Jones Interactive, now known as Factiva.com [30], and Hoovers [41] to provide the supporting contextual information. We find that, while it's not always the case, the for-fee database services tend to have more specialized and a little more reliable information than you can find on the Internet. But a lot depends on the project, as far as the most appropriate resources are concerned.

In our firm, we have to find solutions for internal clients, and those are not just auditing and tax partners. We do a lot for our consulting services groups and information technology consultants. The range of things we do for our clients makes it a real challenge to stay on top of changes in our industry. That requires us to keep up with industry publications like *Consultant's News* [108] and *Public Accountings Report* [166]. Strafford Publications [179], Kennedy Information [143], and Aspen Publishers [93] provide quite a few newsletters covering industry developments and trends affecting professional services firms. I believe it's really important to follow developments in your own industry and understand the issues your clients are dealing with in order to better serve them.

I realize this may be one of those "it depends on the project" questions, but would you say that you use the Internet in an equal balance with the fee-based services, since they both generate leads, information, and context to help support the point you're trying to make?

In general that could be true, but I don't know how you divvy it up because it does depend on the project. In talking with our information specialist, I've found that business research tends to rely most heavily on commercial databases as opposed to the Internet—it's probably a 90/10 split—because reliability of the data is critical. For research on people, the split may be 70/30 because the Internet sometimes has useful tidbits of information not sought out by the for-fee providers. For government-related research, particularly research on the federal government, the split is close to 50/50.

How do you cope when you're in the middle of a search and just not finding what you want or what you believe must be out there in some form?

The biggest thing is to ask for help. Nothing equates to having team members whom you can use as a sounding board. They can provide new ideas or suggest different aspects of the search that you hadn't considered. The researchers on the team have what I call a treasure hunt mentality. They can be extremely optimistic about finding that golden nugget of information that will form the cornerstone of the analysis, and they just can't sleep at night till they find it. That's invaluable. As part of a team, if the researcher hits a wall or is not able to find anything further, he or she can go back to the analyst and say, okay, this is what I've tried and where I'm not finding it. And the analyst may be able to work with the researcher to identify new avenues to approach the problem. Just getting a fresh set of eyes sometimes helps. The team concept is critical here.

Once the secondary research is done, what are your next steps? It sounds like your folks go on to do primary research. Do you have any specific order in which you tackle each stage of the process?

You're probably going to get tired of hearing "it depends on the project," but ideally, we like to do some secondary research initially to become familiar with the subject, identify current trends, and develop some insightful questions. We then interview experts or primary contacts that can give us new leads and unique information that we couldn't obtain elsewhere. Then we go back to the secondary research to fill in intelligence gaps, resolve contradictory data, and really immerse ourselves in the topic, which may again involve going back to primary sources. It's really a back-and-forth kind of thing. Depending on our time frame, after the initial secondary research we try to follow the scientific method, which involves developing a hypothesis that you think is true, and then trying to disprove it. It's easier to *prove* something using the numbers or other information you can find. Trying to *disprove* it is really the challenge, and if you can't disprove it, then there's a pretty good chance there's some validity to your hypothesis. In fact, science Ph.D.s on the team have worked out well, even though conventional intelligence notions probably would not expect people with scientific training to excel at business analysis. But because they are trained to understand and apply the empirical method to solve problems, they bring a lot of talent and rigor in analysis to the team.

How and when do you interface with the process folks? Your earlier description sounds as if your researchers and analysts are co-located. Do you find that the research is carried out and then it goes to the analyst?

No, the communication between the two throughout the research and the analysis stage is essential. I don't want to call it simultaneous, because it really is sort of a handing off, but you never know how many times it's going to get handed back and forth. Initially, when a new project comes up, the researcher will go out and download a tremendous amount of information and hand it all over to the analyst. Then the analyst will sift through the information they've been handed, and if there's enough there, say, "Okay, Researcher, I've got enough," and the researcher can move on to other projects. However, most of the time the analyst will read it and go back to the researcher to find answers to some of the more specific, detailed questions. The analyst will say, "You know, this is a really interesting opportunity we found here," or point out some critical piece of information, and ask the researcher to pursue it a little further. Then the researcher gets back into it. It's a constant handing off and communication back and forth. But we try very hard not to have the researcher get too involved in coming up with analysis, because we don't want them to be biased in their research. We also don't want the analyst to do a lot of the research, because it's very easy to become biased in terms of where the information comes from or how available it is.

What road map would you present to a researcher who's been newly assigned to your function?

Much of it is basic for a lot of jobs. One of the key things I look for in hiring people is a constant yearning to learn, and to learn about all kinds of areas, not just stick within a particular specialty.

They need to push back on requestors and get close to them to understand how the information will be used. Like I said, most of our information is value-added analysis, because we're working for partners who often don't have time to read through a lot of material. So we take a consultative approach, using a lot of probing questions to understand what decisions they're trying to make, and how they want to use the information. Many times we can come up with an enhanced solution for them and give them something much better than they originally thought they might get.

Another thing analysts and researchers should do is to set clear expectations up front for what they can deliver, and then exceed the expectations by finding ways to add some extra value to every project. I think most requestors don't realize how much you can do for them. If you learn what they are trying to accomplish and where they're trying to go, then you can become their business partner to help get them there, and you have a better chance of exceeding their expectations.

One more thing: Always ask the client how they're doing. It's critical that you don't ask "how are *we* doing," because they'll just say "fine." That doesn't help you. Really ask, "How are *you* doing? What are the kinds of things that are troubling you?" As they're telling you, you're out there surveying the landscape. You're working on projects that other partners also find interesting or useful, and if they share those requirements, then you can leverage your projects and your analysis to many more partners.

I can't emphasize enough how important listening and interpersonal communication skills are in this line of work. The researchers definitely have to have way above-average listening skills. And the analysts have to always be thinking about next questions and pushing back to challenge the thinking of the requestor. Many requestors think they know what they need and they ask you for it, and after you provide it, they want to move on because they think that's all that could be done. But as I said, if you can partner with them, you can help them to get something better than what they ever expected when they came to you.

You've got to make friends. One of the great things about being an internal intelligence unit is that everybody is on your team and you're out to help them succeed. When they succeed, they're happy and that keeps you happy.

Generally speaking, how much time do you allocate to the planning, the secondary and primary research, and then the organization and analysis of the results? It sounds as if time is a critical factor, so how do you allocate all the time for both sides of the house to do what they need to do?

We try to let the requestors know about the Catch-22 of intelligence: You have only two out of three options: You can get it fast, you can get it cheap, or you can get it done right. You get two of those, but not all three. We try to get them to come to us as soon as possible, but most of our projects range anywhere from as little as a few hours to perhaps as long as two weeks. It's very rare that we have more than two weeks to complete any project, although we do follow some key intelligence topics on an ongoing basis.

In a broad generalization, I'd say we allocate about one third to one half of our time to the research, another third to the analysis, and the final third to writing and communicating the results. Often there is too little emphasis in intelligence on the actual writing and communicating of the results. My view is that any intelligence you provide, no matter how outstanding or valuable, if it's not heard or communicated well, is worthless. So it's really important to communicate it well, and to not overwhelm the requestor with a bunch of information, or they won't get past the first word. The majority of our products probably fit into a single short email or onto one sheet of paper. We try to design templates for standard products that are just one page. That makes it a lot easier, and people know that when they get something from us, it's going to be just the good stuff.

With regard to those standard templates, are you able to share some of the major section headings or areas that you incorporate in your reports?

The most common requests we get are for general overviews of companies and competitors. But the analysis of corporate strategy is probably the most sought-after and value-added work we routinely do. For instance, if you're doing a business intelligence report supporting sales and marketing, you may want to include what the company does, how the company is positioned within its industry, what differentiates the company, the drivers affecting the industry, the issues that the company is facing as a result of those drivers, and the initiatives that the company is taking or not taking to address those issues. All of those things can be broken down into what you might find in an investment analyst report.

We find this model works well, and the real key to analyzing the strategy is trying to find benchmarks, such as how the specific company is positioned relative to its competitor, so there's some level of comparison similar to a peer analysis. We try to determine if what differentiates the company gives it a sustainable competitive advantage, or whether it is just an industry best practice that was probably learned somewhere else and is easily copied by competitors.

The other thing I wanted to mention was strategy per se. If you can infer what the company's strategy is, which involves some level of leadership analysis of the company's management, that's also very helpful—but it's very hard to do with any accuracy.

Have you found any software products useful, whether for Web page monitoring, post-search processing, or analysis?

We stick mostly with in-house innovations and cost-efficient solutions, and we have tried some of the free software applications, such as C-4-U Scout [196] or PlanBee [220] for specific projects. I've read the Fuld reports [239] and they're extremely helpful; we're always surveying the latest offerings, and we've tried some. But our workload's so dynamic that a single product is hard to stick with over the long term. We usually find something for a specific need, then stop using it when we move on to another project. We just don't get repeats of the same requests coming in. While many of those products are really good for research, I haven't yet found any that are flexible enough to produce good analysis on our projects. We tend to find that, while they may save us a little bit of time, they're not worth the investment. What's most critical for our researchers is to stay on top of the latest search engine developments and best resources for data. We've found some recent search engine innovations, such as Kartoo [52], to be really interesting. The most critical asset in intelligence is our people, not the tools.

Out of all the projects you've performed, which one would you say was your largest coup?

We've had a lot of wins, but each one kind of builds on the last, so I really can't point to a single coup that's been the most significant for me. Much of the work we do is part of a long incremental process. I really enjoy the wins where the research and analysis team is able to help out in an engagement where the client service team felt they were about to lose. Unfortunately, the team doesn't always get pulled in at the earliest possible stage; we may be brought in late as a result of the speed of the opportunity, or as a result of a lack of internal marketing on my part. A lot of times, the internal client will come to us either when they don't feel they can win, the opportunity appears to be slipping away, or they don't have a lot of time.

One recent instance involved one of our partners asking us to help because he felt the competition had an inside track to winning a very large contract with a Fortune 500 company, and our people didn't know much about the software that our competition claimed they could use to meet all the Fortune 500 company's needs. All we had to go on was the reported name of the software as they had heard it; we had to deduce what it was really called. We were able to track down a software engineer who claimed on an Internet resume that he had worked on developing this software. We contacted him and learned a lot about the software. More importantly, we learned that the software was somewhat outdated and that there were better versions available from a company that wasn't affiliated with our competition. That allowed our client to go back to the Fortune 500 company and explain that the software the competition was pushing was likely to be less effective than the initial solution we had provided, and to provide some evidence for that. But if the company insisted on having a software solution similar to what the competition was pushing, then we could implement the latest, most effective version. Needless to say, that helped us win the business.

Those tactical ones where you don't have a lot of time can sometimes be the most rewarding. The strategic ones, while they're critical and very important, sometimes take time to develop, and the process can be so long and drawn out that the value of the contribution the intelligence team has made is harder to measure. People recognize that we were a part of the team, but it's hard to point to clear intelligence wins. They tend more to be team wins.

How about on the opposite side? Have you had any nightmare projects?

The nightmares usually occur when the requestor of the information comes to us with an urgent request and expects an immediate answer. It can make for some really long days when we need to provide a thoughtful, correct response without sufficient time to do it. A big part of the job, particularly for the intelligence manager, is establishing a front-of-mind presence with the requestors so they think of us as soon as possible when they need assistance, instead of getting desperate and realizing they need help. Again, that's mostly the responsibility of the intelligence manager, to get out there and let people know that this facility is capable and available to them.

How do you stay current and confident with your strategies and resources? It sounds like you read a lot!

I read, network, read, brainstorm, read some more. Definitely, a lot of reading. Networking is crucial because often, by the time information gets to print, a lot of others are already using it. So you have to see what's on the front burners. I'd also say that having a creative environment is essential. A big challenge for me was adjusting from a military intelligence environment, where there was a strong hierarchy, to an environment like we have here, with very sharp members on the team in a relatively flat organizational structure. Everybody brings something unique, and to foster that creativity, it is essential that I am more of a peer and teammate than strictly a manager. Then the team is more comfortable being innovative and trying new things that might fail, and learning from any failures. I can't emphasize how critical that is. We are lucky in that we are given the freedom to fail, and that finding innovative solutions is encouraged here.

One of the things that is very fortunate about being in this industry, and particularly at this firm, is that things are constantly changing. What worked last year in the client service business very frequently does not work the next year. And so the people that we serve, the internal senior managers and partners, are in an environment where they know they have to constantly innovate, and therefore they expect you to constantly innovate and come up with new things as well. And they know that they don't get it right 100 percent of the time, so they don't expect you to get it right 100 percent of the time. If I were in a more stable industry where the innovation and change occurred much more slowly, it would be a lot harder to have that kind of freedom.

I'm a member of SCIP (Society of Competitive Intelligence Professionals) [258]. People on the team are members of the American Management Association [226] and the American Marketing Association [227]; marketers tend to be very creative. Some people are involved in individual investor clubs; some of them belong to the National Association of Investors Corporation [252], which helps them analyze companies. That's useful because we spend so much time analyzing the business environment and what businesses are doing.

We read as much as we can get our hands on. For basic reading, *Harvard Business Review* [132] and *Sloan Management Review* [175] are really good. Keeping up with the regular industry journals that I mentioned before, the *Consultants News, Public Accounting Report,* and *Bowman's Accounting Report* [94], is essential. Many of the top strategy consultancies put out some good research and white papers. For example, our own Deloitte Research is extremely useful, and we use that a lot within our own products. Deloitte Research is a long-term think tank group that conducts in-depth research and analysis on business trends and issues and the implications of various trends and issues for our clients. They may spend a couple of months on a project, whereas we turn around projects much more quickly. We serve internal clients and we're much more into immediate problem solving and applying strategy to our own firm's tactics and operations. So leveraging the two is really useful.

What skill set or education do you feel an individual needs to be successful in performing competitive intelligence?

The people I'm looking for tend to have curious minds and lots of energy, which leads them to pursue a variety of degrees. I really look for people who are well rounded and have lots of interests, because we get such a diverse range of projects that someone who is too specialized in one area won't be flexible enough to support everything that we have coming in.

Personally, I'd recommend a business degree in either accounting or finance to start, and then rounding it out with a liberal arts degree such as history or political science. A liberal arts degree helps you hone your thinking and communication skills. I mentioned earlier that we have people with scientific backgrounds. That's very helpful because it gives you a background in how to conduct evidence-based research. That's really what we try to do— discern the real picture and come up with the truth. We try to come up with evidence that leads us in a certain direction. We want, as much as possible, to avoid politics and coming up with answers that we think the client wants. We need to completely separate ourselves from that. So that evidence-based understanding is critical.

If you're going to focus on the research side, you really need to get the master's in library science. That gives you the basic grounding for research. Even if the technology changes, you have a good foundation to build on. But you probably want to round out that library science degree with some English or other courses that will help you communicate the results of your research. We've found that our researcher, who is right at the beginning of the process in developing a product, is often the same person who comes back with a clean set of eyes to review the final analytic product, because that person has good editing skills and has been separated from the analysis and writing phase of the project. Again, you really need the dual benefits of a hard skill, like accounting or finance, that will teach you the language of business, along with the liberal arts education that will give you the ability to think and communicate effectively.

You've obviously been in intelligence for a while; what do you enjoy most about the profession?

Yes, more than 13 years, and I'm thrilled to be in a place where I can leverage what I used to do in the government with the private sector. The private sector has such a huge opportunity to develop effective intelligence units to help them make good decisions. It's no secret that many company managers make decisions by gut feeling, and many CEOs are praised for making decisions on their own, or for having the right instincts. Too often good decisions made that way are the rarity and not the reality. The reality is that people who do the analysis, understand the environment in which they're operating, and make evidence-based decisions that will lead their firm in the right direction are the ones who will beat their competitors.

And what do you like least? Any downsides to working in intelligence?

Just the opposite—what happens when the business leaders follow their gut or make a decision without first analyzing the decision and its implications. I can understand that sometimes time constraints force business leaders to make decisions without fully analyzing them, but intelligence analysts have a responsibility to be on the forefront and always be prepared to address the "what-if" scenarios to avoid being surprised. If something new happens in the industry, or our competitors take an action that I had no idea was coming and I hadn't warned our business leaders about, that's what I like least.

Is there anything I haven't brought up that you'd like to talk about?

I just want to emphasize the team aspect of intelligence work. You need to have a lot of people on your team. You need a good team because you're simply not going to be as effective as a sole researcher or sole analyst. If you build on unique and complementary skills, then you don't necessarily have to be the jack-of-all-trades. You can have a good team, a winning team. It's a challenge to put a good team together and then keep it together, because if you have a really diverse group with unique talents, they're going to be very different kinds of people. I would say building and managing good teams is critical to intelligence analysis. We too often think of analysts as the Jack Ryans of the Tom Clancy world who just come up with insights on their own and run with it. There's much more to be said for the team that builds on each other, looks out for each other and comes through with better and more useful analysis.

Super Search Power Tips

➤ Researchers get too tied to the information they come up with and try to find a way to incorporate it into the final product. But analysts don't have that bias, and therefore they don't have a problem eliminating it. It's critical to have separation between research and analysis, but still keep them working together.

➤ One of the most valuable resources for competitive intelligence is a Rolodex. Spending a lot of time building that Rolodex is really key to a successful CI effort. That's what makes CI one of the most challenging things to develop in a corporation—so often they want immediate return on investment. But it sometimes takes years to develop a Rolodex within your own industry, a repository of information and a collection of individuals that you can network with.

➤   The Internet can be one of the most biased resources;
    it can also provide a lot of unique information that
    can't be found elsewhere. Business research tends to
    rely more heavily on commercial databases because
    reliability of the data is critical. For research on peo-
    ple, though, the Internet sometimes has useful tidbits of
    information not sought out by the for-fee providers.

➤   I can't emphasize enough how important listening and
    interpersonal communication skills are in this line of
    work. The researchers definitely have to have way
    above-average listening skills. And the analysts have
    to always be thinking about next questions and push-
    ing back to challenge the thinking of the requestor.

➤   We allocate about one third to one half of our time to
    the research, another third to the analysis, and the
    final third to writing and communicating the results.
    Often there is too little emphasis in intelligence on the
    actual writing and communicating of the results. My
    view is that any intelligence you provide, no matter
    how outstanding or valuable, if it's not heard or com-
    municated well, is worthless.

➤   Look at yourself and know yourself well. Work on your
    less comfortable attributes. If you're an introvert, seek
    out opportunities to socialize and network. If you're an
    extrovert, then immerse yourself in a project that
    requires really deep, contemplative thinking.

Bret Breeding

CI Artist

At the time of this interview, Bret Breeding was the Global Corporate Competitive Intelligence manager for Compaq Computer. A true believer in "build as you go," Bret was previously employed as Manager of CI for Shell Services International, which included maintaining their knowledge management tool, CI KnowledgeHouse, and with EDS in a variety of areas in their Energy Strategic Business Unit (SBU). Bret graduated with honors from Oklahoma State University with a double major in management and marketing and a minor in geography.

bbreed67@yahoo.com

Bret, can you tell me a little about your background and how and when you started performing competitive intelligence?

I graduated from Oklahoma State University in the late '80s, and started at EDS as an engineer, which was one of the few ways to get into the company at the time. I quickly went over to the business development side of the house, where I found a home in competitive intelligence and worked in that area for about eight years. In 1997, I moved to Shell, which had an IT (information technology) services division called Shell Services. They had what was called a "green field" site, meaning there was nothing in place, and I could create anything that I needed to make an effective CI practice. This is where I really started to develop an approach of my own. I took a lot of things I had learned at EDS, put my own spin on it, and developed it at Shell.

Soon, I started to speak at a lot of conferences. Eventually I wrote an article, which appeared in the book *Proven Strategies in Competitive Intelligence* [165, see Appendix] by Dr. John Prescott, participated in a forum from APQC (American Productivity & Quality Center) [228] on best practices in CI, and worked with Dr. Bob Tait to actually help create a consulting practice at Shell that would help other companies set up their CI practices. In October of 2000, I moved to Compaq, where I took the job of manager of Global Corporate Competitive Intelligence. That basically involves setting the CI policy and standards here at Compaq.

How would you describe your current functions in a nutshell?

I run a team of eight analysts to produce a series of deliverables that are high impact in nature and that are geared toward the executive leadership team, the sales force, product managers, and the strategy teams here at Compaq. I also have process ownership and stewardship over all the other CI functions inside Compaq, in that I help set the process for how we do deliverables and how they all tie in, from a corporate perspective down to the perspective of a business unit that has ownership over the products, over to the geographic perspective that has ownership of sales. And, finally, I help facilitate the communication among projects being worked on by the various CI personnel in the company, and communications among all the CI people.

What types of research have you performed and do you perform now? Do you concentrate on certain subject disciplines, or are requests all over the map?

My specialty has been IT services for the most part. When I worked in the energy business unit at EDS, I had a lot of dealings with oil and gas, chemical, and utility companies. When I moved to Shell it was very much the same thing, but from the perspective of how an oil company uses IT. When I went to Compaq, obviously my approach had to broaden from just the IT services perspective to myriad hardware areas. Now I am concerned with computer products like storage devices and high-end servers as well as PCs. Of course, Compaq has something like the fifth or sixth largest IT services practice in the world, so my background in that area has been helpful as well.

One issue that's been covered in *Competitive Intelligence Magazine* [104] recently is the debate about using the word "intelligence" and the difference between intelligence and pure research. How do you define competitive intelligence and what do you think are the key factors that make it "intelligence" vs. research?

Basically, the work that we do for our customers—which are our executive leadership, our sales force, our product managers, and our strategy people—should help them with *their* customers. It all flows downstream. Our approach is very customer focused; how are we going to help our customers help their customers?

All competitive intelligence starts with a base, and on that base you make a series of incremental improvements. I'll take you through a little bit of process that I went through. At Shell, four people knew who I was when I first joined the company; those were the four people I interviewed with. Over time, what you're trying to do is gain an audience and build an awareness for your information. One of the mechanisms to deliver it is a newsletter. A newsletter creates two types of awareness: 1) an awareness of what the competition is doing in the external environment, and 2) an awareness of the actual CI team that's providing this information. So one of the things I did first was ask my manager who else should get some of the competitive intelligence I delivered.

With those leads, I could now contact, say, 20 to 25 people and distribute a newsletter to them. The newsletter's going to create an awareness of what the competition is doing out in the industry, and about how we need to be prepared to attack and defend. Now, let's say I send that newsletter out once a week, and it comes into your mailbox and it says from Bret Breeding, with "CI News to Go" as the subject. Very soon, the recipients will start to associate competitive intelligence with the person or team actually sending that newsletter. Because I've created this awareness through my newsletter, they will automatically begin to think about who they should call when they need someone to go digging. And soon, the number of people subscribing and the number of requests start to increase. The caveat is—and this is a rut that happens in a lot of CI departments—news requests, news requests, news requests; it just snowballs. Next thing you know, that's all the CI department is doing; they can never get to do the real job they need to, which is simulation and scenario planning. That's the top level, where the big value-add is for CI (see Figure 11.1). The approach I advocate is one where you take your most requested news items and figure out a way to make those sorts of items easily available to an audience. In essence, wean that audience to using automated methods, which usually means the Web, so they can pull the information themselves. We steer our users to intelligence, not merely news items. I'll walk them through our corporate intranet the first few times, and then hopefully by the third time they'll be saying "Brett, I've checked out what's on the Web, now I need to know this extra piece." That's where I want my audience to be.

Once I get this automation going for the more routine kinds of information, I can turn to things such as simulation. Someone calls up and asks what is this competitor likely to try to do on this deal? At that point I can say, based on all of our experiences with this competitor, that we predict that X, Y, or Z will be the tactics this guy's going to employ. The fact is that you'll never build up the experience to be able to answer questions like that unless you get a lot of feedback from your audience. That feedback comes from helping them out; once you've helped them a series of times you can call them up and ask, Bob, you've run up

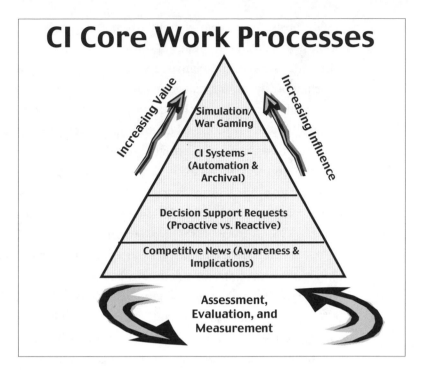

Figure 11.1

against this competitor. Can you tell me what happened? Bob is likely to come back and say, this is what this competitor did. I, in turn, will use that information later on with someone else, when I try to simulate what this competitor's likely to try to do.

We also get what we call decision support requests, which are "as needed" requests that require intelligence to impact decisions. We also produce a quarterly earnings review, which takes a look at the competition each quarter from a variety of perspectives, and a quarterly competitive review that ties up all the competitors we track into one presentation. These are delivered to different executive audiences inside Compaq.

What is essential in your CI toolkit? What couldn't you live without in your daily CI work?

Obviously, I can't live without my newsletter. Must have that, because that creates awareness. I must have my competitor profiles, which are ongoing, cumulative reports that organize key competitor information by several categories including overview, competitor qualifications, competitor clients and offerings, and marketing messaging. Without my profiles, I couldn't guarantee that my staff actually has the base level of information that's necessary to know about a competitor. And I've got to have my playbooks, to actually simulate what a competitor's likely to try to do. The playbook simulations come from Jim Holden's [245] "Strategic Value Selling Methodology," which is a highly competitive-based methodology for making strategic relationship-based sales. The simulation is centered around one of four different strategies a company can take. When several competitors go after a piece of business, one of four things can happen. If Competitor A has the best product or service, it has what is called a direct strategy. A direct strategy is associated with having the best product or service offering of any of your competitors. Now, the rest of the competitors don't just pack up their shop and go home, they use a variety of strategies to counterbalance that. One strategy they might try is to use a relationship to change the buying criteria, to move it away from that product or service superiority to something they do offer. That's called an indirect strategy: Use the relationship to change the rules of the playing field. Another strategy that's close kin to that is called a divisional strategy. It stresses trying to divide the deal up into pieces; that way, maybe you don't have the best suite of offerings, but you have one or two pieces that are best in class, and you can get the client to bite on those pieces. The fourth strategy is a containment strategy. It says, look, I probably can't win this deal, but there are other deals in the area I want to win, so I'm going to try to get this buyer to delay his buying decision. That way I can basically tie up all the competitor's resources on this deal, so I can win other accounts in the area.

You spoke about guiding people to the Internet when they just have a simple question. In your

own information gathering and research processes how much do you use the Internet, vis-à-vis the for-fee and subscription-based online services?

We buy several different services, we have quite a budget, and we exercise a lot of different research tools. I have personal subscriptions that put news in my mailbox that we in turn use for the newsletter. We use sources such as Gartner [35], IDC (International Data Corporation) [48], and Thomson's First Call [81]. We have access to a wide variety of news banks from around the world. We add value to the information we pull. For example, we'll pull a news story on Competitor X. Competitor X may have signed three or four storage deals in the last month. Well, instead of running a story on each of those deals, we tie them all together, and say Competitor X shows strong momentum in the storage industry, along with some little factoids about the specifics. But what we really want to do is present competitive implications and recommendations about what the story really means. We aim to answer four questions in each newsletter: What does this mean to the industry, what does it mean to this competitor, what does it mean to this competitor's competitors, and what does it mean to Compaq and its customers?

Once your data-gathering is done, what are your next steps?

After the data-gathering is done, it's always about finding out "what does this mean"—those four important questions I just mentioned. If you don't deal with those, you're merely a reporting service, and anyone can get that from anywhere. Once the information has been gathered, it has to be summarized, consolidated in such a way that someone can get to it really easily, hit the high points, but then get to the part where it tells them, this is what this actually means.

Do you follow the Porter [163] model, where you start out with planning and then go on to primary and secondary research before you start your synthesis, or have you found a different approach that works for you?

If I had to systematize it, I'd probably agree with how Porter does it. I really don't think about it much in those terms. The fact is that if you dig hard enough and have enough contacts, you can usually get the information you want. I know what needs to be done, I think I know what's cost-effective and what's available to us at no fee, I know what's available through my own personal networks, and I know what it's going to cost me. That's basically how I attack it.

Do you have a standard model or template that you use to organize your research results?

Every one of our deliverables has a standard format. For example, our monthly pricing updates have a standard template that we use. Whatever it was last month, you duplicate it this month. Our bill tracker is the same every edition, always consistent. We actually have what's called a process flow that takes every one of our analysts through our more tricky deliverables like our earnings analysis, all the way from start to finish. Every moment of their week is documented in terms of all the things they have to do. Because a lot of different things go into that deliverable, and every one of those is documented, the way the information should appear on the page is all formatted and it just has to be inserted and it's ready to go. Every one of our deliverables has a process flow that says this is how it should be done during the course of that period, whether it's a week, a day, a month, or a quarter, and every deliverable has a template associated with it that says this is the format that you shall use. I also have a content manager who insures that all the deliverables that come in look like they've been written by the same person.

That's great. It sounds like you also do a lot of training of people whom you bring in or who are assigned to you. When you train someone, is there a basic road map that you present them with?

One of the things we did differently was bring people in from several types of backgrounds—sales, consulting, library, engineering— the reason being that once they learned my methodology, their own perspectives and experiences would take over, and that adds more and more and more to the deliverable. Now when we bring in someone new and they see the deliverable set, they are often intimidated. We recently brought in a lady from Venezuela who thought she would "never get it," but about a month later she stated that, after you go through all the different cycles, it's a piece of cake. Take just one deliverable at a time, get real good at it, and then you go on to the next. If I were starting a CI department, the first thing I'd do is produce a newsletter. I might just start with "what does this news mean to the industry." But I'd slowly improve; I would then add competitor profiles, and so on. It just builds as you go. As you get more sophisticated, you can add other deliverables.

Over time, your approach develops in such a way to adapt to the needs of your constituents. You find, after talking to people like the CFO of the company, that you start incorporating things they think are important. You listen and let things evolve. A lot of my ideas are not my ideas; I've stolen all of these ideas. Everything I've created has come from somewhere else. The ideas really aren't that earth-shaking or revolutionary; they've just evolved with time, experience, and tweaking. I think it was Steve Jobs who said, "Good artists copy but great artists steal."

How much time do you allocate to the planning, research, synthesis, results organization, and communication phases? Do you have a formula to budget your time for each type of request?

Time allocation is totally dependent on the amount of information one can obtain. If information is prevalent, you can spend a larger percentage on synthesis, analysis, and communication. If information is not prevalent, you may spend all your time trying to dig up those few golden nuggets. But everything you get has to be communicated in some way, and I build that into the process for each deliverable. Communication could take anywhere from a few minutes to 25 percent of the total time allotted. What we report and how we report it depends on the audience.

What software products do you use in-house? You mentioned earlier that you use some services that push news information to you. Do you use anything else to help you with either post-search analysis or Web site monitoring?

Our information group actually performs the post-search analysis and Web site monitoring for us behind the scenes. They provide great results, but I don't get to see all that they use behind the scenes. From a source point of view, we try to pull daily news from general business sources such as *Business Week* [97], Bloomberg [9], the BBC [8], Cnet.com [12], Yahoo! Finance Vision [87], and the *Wall Street Journal* [193]. We also task industry sites such as Red Herring [169], IT World.com [50], Upside Today [188], and AsiaBizTech [6]. And we look for updates from market research houses such as the Giga Information Group [37] and Frost & Sullivan [33]. We use Dow Jones Interactive [23], soon to be Factiva.com [30], as a search service, and the Dogpile [22] search engine, which may be a source of daily news alerts as well.

Looking at your career in CI, what do you feel has been your largest coup?

One of my largest coups was that my methodology was considered so good that Shell took it and made a consulting business out of it, devoting a lot of resources to it. The other coup was that several articles I wrote about my experience at Shell were published in a book, *Practical Strategies in Competitive Intelligence.*

On the other side, have you ever had an absolutely horrible nightmare of a project?

No, not really. I would try to manage against that. You should never get stuck on a project that's going to be horrible. Never take on something that you just can't do. Admit you can't do it, even though it might be painful to do so.

How do you stay current and competent with your strategies and resources?

One thing that helps is that we go on road shows all the time. We are constantly visiting our key customers and getting their feedback. We also attend conferences and find that, when presenting a deliverable, someone will say, "You should do it like this"—and I'll be doggoned, they're dead right; I *should* do it like that. It's more or less going out and meeting a lot of people and incorporating all those perspectives, because you really can't innovate in isolation. Analysis really is a synthesis of perspectives. You're taking the perspective of your constituents, market analysts, suppliers, and so on, incorporating, synthesizing, and regurgitating it in such a way that it sounds intelligent.

You mentioned previously that the folks in your department come from several walks of life. What do you look for, in either their skill set or their educational background, relevant to performing CI in your company?

That's a good question. I'll tell you a story. It's about a guy named Warren Bell who runs the CI for Pivotal Corporation. Warren was the first person I ever hired at EDS when I was a manager there. Warren came into my office and sat down for his interview, and we talked for a couple of minutes about the position, and I looked at him and said, "Hey Warren, do you like sports at all?" And he said, "Oh, I love sports." And I said, "Well, what's your favorite team?" He said, "Oh, the Oakland As. I used to be a big As fan in the '80s." And we started talking about sports and one topic led to another. After about an hour and a half, I said, "Well, Warren, looks like I want to hire you." He was just shocked; in fact, he tells this story too. And about a week later, my manager called me into his office and said, "Bret, I'm not going to let you hire anyone ever, ever again." I asked "Well, why, what's wrong?" He says, "A bunch of people outside your office heard that all you did during that interview was talk sports to that guy. I'm not going to let you hire anyone again if that's all you're going to do." I said, "Well, hold it. One, the guy obviously reads a lot to know as much as he did. Two, he remembers everything he reads. Three, he can tell me what he reads and how it fits into the context of an overall picture. Four, he's got a passion about something." That's exactly what I look for in an analyst.

So, when I talk to people, I like to find out what they like in life, if they read, what they read. It doesn't really matter what they read. Tell me what you read and tell me that you're excited about it, because I can translate that excitement into something that we do here. If you don't have an outside interest, if you've got just a ho-hum life, it's going to be very difficult to get you excited and motivated to do this type of work. There's a lot of reading and remembering involved in this job, and if you can't get excited about what you read, there's no place for you in this line of work.

What do you enjoy most about the CI profession?

Change is probably what I enjoy most. As I go to conferences, I get to show what we do and how we are evolving our products and approach. I typically have a lot of repeat people at my speaking engagements. They share spinoffs from what I do to what they've done, which becomes a key learning experience for me. I have my own little set of followers who come back from conference to conference to see each of my presentations and how our deliverables change and evolve over time. They share with me how they've twisted my approach or product in a certain way, and really made it effective for their organization. I'll actually go and steal those ideas back from them. It's a very good way of evolving your own approach.

Are there any downsides to the profession?

A lot of people talk about CI in terms of being a really new profession with no standards in place for how to do it. I think that's another part of the reason why I like to go out and talk a lot about what we do here. The problem is that you have a lot of theoreticians who speak in broad terms about an analytical model, the five forces and all. The five forces is a good model, but it's never ever actually helped a company beat its competitors on a deal. It may help position the company better against its competitors in terms of its strategic plan, but it's limited when it comes to actually helping win a deal. Theoretical models are dormant, a nice way to represent the information to an executive, but not quite there when it comes to actually making decisions.

Because CI is such a new industry it's still very chaotic. Look at Don King, the boxing promoter. Don King is a very shady character, but he's very, very astute in certain areas. He has this idea that a chaotic environment is a good thing, and I actually believe that as well. CI doesn't have a lot of standards yet, and that means you have a lot of room to be flexible. It's not like cost accounting or financial accounting. In CI there are so many different ways to do it, and because the industry's so new, you can actually thrive within the chaos. That's one of the things I like about Don—in boxing, he thrives within the chaos. There's no governing body, there's no regulation that says you can't do this, so he figures a way to make it creative, to benefit him, and maybe I do it that same way. I figure out ways to be creative, so I can actually thrive and prosper in this type of environment.

Super Searcher Power Tips

➤ When starting your CI practice, don't try to do something complex right off the bat. Figure out what you really need to do—profiles, news, whatever it may be—to satisfy your audience. Do it well and then build on it over time.

➤ A newsletter creates two types of awareness: 1) an awareness of what the competition is doing in the external environment, and 2) an awareness of the actual CI team that's providing this information.

➤ Try to help as many people as you can with their decisions so you gain their confidence. That way, when you need to ask them for a favor, you've got it.

➤ Every one of our deliverables has a process flow that says this is how it should be done during the course of that period, whether it's a week, a day, a month, or a quarter, and every deliverable has a template associated with it that says this is the format that you shall use.

➤ Staying current and competent involves going out and meeting a lot of people and incorporating all those different perspectives, because you can't innovate in isolation.

John Wilhelm

Systematic Focus

John Wilhelm is Vice President at Kaiser Associates, a strategy consulting firm in Washington, DC. Prior to joining Kaiser Associates in 1993, John was an analyst for the investment banking division of Salomon Brothers.

JWilhelm@KaiserAssociates.com

Tell me about your background and how and when you started performing competitive intelligence.

I received my undergraduate degree in Finance and Management from the University of Virginia. I then headed to Wall Street where I worked as a financial analyst for the investment banking division of Salomon Brothers for three years. In my final year at Salomon Brothers, I started looking into the field of consulting and chose Kaiser Associates because of the entrepreneurial nature of the firm and the chance to work with leading companies in a number of industries. I started at Kaiser in 1993 as an entry-level consultant. During my tenure in this position, I started to develop the tools for performing competitive intelligence and learning about how I could use competitive intelligence as one of several inputs into developing strategies for my clients. I then moved into a management position where I continued to develop my research skills but also got a chance to work more closely with our clients and to teach competitive intelligence and other strategic skills to other analysts. Over the years, I've earned an MBA from Wharton while building my own practice at the firm. Over a 10-year period, I have been involved in more than 200 projects for Kaiser Associates, many of which have included using competitive intelligence as a tool for delivering recommendations to our clients.

How would you describe your present function in a nutshell?

Kaiser is a strategy consulting firm providing fact-based advice to clients. We work across a variety of different industries. My specific function as a vice president is to develop relationships with clients and lead my own practice. I focus the majority of my effort on a core set of long-term clients. My job combines business development, sales, account management, and project delivery, as well as consultant management and development. We span a lot of functions because we are a small, entrepreneurial firm, so every Vice President chips in to just about everything.

Do you have specific types of research that you perform, or do you find that you cut across several industries, such as manufacturing and consumer goods?

We work across most of the major industries. I personally focus on a handful of clients in industries such as aerospace and defense, technology, pharmaceuticals, healthcare, and consumer products. The firm overall supports core clients that are typically number 1, 2, or 3 in their industries, covering a dozen different industries. Our clients are from different industries and their business issues are diverse. We support their decision making by providing strategic advice based on facts. These facts come from high-quality research that is customized for each client and each project we conduct.

How do you define competitive intelligence?

To me, competitive intelligence is simply a systematic way to collect information about your competition, analyze that information, and then use your findings to make decisions about strategy. Kaiser conveys to our clients that gathering intelligence requires a system that incorporates an entire process, and then we help clients work through the steps. Without a method for approaching competitive research, you can get sidetracked or end up with big gaps in your understanding of the competitive landscape and how that impacts your strategy. It's essential to understand the desired impact of the project. When somebody hands you a competitive analysis project, don't just say, "Great," and go off and do it. Do say, "At the end of the day, when I give you this report, what is it going to be used for? Is this to get into a new market? Is it to position a new product that's coming out? Is this a case where your sales force is underperforming in a certain region? What are you going to do with this information when you get it?"

What do you feel is essential in the competitive intelligence toolkit?

Having specific methodologies and processes to guide the research. Number one, we always develop a work plan that shows us milestones over the course of a project. There are different things that we want to accomplish at each step, or even in each week of the project. I think that's critical to make sure that you're always on track. Number two is to have a list of research resources that you can turn to. When we scope out the project, we start to map out the types of resources that we're going to be able to use to get at the research. That's important for us so that we don't reinvent the wheel.

Everything we do is hypothesis driven. So instead of going out and just getting a lot of information and then coming back and trying to understand where it all fits in, I sit down with my clients in the beginning and develop specific hypotheses about how I think the competitors might be playing in the market or how they might be considering a certain issue. Then we go forward and map the research to either validate or refute that.

How do you stay focused and eliminate extraneous data that is just "noise?"

At the beginning, when we start to talk to our clients about competitive analysis, we make sure that we understand a few things. First, what is the role of competitive intelligence in the overall strategic planning process. Secondly, what is the impact of the research going to be. And thirdly, what kinds of decisions are going to be made on the basis of the results. Then we sit down and challenge them on "the nice-to-knows" vs. "the need-to knows." Everybody, when they look at their competitors, would love to know just about everything about them, but there comes a point where not all of that information is valuable, and it might take up a lot of resources to actually get at the kind of research they're looking for. We come back to them and say, look, what is the end impact? And then, how are these specific points of research going to get us to that answer? By developing a clear scope for the work with our clients, we make sure that we are providing the information that will have an impact rather than information that is nice to hear.

Also, don't repeat what's already been done. Look to see if the client has old reports from your firm, and if they do, whether that work actually needs to be completely redone from scratch, or if it's work that needs to be updated. You don't want somebody who wasn't involved in the key decision-making group to come back and say, oh, we already did that a few years ago.

How do you weigh the Internet and the for-fee database services in your workflow, and in your research process?

The Internet has really altered the way that we go about research. When I started doing research several years ago, one of my first steps was to call up Investor Relations in the company I was studying and have them mail me the annual report. You can now find that same information as well as all of the company's other financial information through the SEC (Securities Exchange Commission) [73, see Appendix] Web site.

The Internet can be a big part of the research process, but there are a few key things to note about how to use it. First, the Internet is a great place to get started because there is such a proliferation of information, and you can sort through it relatively quickly. You have to be focused on what you are looking for and keep track of the sites that are the most useful.

Second, the Internet is a great way to keep up-to-the-minute on what's going on with competitors and with the industry, and you should set up a system that feeds this information to you. We use LexisNexis [56] and Yahoo! News [88] to constantly update the top news stories on our clients and their competitors, and I check those several times each day.

Lastly, it's important to remember that your clients have access to the same information on the Internet that you do. You have to take the information through the next steps. First, you need to build on it through other sources. We use a handful of for-fee services, including LexisNexis and Hoovers [41], as well as others that are very helpful in getting industry- or company-specific information. We then continue the research by contacting primary and secondary sources. Throughout the project, we are pulling the information together from the Internet and other sources to determine the impact for our clients. Our findings are not dependent upon any one source.

What do you do, or how do you cope, when you are in the middle of a search and you're just not finding what you want or what you believe must exist?

Typically, at that point we'll sit down as a group and brainstorm again about where the potential sources of information might be. The other key for us is really understanding and then collaborating with our client. Our clients live in their industries day-in and day-out. There might be some things that the client knows that we don't. We talk to them about the types of information that they're looking for and we try to bounce ideas off them. We ask for ideas on where we can get the information or if there is somebody at this or that association that might be able to help us, and so on. We keep that constant flow of communication going.

Another thing that's critical to the project is managing the expectations of our clients, helping them to understand that there are some things that we're not going to be able to get to a 95 percent certainty level. If there's a specific data point we can't get, we say, all right, what would be some of the potential drivers of that data point? If you're looking at quantitative information, then you would say, we can't get that specific number, but what are some of the drivers of that number? Then we try to get the research done related to those drivers. We are very upfront with our clients. We tell them, these are some of the drivers; we've used our own analytical tools to develop a good representation of what we think the answer might be, but we did not get that number directly from our conversations with people in the marketplace.

Once the secondary research is done, what are your next steps? Do you have any particular process that you follow?

Typically, what we'll do in the secondary research is get all the financial information, as well as analysts' reports and other research reports that are out there. From there, the first step that we take is to actually start talking to industry analysts. These might be some folks on Wall Street or other people who track the industry at market research firms. We talk with them about the report they've done, and then build on that to either get a more updated view or just some additional opinions. We use a back-and-forth conversational approach to say, "Well, your article said this but my take on it is a little bit different ..."

After the analysts, we start to talk with other players in the market. The list might include customers, suppliers, partners, and other competitors. By spreading the net wide, we come up with a robust set of information about the industry overall.

We do all of this before we actually go to the competitor companies themselves to gather their opinions of the marketplace and customer perceptions. And often we find that, if we start with the hypothesis and go through the rigorous process I've just described, by the time we actually get to the conversations with the competitors, we've been able to either validate or refute, with a pretty strong confidence level, the hypothesis that we developed at the front end. There are many instances where we don't even go to the competitors at the end of the day.

Do your clients rely on you to do the entire process or do you perform as middlemen, where clients take your data and combine it with their internal analysis and deliver the final results to their executives?

It varies. Occasionally, there are times where the client has developed a report for somebody higher up and there's a critical piece missing. Kaiser may fill that hole by providing that information and insight. More often, it's a more strategic effort, where they're really looking to us to provide insight on how they should approach an issue. Typically, our work goes straight to the president or vice president of the organization. We collaborate with the client team throughout the process so the end product might either be a joint presentation of the client team's work and ours, or it might integrate their work into our analysis.

It's important to understand who the audience is going to be, who's going to see this at the end and throughout the project, and to make sure that you have a clear line of communication with the people that you're going to be dealing with. Whether it's a small team or an executive group, really understand what the hierarchy's going to be, and whom you need to go to for questions throughout.

Do you have a standard model or template that you use in order to organize your research results, or do you find that it's totally customer- and custom-driven?

We use typical strategic models such as the Porter analysis [107], four-corners model, and those types of things to scope out the findings of the research. Based on the number of studies that we've done over our 20-year history, we've got some pretty successful templates for how different studies can lay out, depending on the variables of the project.

What road map would you present to a researcher who's been newly assigned to a CI function?

There are three things that I would highlight as being critically important. First, it is crucial to develop the lines of communication with the end customer, whether it's internal or external. To deliver a successful end product you have to have the support and interaction of the customer. Up front, you need to have a clear understanding of the scope, expectations, and milestones and the format of the final results. Throughout the project, you need to have a constant feedback loop to make sure that the customer is getting what he or she needs and can comment on it prior to the critical milestones so that adjustments can be made.

The second critical assignment is to front-load the process. Many people make the mistake of receiving an assignment and then immediately jumping into the research. If you take the time to set up the project well at the beginning, you will save a lot of wasted effort later in the process.

Finally, you need to keep track of the steps you are taking in each project and continue to build the system. During your first CI assignment, you might have to develop a lot of the processes, methodologies, resources, and templates, but it should get easier as you continue in your role.

How much time do you allocate to the planning, secondary research, primary research, results organization, packaging, and delivery?

Competitive analysis is a factor in some of the work that we do, but it's not often the sole goal. So there are times when we focus on what is my competitor doing in this area, but other times we do a market analysis where we have to understand the entire competitive landscape. That includes talking to the customers and talking to other people in the market as well as the competitors. Typically, using a 10-week project as an example, we might spend a week and a half to two weeks on secondary research. We would then spend somewhere between five and six weeks on the primary research, and then the last two to three weeks on analysis and final recommendations. We try as much as possible in the first few weeks to establish a framework for how the end deliverable will look, and then we start to populate that with findings as the project moves along.

What types of results do you feel are essential to report? Or does it vary depending on the project?

First of all, you should always define the format for the end result at the beginning of the project. One of the key issues is determining who the ultimate audience will be. Your report is going to look very different if you have 15 minutes in front of the CEO vs. two hours in front of the global sales force. Once you have determined the audience, you should then discuss the formats that have been successful with that audience in the past. For instance, some clients may want to see the detail while others may ask you for "the three things I need to take away from this."

You should also collaborate with the client throughout the project by sharing with them the templates and analytical tools that you will use throughout the process. That way you can work with the client to integrate their style and yours into the final report.

Finally, regardless of the format you use, make sure that your client can act on the information. If you are just giving them information, at the end of the day they might find it interesting but they will be wanting more. Look at the information, analyze it, and be prepared to discuss with your client what the impact to their business is.

What software products do you use in your search or analysis process? Have you found any products that are particularly useful?

The LexisNexis Eclipse service. You can set it up to plug in the names of companies that you're tracking, and it will feed you articles on a daily basis. That's been really valuable for us, because it helps us keep up-to-date on our clients as well as competitors without having to keep checking back. Sometimes I just use a My Yahoo! page where I've plugged in the ticker symbols of my clients' companies and get a scrolling list of the top five stories or press releases or whatever it might be. I'll check that a couple of times during the day to see if there's any major news that I need to be aware of.

What do you feel was your largest coup?

One of the more interesting things we've been able to do is find out and understand more about the pharmaceutical industry. It's crucial to the profitability of pharmaceutical firms to understand and prepare for specific product introductions, modifications, and branded vs. generic offerings, before they occur. We've been very successful on several occasions helping our clients position themselves with a better understanding of the marketplace.

What about the other end of the spectrum— your worst nightmare, or your largest lesson learned?

There have been a handful of projects that haven't gone well. The majority of the time the reason was the communication issue. It was when we didn't force the client to spend time with us. The way we report out to our clients now is to meet with them on a weekly basis to show our progress. We've had instances where the client didn't have the time and told us to just go off and do this and come back midway through and at the end. And when we came back midway through they said, "Well, this isn't exactly what we expected," and we said, "This is what we interpreted as what you told us." They didn't meet with us on a week-to-week basis, so we couldn't change the scope or understand that they had a different expectation. As a result we've become much more rigorous, especially over the past five years where we've said, "Look, we need to get on the client's calendar. If it's not every week then it has to be every two weeks." Because if we continue to research what we think is best, that's where we're going to run into mistakes.

Competitive analysis is tricky because the client says, "Okay, this is what I want," and they can list it in 10 bullet points. But when they start to see the information come back, they think, "Wow, that's actually a lot different than I expected it to be. So, all right, those other couple of data points, we don't need those any more, because I'd rather focus the resources over here." So the scope changes a little bit, and you've got to be flexible enough so that, as the scope continues to modify itself based on the types of information you're finding, you can reallocate your resources accordingly. It all goes back to communication and managing expectations.

How do you stay current and confident with your strategies and resources?

We have a very formalized process for making sure that we have one person responsible for managing our research resources. So everybody knows that one of the first places to go is to a part of our intranet where you can find that type of information. If you're looking for something in the telecommunications industry, here are the trade journals in telecommunications that you should look at, or here are the analysts who are some of the better contacts in the telecom industry.

The other part involves the fact that we at Kaiser focus on a limited set of 15 or so clients who are leaders in their industry. So it's a matter of always keeping your ears open, trying new things, working with the client, and then also keeping a central repository in the form of a Research Resources Database that is accessible through our intranet, that helps us make sure that as new things come up, they get added to the core resource list. For example, just a little while ago, one of my managers was looking up something in the petroleum industry and she found a wonderful site that she loved. She forwarded the link to me, and it was great, and one I hadn't seen before. Somehow she stumbled upon it, and we're going to make sure that we forward it to the research resources person to make sure that other people know about it. Serendipity definitely plays a part.

What skill set or education do you feel an individual needs to be successful in performing competitive intelligence?

The key thing for us is the analytical ability. Secondly, it's being friendly over the phone or face-to-face. The key for our consultants is that when they get people on the phone, they can engage them in conversation, whether it's an industry analyst or whomever. Peoples' time is limited, and they're not going to talk to somebody who's just going to read off a questionnaire in a very flat tone. They want somebody who's going to be passionate about the issue and really understand it. So the ability to understand the issue well, to analyze what's going on in the industry, and to be able to come back with an opinion is really critical for us—especially since, as you talk on the phone with people, the conversation may take some twists and turns that you don't expect initially.

One of the key skills that our consultants have is the ability to formulate a decision tree in their mind that says, as I'm asking these questions, if the person says yes, I go in this direction, if the person says no, I go in this other direction. That's really critical to us. If you're bound and determined to have a standard list of questions that you're going to stick to—a framework I don't suggest—you're not going to get the level of insight that you will if you can be flexible. Really listen well to the person on the other end of the phone, and analyze in real time what they're saying, and be able to go on to the next logical question. It's a throwback to Systems Analysis 601 in graduate school, with the if–then boxes. In the 10 years that I've been here, I've seen a lot of people walk through the door, and the ones who are successful are the ones who can learn quickly, who crave learning new things, and have a passion about what they're seeking.

What do you enjoy most about this profession?

The thing I enjoy most about this profession is that there's always something different. People look at me and say, wow, you've been with one company for 10 years, which in this day and age is not too normal. I've done a couple of hundred projects in those 10 years and every one has had a different tweak to it, whether it's the personality of the client or the issues we're examining, or the industry.

There are times too, when we'll be researching something and it'll show up in the *Wall Street Journal* during the course of the project. So, being on the leading edge of the business world is always interesting as well. Although there are specific processes and models you can put on projects to make the job easier, each audience is going to be different. Each competitor that you research is going to be different, and there will be some things that are going to surprise you. It's continuous learning.

It's also a lot of fun to find out what companies do extremely well and to be able to go back to my client and say, "Hey, the reason they're beating you in the marketplace is that they've figured out a way to do this, and you guys need to figure out your own way to combat this, or else the market share is going to continue to sway in their favor."

And what do you like the least?

When companies don't see the broader application of competitive intelligence, when they don't realize its value overall. When they look at CI more as a means to satisfy their curiosity than actually taking what we find and implementing it and making a real impact on their business. At the end of the day, they're paying us to go out there and get this information, and if it sits on a shelf it's not doing anybody any good. The times that I have most enjoyed are when a client calls me up, somebody that we worked for three years ago, and says "I was in somebody's office and I saw your report, and they obviously got a lot of use out of it because it was dog-eared and a little bit worn." That's music to my ears. I hate to see companies continue to falter based on some of their old habits, and not utilizing what we spent a lot of our effort on, providing good ideas that could change the landscape of their business.

Super Searcher Power Tips

➤ Many people make the mistake of receiving an assignment and then immediately jumping into the research.
If you take the time to set up the project well at the
beginning, you will save a lot of wasted effort later in
the process.

➤ The more you can develop specific methodologies or
processes around doing CI, the better you're going to
be at it. There are always challenges inherent in getting the actual information, but if you develop a
framework for how you're going to get it, it will be that
much easier and have more impact.

➤ Limit the scope of activities to make sure it fits the
resources you have. Separate the nice-to-knows from
the need-to-knows. Make sure the information you're
getting has a purpose. You don't want to throw 30
percent of it away. Each piece must have an impact on
the business.

➤ Collaborate with the customer throughout to ensure
that the process is working and that they are getting
what they need. Consistent feedback, regardless of the
length of the project, is a must.

➤ Manage expectations throughout the project. You've
got to understand that there are some things in competitive analysis that you won't get, or that are just not
possible. Be able to tell your client, "We understand
what you need; this is how we're going to go about it."

➤   Develop hypotheses up front to ensure directed research. Get some opinions about how your client thinks the marketplace might play out, or how that competitor might react to different scenarios. Don't do your research and analysis in a vacuum, where you're getting data and then trying to apply it later.

➤   Use a central repository for research resources. Maintain a list of sources that have worked, including people. Each time you go into a new project, start with the research resources repository and build from there. At the end of the project go back and add new resources to your central repository so that it continues to be a dynamic document.

Ken Sawka and Cynthia Cheng Correia

Leveraging Internal Competitive Knowledge

Kenneth Sawka directs Deloitte Consulting's Pursuit Support Center. At the time of this interview, he was Vice President of Fuld & Company's Global Consulting Practice. Prior to his years at Fuld, Kenneth was senior manager in Deloitte Consulting's global Strategic Planning practice. Before launching his consulting career, Mr. Sawka spent eight years as an intelligence analyst at the Central Intelligence Agency.

ksawka@dc.com

Cynthia Cheng Correia is Director of Information Services for Fuld & Company Inc., a competitive intelligence research and consulting firm. She oversees its information resources, manages literature research functions, consults and trains in competitive intelligence and strategic information management and research, and oversees Fuld & Company's Web-based Internet Intelligence Index. Cynthia's experience and areas of interest include competitive intelligence, global business information resources, knowledge management, library/information services management and marketing, and information and technology literacy.

ccorreia@fuld.com

Can you both tell me a bit about your backgrounds and how and when you started performing competitive intelligence?

KS: I've got a checkered background. I got started in intelligence by spending eight years with the CIA fresh out of college, so I was there from '86 through '94. When it came time to leave government, about five years later than I thought I would, I became aware of the field of competitive intelligence and took a consulting position with a firm called the Futures Group, which was another small niche firm in competitive intelligence. That firm was acquired by Deloitte Consulting. I spent 18 months with Deloitte as a senior manager in their strategy practice and then joined Fuld to take over their CI systems and CI process consulting organization in October 1999.

CC: My interest in CI goes back to my library school days. I took a competitive intelligence course at Simmons College's Graduate School of Library and Information Science and got turned on to CI through that. After graduation, I managed an information service at an economic development organization where we monitored competitiveness of other states and regions and conducted some competitive research, although not anything at the level of research/analysis and the competitive intelligence process at which Ken and my other colleagues are experts. I then worked to build an independent information service with some partners, and moved on to Fuld & Company to oversee their information services.

In a nutshell, what is your current function? Do you focus on a subject specialty?

KS: Typically a client of Fuld has a need for competitive intelligence that can be satisfied with some combination of research and analysis that we provide on an outsource basis. They also need to build some internal capability or infrastructure to enable them to address some of their competitive intelligence issues on their own. That involves helping them leverage internal competitive knowledge that may or may not be written down, that may or may not be in a database, but is at least in the minds and heads of people inside the organization. We then build the tools to collect that information, analyze it, process it, store it, archive it, and ultimately turn it into intelligence for decision makers.

CC: I manage information services that support Fuld's research and analysis, consulting, seminars, marketing, and other activities. Our services include literature research, collection management, consulting, training, news monitoring, Web resource development such as our Internet Intelligence Index, knowledge management, and so forth. We provide company-wide and client information support.

KS: Fuld is organized by industry practice, so we have six industry practice groups that are really channels into our market, so any services we provide for a client get provided through these industry groups. We cover consumer products; financial services; life sciences, which is healthcare and pharmaceuticals; manufacturing; technology and telecom; and energy and utilities. The work is spread across those six industry groups. Certain years some are bigger than others, but if you look at projects we've done over time, they have been fairly evenly spread across those six sectors.

KS: Both Cynthia and I have the luxury—in fact we're a bit of an oddball—of getting to support all of the industries. So it's very common for today to be a pharmaceutical project, while tomorrow is going to be consumer products, and the next day we're going to do telecommunications. We get the entire mix.

CC: As an information professional serving the needs of six major industry practices, information services is my specialty. We keep up with industry news and developments so that we can be knowledgeable in providing our services and be as prepared as we can when projects or proposals come our way. Our research project teams include some talented people who have very deep industry knowledge, and we can always tap into this level of expertise when we have questions. At the same time, we are also ready to help prepare colleagues who are new to our firm or who want to explore areas that are novel to them. For this, we provide training and background information support.

How do you define competitive intelligence and how does that differ from doing business research?

KS: For me, and for the clients that we work with, intelligence suggests the expectation that action will result from the knowledge or the learning or the content that we either give a client directly with the good research and analysis we do, or that we enable the client to learn on their own from the process building that we do. So, when we're asked to provide intelligence in whatever form, one of our first questions always is what are you going to do with the information? We'll turn clients away—we're almost bad to a fault on this—if we don't get a satisfactory answer to that question. We'll say, well, it sounds like you really haven't thought out the purpose or the application for this, so perhaps you're better served by a market research firm such as Gartner or IDC or one of those companies, who provide information without the expectation that there's a decision or an action or strategy dependent on that information.

CC: I've heard the assertion recently that librarians have been conducting CI for years in using their business research skills. I know that many do and do it very well, but I've also encountered librarians who confuse conducting research that *feeds* into CI with CI itself. CI involves more than business research on a competitor. It is a specialty, and there are certain ways that one goes about researching for and practicing CI so that it can be conducted effectively. The idea that CI research is primarily traditional business research is also perpetuated by some information vendors who package, perhaps enhance slightly, and market their business content as a one-stop CI resource, without recognizing the function and components of the intelligence process. This is not to diminish the corporate librarian's role—we are a critical component of a good CI team—but I think that if librarians are truly interested in CI, and are looking to practice CI, it is necessary to understand the CI process in its entirety, how businesses will be able to use information and intelligence, and where librarians can fit in with their skills. I'd like to emphasize that CI doesn't rest with business literature; the primary research and analysis components are extremely important. That's where you often get most of the intelligence that you can use.

KS: I had a client a number of years ago, a big pharmaceutical client, and they engaged the Futures Group to help them build some CI capacity and process. My first day with this client, I was walking through the halls of the company, and I came across their library, and the name of the library was The Intelligence Center. I said to my client, the first thing you've got to do is change the name of the library, because if the organization believes they're getting intelligence directly from the library, they're wrong. I don't know if they did or not; I think they still call it that. But the point is that although secondary research is a very, very important component that goes into delivering intelligence, secondary research by itself isn't intelligence. You're dealing with information that is to a large extent available as a mass commodity, and there's little that's custom about it. Good secondary researchers and, by extension, good CI programs inside companies, take secondary research, combine it with good human intelligence collection, primary research, good analysis. Secondary research is one of three or four or five different ingredients in intelligence that, again, is going to be delivered to a user with the expectation that some action is going to happen as a result of that analysis.

CC: That's not to diminish what librarians do. We are a critical component of a team, and, in fact, may be underutilized in terms of our resources and skills. We help organize and direct research, provide material for human source collection, conduct primary research, provide critical observations and discoveries that we gain through our own research processes, and provide analysis and reporting. We can often make or break a project. But I think that if librarians are looking to get into CI, then it is essential to understand the entire process and discipline so that we can broaden our skills beyond traditional library or online searching skills.

KS: Right, and we often hear, when we're building a process with a client, that the corporate librarians love our being there, because we are providing a channel for them to take what they do and apply it to a process that makes what they do much more valuable. We also advise our clients to find an information researcher who knows the difference between "get me the article on page A3 of yesterday's *Wall Street Journal*" and "get me information that can help me assess my competitor's intent to enter Latin America with this product."

CC: And by understanding the needs and the processes in a given industry channel or business environment, we're able to make decisions about the kinds of resources or techniques that will uncover material and provide analysis that can be used by key decision makers.

What is essential in your CI toolkit?

KS: For me, it really depends on what the client is trying to accomplish and what we're trying to address. We don't necessarily go in to a client with a toolkit. We go in with a methodology to help them build a process, but what that toolkit includes is going to differ for every client.

CC: From my perspective, because I've worked very much on the research and analysis side, we use a lot of the standard business information resources, including the aggregators like Dialog [20, see Appendix] and Factiva [30]. With Factiva, we produce the Competitive Intelligence Center [13] on the Web. This is a Web site hosted by Factiva that features insights from the CI and industry experts at Fuld & Co. And we also use a lot of unusual—I guess, from the standard business research perspective—resources, like monitoring discussion groups, for example. In fact, I'll refer to the interview with Helene Kassler, who was my predecessor at Fuld & Company, in *Super Searchers Do Business* [181], where she discusses some of these resources and techniques, as well as to other articles Helene has written [247]. We're always on the lookout for new resources and building on our techniques as well, because the Web and the information industry are rapidly changing, and we have to constantly keep abreast of that. There are some nice newer search tools like Vivisimo [223] and Teoma [80] for general searching, specialized engines like Scirus [69] for science and technology; the list goes on. I could devote more time to itemizing these things, but there are no magic bullets or tried-and-true recipes. It's probably more efficient to reference Helene's articles and emphasize keeping up with developments in the industry, exercising creativity, and thinking globally about resources.

How do you weigh the Web against the for-fee database services in your workflow and your research methods?

CC: It's something that we constantly have in mind, and it truly depends on the project. Sometimes a project may have a smaller expense budget, so we're not able to use some of the more robust but costlier information aggregators and we have to rely more on free resources. Other times we have a healthy expense budget, so we're able to devote some time to using those vendor resources. But what's most important, I think—and librarians recognize this—is that it's often more cost-effective to turn to a fee-based resource for some key articles, transcripts, or other material than to trawl the Web for something that may or may not turn up in the time frame we have available. I'm working on a project right now for which I've been trying to find resources on a topic that's extremely broad, and there's a lot of noise out on the Web. This is when turning to an aggregator certainly saves a lot of time and, in the end, money.

How do you cope when you're in the middle of a search and just not finding what you want or what you believe exists?

CC: One of my favorite techniques is actually very low tech; I like to sleep on it, if I have the time. I find that by getting away from it, I might wake up inspired—or, if I'm very lucky, with the perfect research solution—the next day. I also turn to my colleague, Frederique Feron. We often bounce ideas off each other to see where we might have missed something. She and I have some overlapping skills and experiences, but we each bring some different yet complementary qualities that allow us to broaden our collective approach and perspective.

It also pays to map out a project ahead of time. Even though we're a component of a larger CI project, we have to plan our work extremely well and know which resources we should and can use given the project parameters; it's essential to stay within budget and deliver what the project manager and client expect. This is where the reference interview is also very important, and why it's key to keep up on new developments and resources on the open and the Invisible Web, the part that most search engines can't get to. It also helps us to be more resourceful and creative in our searching if we read publications written by our fellow info pros and consult wonderful newsletters like *The CyberSkeptic's Guide to Internet Research* [112], and online communities like BUSLIB-L [98], that are out there to support what we do.

Once the secondary research is done, what are your next steps, and do you have a specific order in which you execute them?

CC: Typically, we provide secondary research material to the project manager or the researcher, and they take it and do what they need to do. At that point, it's usually going on to the primary research phase. Once in a while, depending on the duration of the project and our budgeted time, we'll come back into the project to refine our search or to monitor the industry or some target companies. If it's a project that involves mostly literature searching, the information industry, or one of our librarians' areas of expertise or skill, we may also conduct the primary research, supply additional research guidance, provide consulting, or deliver the analysis and reporting.

How and when do you interface with the process folks?

KS: What we've learned over the years is that, no matter what a client says, it's just about impossible for any organization to be truly self-sufficient in providing their own competitive intelligence. Depending on the nature of the industry and the issues you're trying to solve, there are certain degrees of self-sufficiency that a company can achieve, but rarely can a company do entirely without externally provided CI, if they're serious about CI. One of the first things we do in a consulting engagement is conduct a needs analysis; I work with the client to identify the decisions-based intelligence requirements that this CI process ultimately needs to address. Once we do that, we can say, you've got a few needs here that are either of a high degree of urgency or a high degree of impact; it may not make sense for you to wait to have a process built that can address all or part of these issues. Or we might say, there's so much riding on getting the answer to this issue right that it behooves you to have some experts go and work on this problem for you. Then what we wind up doing is building infrastructure.

We have one client now, an enterprise software company, for whom we've built a process. They have figured that the process will cover maybe 40 percent—given their full-time resources—of the intelligence issues that we identified this organization should pay attention to. So they now have a very well-defined set of intelligence needs that their own internal process handles, and any need that comes up that falls outside that system, we handle on a private-label basis. We'll do the research and the analysis and then deliver the results back through the infrastructure that we've built. The end user doesn't always know if it's Fuld & Company or the internal process that's delivering the answer; they're just getting good answers. That's all they care about, and all they should care about.

Do you have a standard model or template that you use in order to organize your research results or present the project results?

KS: Not really, because we answer so many different questions for so many different kinds of companies. We do try to construct the skeleton or the framework of a deliverable, create the outline and major sections of what we think it's going to address, early in a project. But in the end, we're creating custom pieces of analysis every time we do it. It'd be tough to force-fit the same deliverable template to answer a question like "tell me how my major competitor trains its sales force" and one like "tell me how antitobacco legislation is going to affect my ability to expand into North America." Those are two very different questions that will demand different processes that will demand deliverables that look very different.

Another thing is that the people who run our industry practices come from the industry, so it's important for them to go to their clients with the deliverable that's going to be meaningful for them. The report and analysis that is of a high degree of utility for a bank is very different than the one that an e-commerce software company would find useful. For all those reasons, we really create a new format every time we do it. Frankly, it keeps it fun for us, too; if we were doing the same deliverable every time, we'd all get bored.

We've talked a lot about process, and obviously you folks have that down to a fine science.

When you go out and explain the process, what steps do you recommend, and in which order?

KS: What we do is follow Jan Herring's intelligence cycle [243]. Every CI process has to embody every element of the CI cycle. But when it comes time to say "here's what we think your process should look like," we may or may not use the cycle as the way to frame it for the client. We've actually used some work that John Prescott [254] at the University of Pittsburgh put together, that showed four or five steps to how a CI process can evolve in a company. John presented this model at a SCIP conference a couple of years ago, and two of our consultants in London have taken that and have applied it in support of some of our consulting. We may take four to five different approaches. We may say that your process has to address your competitive rivalry or the power of your suppliers, because that's where the highest degree of impact is going to be on your business and on your strategy. We're going to advise the client to build up the elements of that process where they can get the most return quickly. We might possibly say, look, because of the needs that you have, and because of the opportunity to leverage existing knowledge that lives within your company, the first thing we have to do is focus on how to analyze it. The fourth step in the CI cycle may be the first thing we tell the client to focus on, because that's where they're weakest, or that's where they can get the most immediate return.

How much time do you allocate to the planning, secondary research, primary research, and results organization and reporting? How do the percentages fall?

KS: Again, this is very client-need and project-need specific. Generally speaking, the greatest amount of time is spent on the primary research. But, if you were to ask me to put a percentage allocation on where the greatest value is derived in a project, I'd put it on analysis. Primary research takes time. If you're trying to contact busy people, and it takes three or four snail mails, two faxes, and five emails, and then an hour to conduct the interview and an hour to write it up—that's time. And in that whole process there may be 10 minutes' worth of information that's truly valuable; the rest is fluff. So the time devoted to getting that is significant. But when we step back and try to derive meanings and draw conclusions through analysis, that's where the greatest value is added.

CC: I've worked on quite a few projects in which the emphasis was on secondary research, but you still have to have an analysis component. And sometimes primary research will uncover some information that warrants additional literature searching. The way we allocate our time and resources often depends on the client's needs, the project resources, and what the research bears out.

KS: And we so often see somewhat unsophisticated clients who have a practice of delivering what they call intelligence, and it's no more than a summary of what they've pulled off LexisNexis, or what they hear in a salesperson's weekly report. There's no meaning or interpretation or conclusions or implications drawn from that information; it's not actionable, and therefore it's really not intelligence. It's just more information floating around the company.

Have you found that there are specific types of results that you report frequently or regularly?

KS: No; it really varies with the project. A project I worked on some years ago for a gas turbine manufacturer involved telling them how far behind their competitors were in developing a certain turbine technology. There were no financials in that, no marketing strategy—it was all heavy engineering technology stuff. Another project might be, tell me the chances that my biggest customer is going to get acquired; in that case, your results are probably 80 percent financial—there's going to be no technology or R&D involved in that.

Do you use any particular software products or online information services for manipulating research results, Web page monitoring, or manipulating data to aid in the analysis?

KS: Our 2002 intelligence software report [102], which is on our Web site, is our bible on that question. Every 12 to 18 months we publish a review of the major software packages that support competitive intelligence, with a bit of analysis on their value and validity in terms of supporting intelligence. Our premise is that technology supports the process, not the other way around. A number of vendors did and still do claim that technology is the solution, technology is the process, and we couldn't disagree more. Of the packages that we've been reviewing for the past two or three years, there are about a half dozen that we have identified as being truly designed for CI applications and therefore able to cover most, if not all, of the components of the CI cycle. Those are Strategy Software [219], Wisdom Builder [225], Wincite [224], Knowledge Works [203], and Docere [208].

CC: In literature research, of course there's technology behind online searching—processing document output, and so forth. Most professionals who build taxonomies and indexes will agree that you really need the human element, even if you were to use very good software. Good classification schemes, taxonomies, and indexes can be built with the assistance of technology, but the human component is critical for great functional schemes. This component involves one's experience, the understanding of the framework and content, consideration for end users, and so on. This point applies to CI software as well. We cannot rely on software to handle all the variables that the professional understands, particularly tacit and contextual elements.

For news alerting and monitoring, we often use Factiva/Dow Jones Interactive's Custom Clips [199] as well as other products. For Web site monitoring, we had been using MindIt [213], which is now defunct, with some success. We also use Spyonit [218], and we've started using ChangeDetection.com [197]. We use

TVEyes [222] and TracerLock [221] to track media and news-groups, respectively. Many of these Web-based tools have become fee-based, at least for some of the more sophisticated monitoring components, but they still offer some nice free functions. We monitor Usenet, which is searchable through Google [38], and other discussion groups to obtain names of contacts, to find out what people are saying about products, issues, and companies, or just to understand an industry in general. These resources include employment boards, industry boards, medical news groups, and so on. We've also used f*ckedcompany.com [34], which isn't authoritative but can give us a heads-up about company rumors. The boards at sites like Vault [85] can provide some insights into companies' compensation structure and working environment, but you have to be aware that these sites are anonymous and you can't embrace all that you read as gospel truth. There is a universe of resources out there, and we will choose a product or service depending on the project and its duration and budget.

For manipulating results for analysis, we often rely on SmartWrap [217]. It's a wonderful shareware application, a time-saver that allows you to eliminate the need to reformat text that is copied from one application to another.

I feel that, in discussing software, it's important to reiterate that these are tools that assist us. The longer I've been managing research and information/knowledge resources, the more I am convinced that the human component is critical. It's sometimes easy to forget this as we encounter and embrace increasingly sophisticated tools, but these tools have enabled us to work faster and more efficiently so that we can be liberated to perform higher-level functions.

Out of the projects that you've done, was there one that stands out as a wonderful coup?

CC: In one case, we were researching directors and managers of a particular company. Having hit a ceiling, we were having a very difficult time getting further background information on these individuals. I stepped away, thought about it a little bit, and finally realized that for one particular person, the spelling of his name was the key. We had the correct spelling, but not the only spelling. This person is European, and I was relying on the Americanization of his name, rather than expanding the context. So I then searched using characters from what I suspected was this individual's native alphabet. I retrieved a wealth of information, and we ended up plugging most of the holes. Our client, in fact, was almost confident that we wouldn't find this information that they had been tearing their hair out attempting to find. They had exhausted their internal resources and skills, but we were able to apply ours to achieve what they wanted. That was a real lesson for me, and it underscores the value of information professionals—that we employ our training, our tools, and our creativity to help generate and otherwise support business.

We also have on our library staff Frederique Feron, who is a fellow information professional and a native of France. Her search skills and fluency in both French and English have enabled us to tap into a wealth of material, and to make quite a few breakthroughs in our European research. As a native speaker of French, Frederique is able to apply her understanding of cultural and linguistic differences among various francophone cultures around the world. This enables us to provide an additional dimension to our services, going beyond English-language news abstracts. With this success, we've expanded our capabilities by contracting a team of professional searchers who are fluent in Spanish, German, and Italian.

How about the other end of the spectrum, after you had spent all kinds of time and effort on a project that simply didn't pan out?

KS: Never had any of those.

CC: No, but we do have challenging projects that most business searchers can relate to. Finding private company information, and private company financials in particular—ouch. We try to be creative, but sometimes the information is just not out there to the extent that we want and need. That's where primary research comes into play and adds value to the literature search.

How do you stay current and confident with your strategies and resources?

CC: Reading becomes a hobby if not a second job, as I'm sure you can understand. I subscribe to various newsletters like Search Engine Watch [72], SearchDay [72], Search Engine Showdown [71], Research Buzz [170], FreePint [32], and Job Machine's CyberSleuthing [113], which focuses on recruitment research and sometimes suggests some nice software tips. We visit Gary Price's Weblog, The Virtual Acquisition Shelf & News Desk, aka "ResourceShelf" [68], for news and updates as well. Of course we also subscribe to print resources geared toward information professionals, like Information Today's *Searcher* [174] and *Information Today* [136]. Attending information, online searching, and related conferences is very important, too. I find that listening to other people's experiences and exchanging techniques and tools challenges me to think more creatively. Professional exchanges, networking, and camaraderie are very important because, very often, those of us who are in the trenches face similar challenges. Given this ever-changing landscape, it's difficult to stay on top of every development and attend to all the other important aspects of one's work without these interactions. People discover new tricks or tools, and a wonderful thing about our profession is that so many are so willing to share.

We don't limit our professional development and current awareness to English-language material, either. Frederique, for example, monitors European CI developments and resources. We subscribe to *Veille* [191], a French CI publication, Transnationale.org [84], a service by a watchdog group that reports on global companies, and various other publications and services.

KS: Professional societies are also important. We're all very active in SCIP (Society of Competitive Intelligence Professionals) [258] and Cynthia is active in SLA (Special Libraries Association) [259]. Basically, any venue we can find to share war stories or best practices, or ways to show how we can add value, is going to be important. Clients pay us a lot of money; we want to make sure we can deliver good value back to them.

What skill set or education do you think an individual needs to be successful in performing competitive intelligence?

KS: If you subscribe to the premise that the most valuable activity in any CI endeavor is analysis, then that gets you somebody who is a good critical thinker. Somebody who is comfortable with different kinds of data—qualitative, quantitative, structured, unstructured—who is comfortable with ambiguity, who can see the forest for the trees, who can draw conclusions, and who can either write or speak very, very well and very, very clearly. If you look at those attributes, a perfect degree might be an MBA or an engineering or a journalism degree. Actually, I haven't seen any one specific college degree that tells me, yep, that's going to be a good intelligence person. Some of the best intelligence analysts I've ever worked with are in the government, and they just won't leave because they're chained to their desks, they love their work so much. I've seen very good analysts who have come out of sales or market research. It's all over the map. What I've often seen is that certain people's brains seem hard-wired to be able to do this work, and if you can refine that basic pathway of the brain to cope with issues that are specific to an industry or a technology or a company, then you've got someone good.

CC: It's great to have a range of backgrounds. As I look around at my colleagues at Fuld & Company, they come from different areas of training and experience. As a result, each lends a different type of thinking to the process. It certainly is interesting working in such an environment, and it's a great benefit to a project team to have a variety of expertise, styles, and skills.

What do you enjoy most about this profession?

KS: For me, it's the ability to work on lots of different issues and projects. I'm king of the short attention span, so if I were to get caught working on analyzing three competitors' financials every day for years, I would shoot myself. It's the ability to say, today I need to spend eight hours with my pharmaceuticals client helping them to protect against competitor efforts to surpass their vaccine technology. Tomorrow I get to go to my European telecommunications client and alert them to how privatization and deregulation are forming competitive threats that they've never even thought about. That's pretty cool. And to get to do all those things within 48 hours is a lot of fun.

CC: I have to echo that. Certainly, what I do is often more function specific than what Ken does, but we get projects of various shapes and sizes coming across our threshold, and it's wonderful working on them. I also enjoy that many of them involve activities or issues that are at the forefront of their industry. It's pretty exciting to get an idea of a product's impending launch, to see how an industry is being shaped or reshaped, and to witness new directions in which companies may be going. I enjoy being a part of a team, contributing to a valuable end product. The search process can be very rewarding, particularly when you hit on something significant. It's a fantastic feeling when you strike gold. This never gets old because the projects, and the information dynamics and landscape, are constantly changing. We have to update or revise our techniques, tools, and mindsets. These are all factors that encourage professional growth, and the development of both hard and soft skills.

And what do you like the least?

KS: Getting on airplanes. The travel gets a little hectic. But the most frustrating thing for me is when we encounter well-intentioned CI managers in companies that just can't get their organization to give them the legitimacy they deserve. Part of our job is just enabling our clients to embrace CI as an important and necessary discipline and then getting managers to approve adequate resources and budgets to do what they have to get done. A perfect example: We just finished a project for a major consumer retailer, who brought us in to look at the extent to which their existing CI group—a three-person market-intelligence team—was really addressing the issues and doing the stuff that was important to the organization. We came in and said, there's a serious misalignment here. What these guys are being told to do is not helpful to addressing the company's real strategic issues. We gave them a lot of recommendations on how to fix it, and their management said, "Sounds good, start doing it." So our clients were all excited; a new day was about to dawn where they could really do some cool stuff. At the last minute the management said, well, never mind, we want you to just keep doing what you're doing. It was clear to us that they didn't have a good understanding of what CI could bring them.

Anything else you'd like to share that we haven't touched on?

KS: I think CI people like to stress how they do what they do, how important primary research is, or this secondary research technique or this cool analysis process. What we tell clients is, consumers of intelligence inside companies don't care about any of that. You come in and say, look at this really cool Porter five-force analysis I did of your industry. They don't care. What they want to hear from CI are new angles on existing competitive situations, new ways of looking at their competition, warnings of impending threats, potential opportunities they didn't see coming down the pike, and new strategies for dealing with the changes.

Super Searcher Power Tips

➤ Don't lose sight of the ball. Don't get so intrigued by your own research or analysis methods that you forget why you're solving the problems you've been asked to solve.

➤ Always state the benefit of what you do in language that your users understand.

➤ It's extremely important to be organized. Especially when you are juggling multiple projects at once, and each one of them poses different challenges. Preparation is essential, and there are a number of tools and techniques that can assist us to work more efficiently.

➤ Fully understand what the client's needs are, what it is you should be looking for, what the deliverables are, and what types of budget constraints you're working under.

➤ Solid secondary research, primary research, and analysis should be complementary components of a project. Combined with a solid understanding of the client's position and needs, these components are essential to delivering a successful product.

Doug House and Anne Henrich

Decision-Driven Research and Comparative Analysis

Doug House is President of Washington Researchers and is a frequent, highly rated speaker on competitor and market intelligence. Doug has been a business intelligence analyst since 1987. He has designed and directed competitive intelligence studies of hundreds of companies—including private companies, subsidiaries, and other sub-corporate business entities—in numerous industries.

dhouse@winfogroup.com

Anne Henrich is a Senior Vice President of the research affiliate of Washington Researchers. She leads market and competitor analysis engagements for clients in the financial services, information services, and IT hardware fields, among other industries. An energetic, animated speaker, Anne regularly trains clients and seminar groups on telephone data collection, research strategy, and competitive analysis.

ahenrich@winfogroup.com

Doug and Anne, can you each tell me a little bit about your backgrounds and how and when you started performing competitive intelligence?

DH: My first job out of college was with a law firm here in Washington, DC. Among other things, I did market analysis and pre-merger and acquisition due diligence research, and that included some primary source telephone work. From there, I went to Marriott in the corporate strategy group, where I did business development research and competitor research and analysis. Then I joined this firm in 1990, so I've been doing research on the vendor side since then.

AH: My experience is less broad than Doug's. I didn't enter the field until I actually started working here. I joined the company in '95 as a research analyst, so I was on the phone and poring through documents, trying to get data for our clients, and then worked up to managing projects. I didn't come from a research background; I was previously a property administrator for a big vacation resort in Williamsburg, Virginia.

DH: Over the years, we've found that there isn't really a good correlation between what people did in their last couple of jobs before they joined us, and how successful they are as a primary source competitive intelligence telephone researcher. It has more to do with a set of characteristics and a general outlook toward what you do, and curiosity, and a knack for making people want to talk to you. So we hire a lot of people who have no prior research experience.

Could you each describe your current function in a nutshell?

DH: We sell, scope, manage, and direct competitive analysis and competitive research projects for clients. We work with clients to define what their business problem is and what information about the external environment they need, or what conclusions they need to draw about the external environments in order to make a good decision. Then, working with a team inside our organization, we translate what we call intelligence objectives into research objectives and data collection objectives. After we coordinate that process, we do an analysis of the findings and present them to the client, showing them how we reached our conclusions, what the outside world looks like, and how it matters to the decisions they're trying to make. The organization does everything from the background and research steps all the way to the finished product.

AH: I would also emphasize that what we do is not just competi*tor* focused. It's focused toward helping clients understand their competitive environment and all that entails. Sometimes it's understanding an opportunity, be it an acquisition or a chance to partner or ally with someone; sometimes it's a chance to understand a new market in which they may want to play, or that they're currently playing in but in which they want to expand their presence; and sometimes it is a head-to-head competitive picture. But it's not just what I would call CI; it's really competitive *assessment*.

We are not an industry-specific firm, so we work in just about any kind of business environment. We don't do business-to-consumer research on any kind of regular basis, although we might look at a business whose end product is ultimately distributed to consumers.

DH: The fundamental competitive analysis–competitive research toolkit translates very well from market to market and industry to industry. While there's certainly some advantage to having a vertical market focus—a certain depth, especially when it comes to secondary sources, that you get when you've been working a particular vertical for a number of years—there's an equal advantage in having experience in using your skills against the same set of business problems in a lot of different environments. By choice and by policy, we work in a lot of different markets. Unlike some firms, we have a nonconflict policy that tends to force us into multiple markets. If we perform research for a client, we won't research them for somebody else.

Like you, I think of CI as competitive intelligence, not just competitor intelligence. How do you define competitive intelligence, and how do you feel that it differs from competitor intelligence and business research?

DH: To me the term "competitive intelligence" implies looking at all the factors in the market environment, typically excluding customers, that could influence or have an impact on your business, and doing that in a systematic, rigorous way. Now, here's the catch. What we do is not competitive intelligence based on that definition, because the key idea in that definition is "in a systematic or process-oriented way." My firm actually is positioned a little differently in the market. We do fact-based decision support. We do a lot of work for competitive intelligence organizations that need someone to help them analyze a particular competitor, or get some data they can't get in some other way, or synthesize things in some creative way. But we also do a lot of work for firms or individuals who wouldn't consider themselves competitive intelligence users or competitive intelligence professionals. We like to think that our value-add is helping any business decision maker who faces a situation where a clear and accurate understanding of the external environment is essential. So what we do is related to competitive intelligence, and this fits with what a lot of CI people do, but it's not quite the same thing.

One of the reasons that we've chosen to draw that distinction is that there *are* people out there who do competitive intelligence, meaning the whole process thing. We're a project research and analysis shop, and it's a different toolkit. Frankly, I think a lot of the people who are members of SCIP or another CI organization in fact spend more of their time doing what we do rather than doing processed, systematized competitive intelligence.

What do you include in that toolkit, and what do you feel is essential to helping you add value in your decision-support process?

AH: I would say that our toolkit has two big compartments. There's a research toolkit and there's an analytical toolkit. I'll talk about the research toolkit first. The most important resource in our research toolkit is the telephone, meaning access to people sources who can help us understand what hasn't been put out there in print or document sources, and who can help us make sense of the data that we've already gathered. In the course of any project, we use the phone to contact industry observers; securities analysts; journalists; experts; and employees of suppliers, customers, and the targeted companies themselves. We also use the Internet extensively, and we use commercial online databases. Finally, we spend a fair amount of time looking for what I call offline document resources, documents that haven't made the transition to the electronic world. We also rely on public records, court filings and the like—plans, state department of corporations records, annual reports, local papers that aren't online yet, things of that nature.

In the analytical toolkit, the fundamental model for how we do analysis is Michael Porter's four-corner competitive assessment model [107, see Appendix]. For industry assessment, we also use his five forces model, and we've been playing around with something called the Value Net, which was a model presented at SCIP by a guy named Barry Nalebuff. He, along with Adam Brandenburger, wrote a book called *Co-opetition* [109]. Within all of our presentations in the analytical realm, we really look hard for ways that we can make explicit comparisons between our client and everybody else. By making those comparisons explicit, it becomes clear where the opportunities lie, where the threats are posed, and what you should quit worrying about because they're really not an issue.

DH: I've been doing this work, if you count the time at Marriott, since 1987, and I would say the single most important thing I've learned about competitor intelligence is to put your competitor next to yourself, or next to your client if you're working for a third party. The simple exercise of listing "here's what we do and here's what they do," and then asking, "hmm, why is *that* different, and what is the implication of it being different" yields, I'd say, 50 or 60 percent of the value you get out of the competitor analysis process. I can't say strongly enough how useful just building straightforward and not terribly sophisticated comparison tables can be in extracting meaning from data about competitors.

AH: Comparison tables work for market assessments as well. By simply listing all the players next to one another, you have the opportunity to identify where there may be gaps in serving the market, or where competitors may be competing on operational effectiveness vs. on a truly differentiated strategy that presents an opportunity for you, and things of that nature.

You were saying earlier that the Internet and the for-fee database services are definitely part of that research toolkit. How do you weigh the Internet vs. for-fee or subscription services? Does the percentage of use vary with the project at hand?

AH: I think it's critical to use both; there is some content that is Web-only and some that is commercial online-only, and they're indexed differently, and they're used differently for varying purposes. Companies use the Web to promote themselves, to get information out. But coverage of press sources, for example, is so much better in commercial online databases; it's simply not searchable in the same way via the Web. So we certainly use both, and I would say that we probably use them about equally.

DH: If you go back even two or three years, our information collection was probably 70 percent online databases, 30 percent Web. It's changing, and I would say that it's now more like 60 percent Web and 40 percent commercial online, much more Web than before. A big reason for the changing ratio is that we often use secondary sources to identify the names of people to call. The Web is especially good for that kind of source sleuthing. It also provides some good substantive information. As Anne said, the key to effective use of sources is to know when something you're looking for is simply not on the Web, or so much easier to search in a commercial online database. You can more than earn the search service fees back by using something that's indexed or has a better Boolean search capability or whatever.

AH: There is some Web-only content we're using more and more frequently—things like resume databases to find names of people to talk to. We don't happen to use, for example, analyst coverage through a commercial online service like Investext. Instead, we purchase analysts' reports separately from Intelliscope [47], which is the Web version of the same service.

How do you cope when you're in the middle of a search and you're just not finding what you want, or what you believe must exist? What strategies to you employ?

DH: Want the honest answer? I call a professional and have them do the search for me.

AH: One thing that we've really pounded into our researchers, and that we also present in the seminars we give, is that it's important to have a strategy before you go out and start searching. We recommend that you take some time and say to yourself, "This is what I'm looking for; what resources on the Web are going to generate those things for me, what search strings should I try?" and write them down. Then you go back and say, "Okay, I got these results from this one, and those results from the other," and about 15 minutes into it, we say "stop," and by that, we mean really stop. And then you say, "All right, how's this going to be a good resource for me, am I doing the right thing?" Like any problem-solving exercise, we either brainstorm or we get expert advice. We may call an industry association librarian and ask for some suggestions, or whatever source makes sense, given the problem.

DH: We do two other things that help us a lot. One is that we invest a lot of energy before we start any data collection in trying to identify the proxies and substitutes for the information we really want. Many times we realize that the exact information that we want to find isn't going to be available, but we will be able to get two or three pieces of information that can be added together or used to estimate from. So, before we go online or do any kind of research, we want to have a clue about what to look for.

But I also think that we are faster to give up on searches than most other researchers are. We give up faster because, in our experience, most of what we really want to know isn't available in any kind of print or online source. So, we move away from those tools to the phones much more quickly than a lot of people would.

AH: Right. And during the course of my own projects, and I have a feeling Doug does this too—most of our engagements are eight weeks or so—we go back out to the published sources just to make sure that nothing new has been revealed in the interim.

DH: Because you hate to deliver that final report to the client and have them say, boy, did you see this article, and then have to say, duh.

Once the secondary research is done, what are your next steps? You mentioned "source sleuthing" earlier; can you tell me more about that?

AH: From a process standpoint, you have to do some extraction and synthesis of that secondary data, and ask yourself, okay, what have we learned from this? You need a checkpoint so you can say, these were our overall objectives; how close did we get using the secondary sources? Then we use that information to inform where we go next. Usually, for us, that's to the telephone. Whom we call at that stage is heavily dependent on where we believe the very specific information lies that our client is seeking. Sometimes we go straight to the target companies. Sometimes we spend some time talking to associations or securities analysts or journalists. Sometimes we go right to the customer, sometimes we go right to suppliers.

DH: Our rule of thumb, as you may have heard us say in seminars and in public many times, is that the best secondary source research in the world will yield no more than 30 percent of what you can learn about any company or market. The other 70 percent is only accessible to you on the telephone. That's not to say that in every engagement it's worthwhile to learn that other 70 percent, or that the 30 percent you *can* learn isn't everything you need. But the majority of what you can learn, especially when you start talking about data that can really drive decision making, isn't in print or online; it's in somebody's head, and you have to go out and get it.

It sounds as if Washington Researchers does the entire process, from planning the CI project to communicating the results. Do clients ever ask you to go up to a certain point and then hand off the research to their in-house analysts to combine it with internal company information?

AH: I have a client in the financial services industry who takes the outward-looking piece that I do and combines it with internal assessments that she runs of her own company's capabilities, and with more in-depth win-loss assessments that they outsource to another firm. For example, she will combine the data from these three different sources to create very robust profiles of where her company fits vis-à-vis the rest of the world. But I think most of our products are used as is; they are presented in virtually the same form in which we deliver them, and often we are the ones doing that presenting. From there, the studies may be cut up; different chunks may go to various divisions inside the organization, depending on who's interested in which parts. But we are typically asked to deliver a holistic product at the back end.

DH: If you go back around 10 years ago and look at our business then, a much higher percentage was just delivering data to clients, who would then use it for whatever they would choose to use it for. In 1993 we made a conscious decision to try to minimize the proportion of the business that was pure data. What Anne's talking about now isn't pure data; it's analyzed, even if it's only part of an overall assessment that they're doing. The big driver in our moving away from just delivering data is that we discovered when we talked to our customers that most people, even competitive analysts, didn't really know how to use primary source information effectively, since they didn't work with it every day. So if I deliver raw data from interviews, often the people I'm delivering it to aren't sophisticated in how to read meaning into an interview, they're not sensitive to how the question was asked, who the person was, how much credibility to assign to that source vs. some other source. With that discovery we finally decided that, in order to create a product that our clients were really happy with, we had to handle the entire process most of the time. And, as we expected, when we started telling clients, essentially, "you *could* just buy pure data from us, but we're going to try not to let you do that if we can," our client satisfaction went up a lot. Our clients are no longer interested in the broad data; they want to know what it means.

Do you have a standard model or template to organize your research results?

AH: No. We're both shaking our heads. In terms of how we present it, our research is customized, client driven. We're always looking for ways to contrast our client with the competitor. That might be a matrix, it might be two columns on a PowerPoint slide, it might be an action–reaction presentation, whatever the right tool is. Internally, our project managers have developed some tools that they use just to understand where they are vis-à-vis the project objectives. If we're researching a fairly complex or extensive set of questions or issues, they have developed some methods to keep abreast of where they are, vs. where they're hoping to be at the end. They know where the holes are, and can track progress.

DH: Part of not having a standard template is our commitment to doing decision-driven research. We try to do work that is very relevant to a choice that somebody's trying to make, which means the information they need pretty much formulates the way the information should be organized and the kind of analysis we should be doing. We have an ongoing internal conversation about how much standardization we should try to impose on what we do, because there are some operational benefits to standardizing, but Anne and I tend to sit in the camp that says standardization is more harmful than good, and so far we're winning.

Do you have a standard road map for training someone new in CI in an organization?

AH: Before you do anything else, find out who values what you do, and then try to build on that base. Don't feel like you have to start off being the CEO's best friend. Find a champion.

DH: Understand your company first. Much of the value of competitive analysis is comparative analysis. It's looking at your company versus the outside world, and you can't do that until you understand how your company makes money, your key strategies for differentiating yourself, your strengths and weaknesses operationally, your management's key assumptions, your business goals. Every time we do a project where a client is asking us to compare them to competitors and we go in and ask them to tell us what are your goals, what are your assumptions, what are your strategies, what are your capabilities, it always shocks me how much work it takes to assemble that information. Without an understanding of those four factors, how am I going to tell you how the world looks compared to you? Do your homework.

How much time do you allocate to the secondary research, primary research and the results organization? Have you come up with a formula?

AH: No, it really depends on the nature of the project. In general we spend more time in primary than secondary; I would say generally somewhere between 10 and 20 percent for secondary, 50 to 60 percent primary, the remainder in reporting and analytical.

DH: Planning is also important, which on most of our projects is about 5 percent of the hours budgeted.

AH: And I would throw in another 2 to 5 percent for client communications. You have to interact with them during the course of the project; you can't go away and then just come back eight weeks later and say here it is.

Do you have a standard template for reporting results? You've mentioned that the expected outcome drives the data collection focus. Are there certain types of results you report consistently?

AH: It's really so client-driven that there is no norm; we report what they need in order to make the decision they're trying to make.

Do you have any software products that you find particularly helpful in the research, data organization, or analytical phases?

DH: Microsoft Office [210].

AH: The Web tools we use are extensive. We like the sophistication of the search engine Google [38]. For Web page monitoring there are two services that we have found useful, Archive.org

[5] and NetMind [215]. But in terms of specialized software for tracking results, presentation, and things of that nature, no.

DH: I run a monitoring project that looks at a very large and diverse market. We monitor something like 350 publications for this study. What works really well is tearing things out of publications and putting them in files. It may seem fairly low tech. Our philosophy is that we don't automate anything until we can't do it manually any more. Not because automation doesn't offer value, because it can, but because most automation projects fail, and they all take a lot of energy and time that we just don't have. The thumb is faster than the search engine. And there are things that you pick up with the eye, just scanning, that machines can't get with a word-to-word matching algorithm.

What would you say was your largest coup?

DH: We have stayed in business, which is nontrivial! My largest coup isn't really a research coup; it's that when I started with the company, less than 30 percent of our business was repeat business; 70 percent was from new clients. Today, 70 or 80 percent of our business is from existing clients coming back to us multiple times, and I think that's because of the quality of our work and the insight we provide.

AH: There are times we've gotten great data out of people we never thought we'd get great data out of, because we were tenacious and skilled. We work really hard to exercise legal and ethical research techniques in the most perfect way possible, using all the skills at our disposal.

How about your worst nightmare?

DH: My worst nightmare is one that we're seeing some signs could happen—people on the fringes of this industry, who have used less than completely ethical techniques to learn information, get caught, get in trouble, get their clients in trouble, and cause a lot of people in corporate America to decide that doing this kind of work is too risky, even when it's done completely ethically and above board. I think that would be a terrible disservice to corporations, which really need this information to create value and to build strong strategy, and also, obviously, a terrible disaster for people like me who make their living doing this kind of work for clients. There are some things happening within the profession that I hope will address the problem, but if I were to name one thing that sometimes wakes me up in a sweat at night, it's the thought of people doing sleazy, slimy, unethical research and getting caught.

How do you stay current and competent with the strategies and resources that you employ?

AH: We read *a lot*. And because we have a limit in terms of how much stuff we can read individually, we have created forums where we share with each other what we've read.

DH: We cheat, though. We publish a newsletter and do training about online information sources so we really have to be reasonably current with regard to basic data collection techniques. But then, as Anne points out, we do a lot of internal learning. One piece that gets omitted sometimes, in terms of staying current, is staying current with the overall business environment. I can't tell you how valuable it is to invest the time every month or every other month to read *Fortune* [126], to at least scan the *Wall Street Journal* [193] for general business information. I've found, over the years, a lot of value reading the *Harvard Business Review* [132], which constantly provokes me to think about how to think about what I do.

AH: I learn a lot by talking to people from other organizations who are doing this kind of work. I deliver the bulk of our seminars now, and I never walk out of one of those seminars without having learned about some new tool or technique or way of thinking about a problem. I would say that brainstorming is essential to long-term success, as well as networking and interacting with other people who are in this business.

What skill set or education do you feel an individual needs to be successful in CI? You mentioned earlier that lots of folks you hire have come from very different walks of life. What do you want to see in a person you're going to hire to do CI?

DH: That's right; we've hired people who in their previous jobs were social workers, pastry chefs, reporters, property managers. We've pulled from a broad range of interests and careers, and they have all been terrific researchers. What they all have in common is, first, a powerful curiosity; they wonder a lot about how things work. Second, they have a terrific amount of tenacity; when they do something and it doesn't work, it spurs them to do more, rather than to give up. Third, they have the knack of making other people want to talk to them, making other people feel important, or making other people feel like they are interested. They have a connective ability, either because they're just naturally that way or because they've developed technique; you can learn how to do this stuff.

Another thing is that they are connective thinkers. Effective business research requires that you be able to take a bit of information over here and mentally draw a line to another bit of information over there, and have it pose a new question and drive you to ask something that wasn't part of the original question set, for instance. Our best researchers always see things hooking up with each other, and that helps them ask better and better questions.

Finally, there's no substitute for pure mental agility. You have to be nimble. All business researchers, even in a vertical market, are asked to look at so many different things, one right after the other, that you need the ability to learn about stuff quickly and effectively.

AH: I can add a few rules of thumb. You're never going to have enough data, so you have to get over that before you start. You have to be willing to make intuitive leaps. You have to understand that competitive analysis or assessment is a process, not a product; it's ongoing, it's iterative, and it seldom yields *the* answer. What it yields is a series of potential scenarios, some more likely than others, that you can plan against and then monitor for change. You have to realize that you're never really done. And, best of all, you have to be forward thinking. You have to be thinking 6, 12, 18 months down the road, because that's when your actions are going to take effect and when your competitors are going to react to you.

Tell me what you like least about the profession.

AH: In the bucket of what I would never do and what my worst nightmare would be, is cost studies. It's the most horrible work on the face of the planet.

DH: I'm sure everybody's been in this boat—it's those times you can't find the right data. We all know, as people who do this line of work for a living, that no matter how good you are, or how hard you work, or how brilliant you can be, sometimes the data just doesn't happen. It's such a horrible feeling when you have to call a client and say, "I know what you want to know, I know how to go about finding it, I did all of the work, and I don't have squat."

And what do you enjoy most?

DH: I love it when I'm standing up in front of a client or talking to them on the phone, and I'm telling them what we found, and this expression goes onto their face, where first they're like, puzzled, and then gradually their eyebrows kind of come together, and then suddenly their whole face opens up and they say, "Oh, that's how it works!" I live for that; it is so thrilling when I can say this is what it all means, or that's how it fits together. God, I love that!

AH: I also get personal satisfaction when the "a-ha" hits. I'm doing a large market overview of an emerging market, and I was stepping out of the shower this morning, literally, putting a towel around my head, and I went, "Oh my God, I see it, I see it! I see the whole market map, I see where they all fit, I know what their differentiation strategies are—I'm not even done with the research, and I get it!" It was thrilling. It really is thrilling to create insight where formerly there was none, and then convey that insight to your client and have them say, "Oh, wow, you guys are great; you're so smart." It's awfully fun.

Super Searcher Power Tips

➤ For competitive analysis, "why?" drives "how?" and "how much?" Spend time trying to understand what's really driving the requestor's need.

➤ Understanding your own company or client is a prerequisite for understanding a competitor.

➤ You will never have enough accurate, sourced, unambiguous data; get over it before you start!

➤ Always have a strategy and a time limit before you go online.

➤ People sources are key, and the phone is the best way to reach them, because most of what you want to learn lives only inside someone's head.

➤ When researching challenging or "hidden" companies—private firms, divisions, subsidiaries, and so on—remember that you can't learn everything, but you can always learn something.

John Prescott
CI Teacher

Dr. John E. Prescott is Professor of Business Administration at the Joseph M. Katz Graduate School of Business at the University of Pittsburgh. His research interests focus on the network of relationships among a firm's industry, strategy, organizational processes and performance. A specific focus is the design and implementation of competitive intelligence systems. John is a founder of the Society of Competitive Intelligence Professionals (SCIP), as well as a past president and meritorious award winner. He has published numerous articles in journals, is the editor of three books on competitive intelligence, was the executive editor for the *Competitive Intelligence Review*, and is currently the co-editor of the *Journal of Competitive Intelligence and Management*. He is an internationally recognized consultant and designed the first competitive intelligence course. John earned his Ph.D. in Business Administration at The Pennsylvania State University, and his undergraduate and masters degrees from Indiana University of Pennsylvania and Stevens Institute of Technology, respectively.

prescott@katz.pitt.edu

Can you tell me a little bit about your background and how and when you started performing competitive intelligence?

I developed an interest in CI during my doctoral training because my major was strategy and my minor was industrial organization economics. Both disciplines examine topics of how industries affect company behavior. I noticed that, for almost all decision-making models, we assume that firms have high-quality data, that they actually use that data, perform analysis on that data, and incorporate it into their decisions. When you check on that assumption, you find that it's not an accurate one, and so I started to look at who were some of the firms that actually help companies understand the marketplace. At that time the companies that primarily were into CI were consulting organizations such as Washington Researchers [261, see Appendix], which was headed by Leila Kight [249]. Thus, my research interests centered on answering the questions "how do CI programs get designed in organizations, how do you manage those processes, and how do decision makers actually use CI once it's provided to them?"

You are a consultant as well as a professor of business administration. Can you describe your functions in a nutshell?

I use a term from Sherlock Holmes, "the practicing consultant," to describe my passion for linking business practice with academic rigor. I like to view myself as a practicing academic, and that involves the intersection of four areas. I'm a professor, and in that role I think as professors do about why and how phenomena evolve. I am a researcher, using typical academic research models and frameworks to study what CI is all about and how we can study it in scientific ways, to get past ad hoc stories to find if there's any science in CI-related relationships. My third role is that of a teacher. I actually designed the first CI course in the United States, if not in the world, and I've been teaching that for over 20 years at the graduate level where I practice CI frameworks and techniques with my students. Finally, I'm active in consulting with companies on how to set up and manage CI processes, how to perform analyses, interact with intelligence users, and design human intelligence networks and on the impact of CI on organizational effectiveness.

What types of research have you performed? Do you emphasize any particular subject area, or are you devoted to company or industry studies in general?

I have traditionally not focused on specific industries, although I do spend a quite a bit of time with the steel industry. In the past I've spent time with industries such as the airline industry. Recently, I've been spending a lot of time with the electronics, computer, and pharmaceutical industries. Rather than specialize in industries, I focus on what I think are interesting CI questions and then see how firms are addressing those questions across a diverse set of industries. The reason I like to focus on this diversity is because I uncover relationships that I wouldn't if I had focused on a specific industry.

I will give you an example of the benefits of this approach by using a recent study on science and technology intelligence. In addition to examining business organizations, I wanted to look at a government agency as well. We gained access to a quasi-governmental agency, the National Technology Transfer Center (NTTC). One of the interesting things we found was that they had a model of science and technology intelligence that we would most likely not have found if we had just stuck to private sector organizations. NTTC has a mandate from the government to commercialize technologies developed by NASA and other federal laboratories. As a result, they focus on leveraging existing technologies into new businesses as their primary focus. This type of discovery is one of the reasons I like studying a diverse set of industries.

Currently I have a best practice study underway that examines how, as a CI professional, one gets intelligence users to implement the CI that is being produced. A second area that I spend a lot of time on is network analysis, where I'm looking at two things. The first aspect is how do you design and construct human intelligence networks for the collection of information in organizations, using principles of network analysis to examine this in a scientific manner. The second aspect we're investigating is strategic alliances. I examine questions such as "How do you evaluate the network of strategic alliances?" and "How do they affect outcomes such as performance of a firm, over time?" A third area relates to how firms design CI programs. I've developed a framework named 'Intelligence Driven Strategy' (see the figure on pages 250–251). It's what I call a decision-oriented approach that allows you to look at 10 key decisions that any CI group needs to consider. From that you can get a pretty good understanding of how to design and evolve a CI program to increasing levels of sophistication. The science and technology intelligence notion is the fourth area, in which we're getting at a topic that's under-developed in businesses: How do we actually do science and technology intelligence? Extending this work, Sue McEvily, Kathy Eisenhardt, and I are editing a special issue in *Strategic Management Journal* [180] on the global acquisition, protection, and leveraging of technological capabilities.

My research thrusts can be traced back to my doctoral work at Penn State. I have always been interested in the question "How do industry structures shape, and become shaped by, firm strategy?" Traditionally, if you take an economist's perspective, industry structures dominate firm conduct. If you adopt a strategy perspective you say, no, conduct dominates industry structures. The truth lies somewhere in between. So I like to look at both industry structure and firm conduct and how their interactions influence outcomes, particularly performance outcomes.

I have extended this area of research into international competitive intelligence. Recently I've been spending more of my time in China, understanding how the Chinese view business intelligence and, in particular, their science and technology efforts. Institutional impacts on industries and firm strategies have significant implications for the CI profession.

How do you feel competitive intelligence differs from business research?

This is one of the areas in which the field of CI needs clarity, since business research has not been precisely defined. There's been a lot of discussion, arguments, and disagreements over the domain of CI. When I examine the domain of CI, I think of four dominant areas. One is market intelligence, which is how you understand the industries that you compete in, the countries in which you compete, and the institutions that constrain or shape strategy within countries. Those individuals involved in market intelligence tend to be located in planning groups. The second area of CI closely relates to marketing and is called customer intelligence. Customer intelligence tends to be done much more in marketing and market research groups and looks at the notions of who our customers are, what we know about them, how we can help satisfy their needs, and so forth. The third area is science and technology intelligence, which examines a firm's underlying technologies, where they're moving, and how they contribute to competitive advantage. The fourth area is competitor intelligence. That is, how do we understand what our competitors are doing, and their moves and countermoves? There are at least two related areas, counterintelligence and regulatory intelligence. So that's how I divide the field.

Now, I would say that business research underlies all of those areas. I view business research as how I frame problems, how I then structure my data collection methods, and how I do my analysis. That underlies and is fundamental to all areas of CI. CI is applicable and should be embedded throughout the firm. The key questions ask how do we ensure that the firm is competitively aware, that information flows to those that need it on a timely basis, and that CI is used in decision making and implementation.

What skills do you feel are essential to the CI toolkit?

A few years ago I was doing a consulting project with Texas Instruments that lasted about three years. They made me the Dean of their Business Analyst program. Part of that role was to develop a training program for analysts. We wanted to look at skills necessary for success, because I believe that CI skills can be taught. With the assistance of Texas Instruments employees, we did a lot of research, interviewed a lot of people, and decided

Intelligence Driven Strategy™

Administration and Structure

1. Role/Focus
2. Location(s)
3. Information Technology
4. Ethics and Intellectual Property
5. Core Work Processes
   - Request Handling
   - Priority Setting and Referral
   - Analytical Framework
   - Vendor Relationships
   - Counterintelligence
   - Relationships with other CI Units
   - Training and Awareness
   - Network Development
   - Building Trust and Credibility

Portfolio

7. Products (Timely, Actionable, Reliable)
   - CI Web Page
   - Newsletters
   - Information Searches
   - Human Intelligence Reports
   - In-Depth Intelligence Assessments
   - Real Time Analytical Alerts
   - Training/Cross-Functional Team Participation
8. Projects

Request — Collection — Analysis — Dissemination

6. CI Personnel

Types	Skills
• Information Specialists	• Understanding Client Needs
• Analysts	• Analytical Frameworks
• CI Managers	• Statistics
• Champions	• Design & Implement Collection Plan
• Human Intelligence Network	
	• Drawing Conclusions
	• Communicating Results and Eliciting Feedback
• Thought Leadership	

Evolution

9. Evolution, Quality Enhancement, and Evaluation Processes
   - Drivers
   - Meaning, Management, and Measurement of Evaluation
   - Stages of Development – Prestartup, Startup, Established, World-Class
   - Social Capital of CI Professional and CI Group
10. CI Community of Practice Initiatives

The Ten Key Decisions of a Competitive Intelligence Program

Conventional wisdom states that at least 80% of the information necessary to make an effective decision resides within the confines of an organization and with its employees' networks. This wisdom also acknowledges that less than 20% of said information is available to and used by decision makers. Intelligence Driven Strategy™ reverses these percentages. Intelligence Driven Strategy™ (IDS) is an upward cascading process in which high levels of competitive awareness, information flows and decision impact result in sustainable and profitable growth. High levels of competitive awareness results in knowledgeable individuals allowing for high levels of information flow between groups, which when institutionalized into the decision-making process significantly impacts strategy and tactics. A competitive intelligence (CI) program is an essential part of IDS. CI can be defined as a

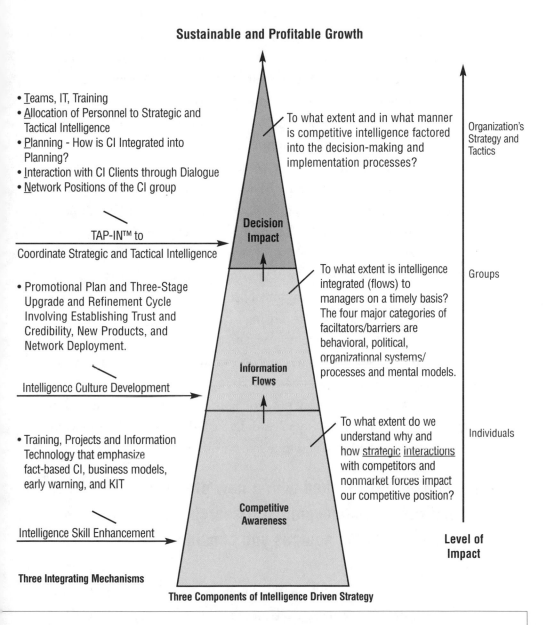

Sustainable and Profitable Growth

Teams, IT, Training
- Allocation of Personnel to Strategic and Tactical Intelligence
- Planning - How is CI Integrated into Planning?
- Interaction with CI Clients through Dialogue
- Network Positions of the CI group

TAP-IN™ to
Coordinate Strategic and Tactical Intelligence

- Promotional Plan and Three-Stage Upgrade and Refinement Cycle Involving Establishing Trust and Credibility, New Products, and Network Deployment.

Intelligence Culture Development

- Training, Projects and Information Technology that emphasize fact-based CI, business models, early warning, and KIT

Intelligence Skill Enhancement

Three Integrating Mechanisms

Decision Impact

Information Flows

Competitive Awareness

Three Components of Intelligence Driven Strategy

To what extent and in what manner is competitive intelligence factored into the decision-making and implementation processes?

Organization's Strategy and Tactics

To what extent is intelligence integrated (flows) to managers on a timely basis? The four major categories of facilitators/barriers are behavioral, political, organizational systems/processes and mental models.

Groups

To what extent do we understand why and how strategic interactions with competitors and nonmarket forces impact our competitive position?

Individuals

Level of Impact

process of developing actionable foresight regarding competitive dynamics (nonmarket factors, industry, (potential) competitors and one's own organization) that can be used to enhance competitive advantage. There are three sets of mechanisms that link a CI program and IDS: (1) intelligence skill enhancement through training, projects, and IT designated for organizational members to enhance their competitive awareness, (2) the development of an intelligence culture to facilitate information flows, and (3) a TAP-IN™ process to coordinate strategic and tactical intelligence. A CI program is comprised of four main components: (1) administration, (2) personnel, (3) portfolio of products/services, and (4) program evolution. Across the components there are 10 key decisions that determine the effectiveness of the linkages between the CI program and IDS.

upon six core skills. The first one is understanding client needs; that is, how do you understand what the intelligence user really needs or wants and engage them in a process that is productive? The second skill is what we call analytical frameworks. What are the analytical tools and techniques to assist in finding and solving problems and implementing their solutions? There are three types of frameworks, including theoretical frameworks, analytical frameworks, and communication frameworks. We wanted to expose analysts to all three types. The third set of skills is statistics—understanding what basic statistics are, how to use them, and how to look behind them to say "this is good" or "this is really based on faulty assumptions" when somebody presents you with statistics. The fourth skill is the design and implementation of a collection plan. How do you, once you have an assignment, actually pull it off from a project management perspective and keep those projects moving in a positive way? The fifth set of skills is drawing conclusions. Once you've collected your data and done some analysis, how do you sit back and reflect on what it is saying about the questions that you're trying to answer? The last set of skills is about how you communicate those results and elicit feedback once you've delivered the intelligence to your internal CI clients, and then learn from that process.

When you've been tasked with a new project that requires some background research, what are some of the sources you consider to be key?

I always start with what we know academically about the subject area. That research is going to tell me the individuals I should talk to, what sources I should look for in different journals or on the Internet, and so forth. This process launches me into the variety of sources, but the process itself drives me more than the particular sources.

How do you weigh the use of the Internet in your mix as far as your workflow and research methods are concerned? Do you find that you turn to the Internet for every project, or does it vary with each topic or case that you work on?

It does vary, but I find that I'm using the Internet more and more to provide me with background information and interesting insights that you're typically not going to find in other places. I use search engines when I'm working on a project; I throw in creative words or combinations, or just link from one site to the next to see if there are threads that can provide a different perspective than the traditional one. I can give you an example of this process. I was working with a candy company recently. We were working with some of their managers and key sales people to explore why and how CI can assist them. I used the Internet to locate information for an exercise to demonstrate the concept of competitive awareness. This is a simple exercise that Professor Russo [255] from Cornell developed to demonstrate overconfidence in managers. It goes something like this: "I'm going to present you with a set of questions about your industry that have quantitative answers. I am not interested in the exact number; rather give me a range, an upper and a lower number that you think the real answer lies between. Make sure you're 90 percent confident that the answer's in that range." I used the Internet to find, for the candy industry, 10 or so of these questions that we could then use in the workshop. Based on the 90 percent confidence range designed into the answers, a person should miss only one in a set of 10 questions. In reality, we tend to miss many more than one. In a very polite and fun way the exercise humbles most of us, in that we don't tend to know as much about our competitors and our industries as we might need to; it's a good rationale for demonstrating that we should be more competitively aware.

One of the questions I used for the candy industry is related to cocoa, a key raw material. I found on the Internet that 70 percent of the cocoa is produced in West Africa. So one of my questions was, "What percentage of the cocoa used in your industry is produced in West Africa?" But the exercise is not merely to identify some relevant and interesting facts about an industry but rather to discuss the implications of the fact that 70 percent of cocoa production is concentrated in a very small part of the world, and if this or that happened, what would that mean for the candy industry. So we take it to the logical next steps as well.

From what you've said, you don't always start with the secondary research. Could you expand on that a little bit and share what works for you?

I would credit Leila Kight [249] from Washington Researchers, who has done a lot of the foundation work in the CI area. She discusses learning curve sources, which are often secondary, and target sources, who are individuals who will have the answer. Depending on how much time, knowledge of the topic area, and other constraints you have, you might go to one or the other. My general approach is, unless it's something very scientific where you have to learn terminology, I tend to go and ask the person directly, and then ask them about the best sources, best articles, best Web sites to go to. After that I use the scientific method of addressing a problem. I ask myself who should know the information I am looking for, and why should they know it. This lets me structure the problem in a logical way. Of course, serendipity and luck are always good allies as well.

In your work, do you do mostly data gathering and some filtering and then pass it on to somebody else to do the analysis, or do you follow a project through the entire process? In other words, which steps of the CI process

do you cover, and what do you hand off to somebody else?

I have to answer this in two different ways. When I'm doing my academic work, a lot of which is with doctoral students, I tend to be involved because there is a mentoring relationship that is very important. However, I now tend to manage a lot of projects rather than actually doing them. When I'm managing a project, I'm involved with all steps, but the extent to which I collect data is low, whereas in the past it used to be pretty high. I am very involved in structuring the problems, designing the methodology, interpreting the results, performing the analysis, and in the writing and the review process.

When I'm working with clients, it's very similar in that I help with the design and structure of the problem; other people tend to do more of the collection, and I then become a primary analyst. When I'm working with businesses, they do rely on me as an analyst for helping them draw conclusions, and often I'll present or co-present the findings with other individuals. It's a team effort, but I like to have my hand in all the steps so that I am aware of the strengths and the limitations of the project and I can plot intelligently.

Do you use a standard model or template to organize your research results?

I prefer to use the scientific model. In CI, the standard approach is to use the intelligence cycle. The intelligence cycle has several variations but, essentially, you ensure that you understand the assignment, collect information from—ideally— multiple sources using multiple methods to ensure triangulation of results, conduct analysis to interpret the results, report the outcome to the person or group that requested the intelligence, and receive feedback. I add two other aspects to the traditional intelligence cycle. First, it is important for CI professionals to be involved in the decision-making process. Secondly, I believe that CI processionals should be involved in implementation efforts that result from their CI. I am currently working on a project in this area.

What road map would you present to a researcher newly assigned to the CI function?

You must start with a promotional plan for your CI activities. This is critical. Rather than being order takers, best-practice CI organizations and individuals tend to say, I understand the CI process, but let me sit back for a moment and think about what I really want to achieve with our CI group. If I know what I need to achieve, then how do I put together a structure that allows me to achieve our objectives? A significant aspect of this process is a promotional plan. How am I going to let people know that CI can help add value? Interview all the intelligence users you can and see what they really desire and need; develop simple intelligence products and upgrade them over time based on feedback from users; provide added value so that you're invited to be on key teams, and in this way get to infuse the team with intelligence mentality. The Intelligence-Driven Strategy' framework identifies 10 key decisions that a CI professional needs to consider and is used for assisting CI professionals in this regard.

How much time do you allocate to the secondary research and primary research —or, as you would say, your learning curve research and your target research —and then to your results organization, analysis, and report writing?

I'm overwhelmingly a primary researcher but also spend a lot of time with secondary sources. Often I am creating a new database, which is why I would say that a lot of what I do is primary research. For example, we track every alliance that's occurring in the steel industry. The way we do the tracking is primarily through their trade magazine, *American Metal Market* [91]. We supplement our database with other sources including interviews and other archival sources.

In terms of time spent on activities, I'd have to say background and data gathering is 30 percent, reevaluating is 40 percent, and then 30 percent of the time goes to the synthesis and the results.

What software products, if any, have you found that help in either the research process or the synthesis, analysis, or presenting stages?

When I am doing any type of search I tend to go to Google [38], unless I directly know the site that I want to access. Embedded in our university system is a way to get into the Internet. We also use Lotus Notes [206]. I'm increasingly using visualization techniques [248, 101], which are embedded in some software. Visualization techniques are a way to organize symbols, words, data, and other media to represent the world in a multivariate way. I'm leveraging the work of Professor Tufte [260] from Yale, who's written his own books on visualizing data. He stresses that we live in a multivariant world and we should be able to present and communicate our findings in multivariant ways. You combine words with symbols, with pictures, with diagrams, trying to show interconnections and causality whenever possible, and communicate it in a visual format. I find visualization useful as both an analytical tool and a presentation tool. Recently, I have been experimenting with visualization techniques in my MBA CI class. For example, I give them an 11″ X 17″ electronic space, and then assign the following: "On that sheet, do a competitor assessment so that if an executive wanted to know everything they needed to know about Kodak, they can view all these things on one sheet." Some of the students are very creative. They put in diagrams, pictures of the board of directors or chief executives, what alliances they're in, how various strategic initiatives are linked to each other, financial performances, with hyperlinks and so forth. It gives you a very quick snapshot of what's going on in a company. We use colors and computerize the process to facilitate making specific points and ease of modification. In one place we can convey significant causal relationships and implications. Most executives would prefer this approach to a thick binder of information. There are an increasing number of software products that allow you to do visualization that can be found on the Internet.

What would you say was your largest coup?

Helping to start and leverage the Society of Competitive Intelligence Professionals is my largest coup. SCIP has had a significant impact on solidifying and institutionalizing the field. I like to say that what we did was get a lot of people to come out of CI closets. People and firms were doing CI long before we started SCIP, but it provided a legitimized forum for them and helped professionalize the field. The fact that it's been in existence since 1986 shows that we have staying power. Also the fact that other organizations such as Competia [233] have emerged shows that CI as a profession is becoming increasingly institutionalized.

What about your worst nightmare?

My academic colleagues' failure to embrace CI as a research and teaching area in MBA schools is my worst nightmare. Every business school at both the undergraduate and graduate levels should have a CI elective. What's really interesting to me is that many academics do not understand or accept CI as a legitimate research field or an important area of research. CI raises images of information collection and practitioner orientations. However, many academics across several disciplines are studying CI-related topics; they just don't realize it. For example, there's an extraordinarily large stream of research on decision-making processes that spans disciplines and methodologies. This stream of research has a lot to say about one of our most fundamental questions, "How does a CI professional get users to implement the CI being produced in their organization?" There's also more literature emerging on information flows within organizations and between organizations. They tend not to think about that in CI terms, but rather in knowledge transfer and coordination terms. One of the things I've been trying to do with some success is get my colleagues to see how what they're doing really applies to the CI profession. Part of my rationale for starting the *Competitive Intelligence Review* and the new *Journal of Competitive Intelligence and Management* is to have a forum for academics to convert some of their research into articles that explore CI-related topics for practitioners, academics, and public/governmental organizations. Thus, my biggest nightmare is being addressed but in a limited way. I hope that the increased number of CI dissertations, especially from countries outside the U.S., will spur the growth of CI among academics.

How do you stay current and confident with your strategies and resources?

Always be open to learning—through reading, training, doing, listening. I'd add to that, always be a little afraid. If you keep a slight edge of fear that somebody else is going to come up with ideas to make yours obsolete, you will be receptive to learning. Personally, it helps that I work in an academic institution where we have a strong Ph.D. program. New Ph.D. students arrive with lots of energy and new ideas, and you always say to yourself, gee, they're a lot smarter than I am.

What skill set and/or education do you feel an individual needs to be successful in performing competitive intelligence?

My position is somewhat controversial, although I can't understand why. Earlier, I outlined the CI program I developed for Texas Instruments. In addition, or as an alternate, I think an MBA degree is essential. If you're going to do CI for a business organization, the MBA package is fundamental; it says I understand what organizations do, I understand accounting processes, I understand finance, I understand human resources, and so on. I believe that CI professionals need the well-rounded package they get with an MBA. But MBA education also has limitations. There's a set of skills such as collection techniques, networking, project management, and implementation that are not well taught in MBA curriculums. We tend to spoon-feed MBAs all the data for a case or exercise. Some students complain that we don't give them enough data, and some of them don't even believe that in the business community you're often provided with even less data than presented in our cases and exercises.

I believe that journalist skills are essential. Journalists know how to talk to people, ask questions; they know how to dig through information in a variety of ways and find new or creative sources. Investigative journalism is particularly relevant for CI professionals. Journalistic skills are also important with regard to being able to write in a very succinct way.

Negotiation skills are critical to develop rapport and interact with intelligence users. Imagine a merger negotiation in which one party has done their CI and the other has not. I can't stress too heavily the importance of developing close interpersonal relationships with intelligence users. You might be a great analyst, but if you can't communicate with an intelligence user or develop a good working relationship with them, you're not going to have much of an impact.

MBA programs do frequently have electives related to several of the areas I've mentioned, and if one goes outside of the MBA school to other parts of the university, there is an even wider selection of courses.

What do you enjoy most about this profession?

The people. Recently I was working with a large multinational company in the Midwest. I was just amazed at how bright the people are, their enthusiasm, and the diversity of the issues that they have command of that are related to their competitive situation. This is not an uncommon situation. Working with bright individuals leads to interesting assignments and opportunities for learning. This is what I like, meeting people and trying to understand and help solve their CI problems. The other part that's most enjoyable is my academic position. I have a lot of freedom and opportunities in being able to research topics of interest to me that I hope will help businesses, governments, and academics.

What do you like the least?

The misunderstanding of what CI is all about and the constant references to spying diverts attention from really important issues. We are constantly fighting the ethics-vs.-spying battle. CI is not rocket science to me; there are tricks to the trade and there is a craft in learning CI, but the constant turf battles between market research, competitor analysis, strategic planning, counterintelligence, regulatory intelligence, manufacturing intelligence, and customer intelligence are counterproductive. Managers need to develop and internalize a better understanding of what CI is, and end the paranoia regarding the spy image. Part of that paranoia is real and justified, because for many countries there was and is a very close relationship between national security intelligence and business intelligence. But in general, I don't think that most CI professionals view themselves as spies; they view themselves as employees trying to help their organization compete in the marketplace.

The field of CI needs to move beyond merely discussing CI as a product as well as a process, although that is a useful distinction. I think it is even more productive to talk about CI as an art, a science, and a craft. CI needs to be thought about as a philosophy. It's a way of thinking about how decision processes should be made and implemented in organizations, and that's the art of CI. Most good CEOs have an art or philosophy about how they believe a business should be run, or how a business should be turned around, and that's what I'm saying about CI. You need to have a philosophy of CI. The second leg is CI as a science, and that is concerned with the variety of tools and techniques for collection, analysis, presenting, and so forth. I think it's incumbent upon the CI professional to articulate and develop its bag of tools. The third leg is the craft of CI. As with most crafts, a fundamental set of skills are learned and improved through actually doing CI. I view this aspect as similar to a carpenter or electrician. They have apprenticeship programs where they not only learn fundamentals from experts but they also begin to gain the tacit knowledge of their craft that develops through experience on the job. So, I conceptualize CI as composed of these three components: think about it as an art/philosophy, as your tool kit, a science; and then learn and apply the craft on the job.

Super Searcher Power Tips

➤ Provide implications with every intelligence product you deliver.

➤ Develop your CI information technology databases and/or Web page only after you know how you will manage them on a daily basis.

➤ Never stop learning about new techniques and perspectives that can be used to constantly evolve your CI processes.

➤ As an exercise, write down three to five of your typical CI assignments. Are you primarily being asked to locate data, answer an information/intelligence question, or help with a decision? When assignments are dominated by being involved with decisions, actually sitting at the table, you know you are making an impact.

Appendix
Referenced Sites and Sources
http://www.infotoday.com/supersearchers

This is a listing of resources mentioned or recommended by interviewees and is not intended to serve as a comprehensive directory of competitive intelligence sources.

RESEARCH/INFORMATION SOURCES

1. **6FigureJobs.com: http://www.sixfigurejobs.com**
   Site for executives and experienced professionals seeking jobs.

2. **10K Wizard: http://www.tenkwizard.com/**
   Powerful engine for searching company literature filed with the Securities and Exchange Commission (SEC). Search engine use is free. Useful for searching companies, people, and industries. Subscription required to pull company filings. Subscriptions start at $125/year.

3. **Adis Insight: http://www.adisinsight.com**
   Provides news and market research services for the pharmaceutical industry. A customized desktop is available with registration. The Web site links to news from the Adis Clinical Trials Insight database, Industry Alerts (updates on mergers and name changes within the pharmaceutical industry), a calendar of scientific meetings, newsletter articles, and links to other clinical trial and disease management Web sites.

4. **Air Transport Intelligence (ATI). Reed Business Information.**
   http://www.reedbusiness.co.uk
   ATI is a fee-based online news and specialist service for the global airport industry. ATI also delivers monthly news in modules, including airlines, aircraft, and airports.

5. **Archive.org: http://www.archive.org**
   Maintained by the Internet Archive, a 501(c)(3) public nonprofit founded to build an "Internet library." Offers permanent access for researchers, historians, and scholars to historical collections that exist in digital format. Links to digital collections of Web pages, books, films, moving images, software, and audio.

6. **AsiaBizTech: http://www.asiabiztech.com** or **www.nikkeibp.com/neasia**
   Now NE Asia Online. Online version of the Hong Kong–based magazine *Nikkei Electronics Asia*, which serves readers in the electronics industry in the Asia/Pacific region.

7. **AviationNow: http://www.aviationnow.com**
   Portal to news articles and publications in the aerospace and defense industry. Top news and selected articles are available free to the public. Many portions are accessible by members only.

8. **BBC: http://news.bbc.co.uk**
   Offers a multilingual hub for global online news, information, and interaction in 43 languages.

9. **Bloomberg: http://www.bloomberg.com**
   Real-time financial and investment information. Bloomberg's primary service—Bloomberg Professional—delivers news on world markets, financial data, and third-party analysis. Prices start at US$1,250/month.

10. **Brint.com: http://www.brint.com/km/**
    Business- and technology-oriented Web portal. Focuses on e-commerce and knowledge management issues, with links to general business resources such as company directories, associations, news services, and related information.

11. **Census Bureau: http://www.census.gov/indicator/www/m3/hist/naicshist.htm**
    Contains historical statistics on manufacturers' shipments, inventories, and orders. Historic time series are searchable by NAICS code.

12. **Cnet.com: http://www.cnet.com**
    Provides news and information for the information technology sector. Highlights major news and product reviews. Also offers software for download.

* **Compendex** *see* **Ei Compendex** [25]

13. **Competitive Intelligence Center (Factiva and Fuld & Company): http://www.factiva.com/cicenter/**
    This Web site contains links to recent articles on CI and the evolving field. Also offers an article archive and an email alerting service.

14. **Datamonitor: http://www.datamonitor.com**
    Provider of premium business information for the automotive, consumer

market, energy, financial services, healthcare, and technology sectors. Market research reports start at US$1,925.

15. **Decision Resources: http://www.decisionresources.com**
    Decision Resources is a market research firm providing primary and secondary research publications, multiclient advisory services, and customized consulting for the pharmaceutical, biotechnology, diagnostics, and managed healthcare industries. Market research reports range from US$1,800 to US$8,000.

16. **DefenseData: http://www.defensedata.com**
    Online information system for accessing national stock numbers, suppliers, price, logistics, and technical and cross-reference details for supplies and parts in use by the U.S. Department of Defense. Also issues daily purchase requests (solicitations) by the DoD. Interfaces with the RFQeXpert system. Access by credit card available.

17. **Defense Technical Information Center (DTIC) databases: http://www.dtic.mil**
    An online information system with databases covering research programs past and present in the U.S. Department of Defense. The STINET portion of the site permits searching by the public. Separate databases for scientific and technical reports, project R&D summaries, full-text documents, and the Research & Development Descriptive Summaries (RDDS) with line item budget detail. Some reports are viewable in PDF; others may be purchased.

18. **Deloitte Consulting Research: http://www.dc.com**
    Research papers covering a wide variety of business issues. As of 2003, Deloitte Research was to be called Braxton Research and spun off from Deloitte & Touche.

19. **Department of Energy sites: http://www.energy.gov**
    The official Web site for the U.S. Department of Energy. Issues covered include data and prices, efficiency, environmental quality, national security, resources, and production.

20. **Dialog: http://www.dialog.com**
    One of the major commercial online services. Wide variety of databases. Subscription costs vary; there is a one-time sign-up fee of US$295 for U.S. customers, an annual subscription fee of US$72 to US$144, plus a US$75/month minimum charge; transaction-based pricing and flat-fee accounts are available. Dialog also offers Open Access, which lets nonsubscribers use the service and pay by credit card.

21. **DialogSelect: http://www.dialogselect.com**
    A selected portion of the major commercial online service, Dialog, combined

with an easy-to-use interface. Provides access to 50,000 publications and documents online. Many articles available in PDF. Dialog subscribers automatically have access to DialogSelect; must be a subscriber to access.

22. **Dogpile: http://www.dogpile.com**
Popular metasearch engine that searches various search engines such as About, Ask Jeeves, FAST, FindWhat, Google, LookSmart, and Overture.

23. **Dow Jones Interactive: http://www.djinteractive.com**
One of the major commercial online services, focusing on international business and financial news and information. Annual subscription plans as well as transaction-based pricing and flat-fee accounts are available. Note: Dow Jones Interactive customers are being migrated to **Factiva.com** by mid-2003.

24. **Dun & Bradstreet (D&B): http://www.dnb.com**
Major commercial online service offering company credit reports and public records searches. D&B also produces online databases and print directories. Some information is available through its Web site at no charge; other information can be purchased from the site with a subscription or credit card. D&B financial databases are also searchable on commercial online services such as Dialog, Factiva.com, and LexisNexis.

25. **Ei Compendex (Engineering Information, Inc.): http://www.ei.org**
Engineering and technical literature database equivalent to the print *Engineering Index*. Provides abstracted information from approximately 4,500 journals, selected government reports, and books.

26. **EIU (Economist Intelligence Unit): http://www.eiu.com**
Online information product developed by the publisher of *Economist* magazine. EIU records include analysis and forecasts of the political, economic, and business environment in more than 180 countries. EIU has companion publications *Country Profiles, Country Reports*, and the premium *Country Risk Service* and *Country Forecasts* covering 90 and 58 countries, respectively. The databases are available through commercial online services and directly from the publisher.

27. **Electric Power Research Institute (EPRI): http://www.epri.com**
EPRI is a science and technology consortium. Offers products, services, and training to the energy industry. EPRI also publishes the *EPRI Journal,* a bimonthly publication providing information on the affordable, efficient, and environmentally safe generation and delivery of electrical power. Selected articles are available free at www.epri.com/journal/default.asp. For hard-copy pricing, contact orders@epri.com.

28. **Espicom Company Profiles: http://www.espicom.com**
   A product of Espicom Business Intelligence. Tables of contents for recent
   reports may be viewed for free in PDF. Company profile reports in the
   US$350 range. Espicom concentrates on the telecommunications, medical
   devices, and pharmaceuticals industries.

29. **EvaluatePharma: http://www.evaluatepharma.com**
   A healthcare industry analysis firm offering a financial database of global
   pharmaceutical and life sciences company information. EvaluatePharma
   tracks the past and future performance of leading pharmaceutical and
   biotechnology companies worldwide.

30. **Factiva: http://www.factiva.com**
   A joint venture of Dow Jones and Reuters, Factiva produces enterprise
   integration tools as well as Factiva.com, an integrated database that combines
   the sources from Dow Jones Interactive and Reuters Business Briefing.

31. **FedLog: http://www.fedlog.com**
   Searchable database facilitating search and cross-reference to spare parts from
   four military databases and the Federal Logistics Information System (FLIS).

32. **FreePint: http://www.freepint.com**
   Web-based portal for information professionals. Site includes links to an
   electronic bulletin board (Free Pint Bar), a biweekly electronic newsletter,
   jobs, and a company profile search utility.

33. **Frost & Sullivan: http://www.frost.com**
   Frost & Sullivan is a multi-industry market research service. Also provides
   custom consulting. A "Watch Profile" service is available for free with email
   registration.

34. **F*cked Company: http://www.fuckedcompany.com**
   Web site that collects and posts rumors and comments about companies,
   people, and products. Also offers three subscription-based services: Rumors
   and Comments (US$75/month), Just Comments (US$25/month), and Rumor
   Alerts (US$12/month). Each subscription covers monitoring up to five
   companies.

35. **Gartner: http://www.gartner.com**
   Consulting firm that produces market research reports. Particularly strong in
   the information technology and communications industries. Executive
   summaries and briefing papers are available on the company's Web site.

36. **Genesis/POV reports: http://www.adisinsight.com**
   Series of "Point of View" market research reports. Topics include:

Antibacterial, Antiviral, Autoimmune/Inflamation, Cardiology, CNS Disorders, Dermatology, Diabetes, Oncology, Pain, Respiratory, and Women's Health. Reports are in the US$13,000 range.

37. **Giga Information Group: http://www.gigaweb.com/homepage**
Giga Information Group is an IT advisory firm providing various research and consulting services and products, including Giga Advisory (research and advice), Giga Council Membership (a networking service), TEI (Total Economic Impact advice), Security Action ReportCard, ForSITE (for senior IT executives), Web Site ScoreCard, and GigaConsulting.

38. **Google: http://www.google.com**
One of the largest and most popular Web search engines. Google also offers news and image searching, access to Usenet newsgroup discussion, and human-compiled links via Open Directory. Google also provides cached links for older versions or "dead" pages.

39. **Haystack (IHS): http://www.ihserc.com/haystack/databases.html**
Haystack is promoted as having the world's largest collection of information on U.S. and Canadian government purchases and stocked parts. Combines and cross-references information from government data tapes and IHS databases. Most databases are available in Windows desktop, Web, CD-ROM, and DVD formats.

40. **Headhunter.net: http://www.headhunter.net**
URL now links to careerbuilder.com, a site designed for job seekers. Searchable by company in the "keyword" search box.

41. **Hoovers: http://www.hoovers.com**
Public and private company profiles and industry overviews. Its strength is in U.S. and large multinational companies, but it is expanding coverage outside the U.S. with country-specific sites for the U.K., France, Germany, Italy, and Spain. Includes IPO news and useful links. Basic company information is available for free. Individual and business subscriptions start at $US399/year.

42. **IC Insights: http://www.icinsights.com**
Providers of market research reports and seminars for the integrated circuit industry. Coverage includes current business, economic and technology trends, capital spending and wafer capacity trends, and the impact of new IC products on the market. Also produces *Strategic Reviews*, which are company profiles available in print, CD-ROM, or online starting at US$1,490/year.

43. **IdDB Database: http://www.iddb3.com**
The Investigational Drugs database is produced by Current Drugs, Ltd, now part of Thomson Scientific. The database is updated daily. It contains news

and evaluated information on all aspects of drug development, from first patent application to launch or discontinuation. Geared for the biotechnology, chemical, and pharmaceutical industries. Main topics are licensing, strategic planning, discovery research, clinical development, business development, knowledge management, and marketing/market research.

44. **IMS Health Market Reports: http://www.imshealth.com**
    Market research reports from market assessment through product launch and life cycle to product promotion strategy. Titles in the series include: Pharma Pricing, National Prescription Audit Plus.

45. **IMS Market Prognosis: http://www.ims-global.com/products/studies/pharma.htm**
    Country profiles in PDF or HTML format. Each entry provides five-year forecasts including economic and political trends. When available, profiles include local medical practices, healthcare systems, insurance programs, number of medical doctors and hospitals, etc. Useful for baseline profiling data and when examining geographic issues in the healthcare field. Cost per country profile ranges between US$3,000–$4,500. Regional profiles cost US$18,000–$20,000.

46. **Inspec: http://www.iee.org/publish/inspec/about/#content**
    Database aimed to provide comprehensive coverage of the literature in physics, electrical/electronic engineering, computing, control engineering, and information technology. Also covers significant literature in the materials science, oceanography, nuclear engineering, geophysics, biomedical engineering, and biophysics areas. Indexes and abstracts over 3,500 scientific and technical journals and some 1,500 conference proceedings, as well as numerous books, reports, and dissertations. Available in several formats, including CD-ROM, and online through several commercial search systems by subscription and pay-as-you-go.

47. **Intelliscope: http://www.intelligencedata.com/product/intelliscope.html**
    Subscription database with access to Wall Street analyst studies, market intelligence reports, and association research. Part of the Thomson Financial family. US$1,100/month.

48. **International Data Corporation (IDC): http://www.idc.com**
    IDC publishes market research reports and binder series mostly in the computer and information technology industry. Also sponsors seminars and offers custom consulting. Business areas include Applications and Application Development, E-Commerce, Infrastructure, and Security.

49. **IRI Studies: http://www.infores.com**
    Information Resources, Inc. (IRI) supplies scanner-based market research data

on consumer packaged goods (CPG). Clients can access detailed information on sales, share, distribution, pricing, and promotion data for hundreds of product categories. IRI also provides consumer behavior tracking data and in-store observation statistics.

50. **IT World.com (Accela Communications, Inc.): http://www.itworld.com**
Web site contains current information technology (IT) news, Webcasts, newsletters, and white papers. Newsletter topics include data management, e-business, e-commerce, remote and mobile computing, and security strategies.

51. **James J. Hill Reference Library: http://www.jjhill.org/index.asp**
The JJ Hill Library is a renowned nonprofit business reference library located in St. Paul, MN. It is considered one of the world's largest business reference collections, boasting over 400,000 volumes. A HillSearch Membership is available for US$595/year or US$49.95/month. A fee-based service is also available.

52. **Kartoo: http://www.kartoo.com**
Kartoo is a multilanguage metasearch engine that presents the search results in a map showing the interconnection between your chosen keywords. Kartoo offers a natural language option, in addition to keyword searching.

53. **Knowledge Management Research Center (CXO Media, Inc.): http://www.cio.com/research/knowledge**
This Web site contains several knowledge management articles, including those published in *CIO Magazine*. Additional categories include Upcoming Events, CIO Radio Spot, The Reading Room, and CIO Forum.

54. **Knowledge Management Resource Center (KM Corporation): http://www.kmresource.com**
This site is a portal to dozens of knowledge management resources. The "What's New" section announces sources as diverse as articles, case studies, conferences, interviews, and newsletters.

55. **Knowledge Management Server (Graduate School of Business, University of Texas at Austin): http://www.bus.utexas.edu/kman**
Web site provides listings of publications and resources for knowledge management.

56. **LexisNexis: http://www.lexisnexis.com**
One of the major commercial online services. Wide variety of databases covering business, news, and legal sources. Also allows searching of current news items on the Web. Subscription costs vary; transaction-based pricing and flat-fee accounts are available. *See also* separate listing for **Nexis.**

*   **Liszt: http://www.liszt.com** *see* **Topica** [83]

57. **L-Soft: http://www.lsoft.com**
Producers of list management software. The L-Soft Web site links to *Catalist,* the catalog of all LISTSERV™ mailing lists. Search by topics, host name, list name, or country.

58. **MarketResearch.com: http://www.marketresearch.com**
This site is an aggregator of market research reports from more than 350 publishers. Offers complete text of reports as well as individual sections or chapters for selected items. Searching for available reports is free.

59. **Mindbranch: http://www.mindbranch.com**
Web site offers market research reports from a number of different sources.

60. **Monster.com: http://www.monster.com**
Designed for job seekers, this site is searchable by company name in the keyword box. Also links to a salary wizard.

61. **Myers-Briggs Personality Types:
http://www1.cpp.com/products/mbti/index.asp**
The MBTI is a well-known branded set of personality profiling products trademarked by CPP, Inc. The testing instruments summarize personality types into four dichotomies: Extraversion–Introversion (describes where people prefer to focus their attention and get their energy—from the outer world of people and activity or their inner world of ideas and experiences); Sensing–Intuition (describes how people prefer to take in information—focused on what is real and actual or on patterns and meanings in data); Thinking–Feeling (describes how people prefer to make decisions—based on logical analysis or guided by concern for their impact on others); and Judging–Perceiving (describes how people prefer to deal with the outer world—in a planned orderly way, or in a flexible, spontaneous way).

62. **National Security Agency: http://www.nsa.gov**
Described as the nation's cryptologic organization. The NSA coordinates, directs, and performs highly specialized activities to protect U.S. information systems and produce foreign intelligence information. NSA releases three major types of documents to the public: Press releases, public speeches and briefings given by senior leaders; Freedom of Information Act (FOIA) releases; and declassified documents. Limited information is available on the Web site. Inquiries may be submitted by email or in writing.

63. **Nexis: http://www.nexis.com**
The news and business publications portion of **LexisNexis**, listed separately [56].

64. **Nielsen Studies: http://www.acnielsen.com**
ACNielsen, a VNU company, is a market research firm providing continuous

tracking of consumer purchases at the point of sale through scanning technology and in-store audits. Clients receive detailed information on actual purchases, market shares, distribution, pricing, and merchandising and promotional activities. Nielsen also provides consumer attitude data. The ACNielsen EDI service provides continuous tracking of box office receipts from more than 45,000 movie screens in 11 countries for the motion picture industry.

65. **Northern Light: http://www.northernlight.com**
Search engine for an extensive collection of full-text articles, market research reports, and investment analysts' reports. At press time, it appeared all but certain that NL would soon cease to exist.

66. **Pharmaprojects (PJB Publications, Ltd.): http://www.pjbpubs.com**
Worldwide information on drugs in R&D and product development. Pharmaprojects monitors new drugs currently under development, tracking all new drug candidates under active international R&D, approximately 6,000 at any one time. Archive extends back to 1980. US$10,450 for one U.S. location with 3 simultaneous users. Additional levels and pricing available.

67. **Platt's Global Energy (a division of McGraw-Hill): http://www.platt.com**
Platt's covers the following energy groups: oil, natural gas, coal, electric power, nuclear, and petrochemical. Web site contains indicators; market commentary; news highlights; and links to news, commentary, and analysis from Platt's Business Technology, Engineering & Risk Management groups.

68. **The Resource Shelf - Resources and News for Information Professionals (aka Virtual Acquisition Shelf & News Desk): http://www.resourceshelf. com**
Gary Price's Web site lists daily news, notes, and links to information sources such as Web search engines, subject-specific sites, reference books, and more. Supplemented by free weekly email newsletter.

69. **Scirus (Elsevier Science): http://www.scirus.com**
A comprehensive science-specific search engine. Scirus searches thousands of peer-reviewed articles and both text and nontext files often invisible to other search engines. Focuses on university Web sites and author home pages. Searches both free and fee-based sources such as ScienceDirect, IDEAL, MEDLINE, Beilstein, Neuroscin, BioMed Central, U.S. Patent Office, E-Print ArXiv, Chemistry Preprint Server, Mathematics Preprint Server, CogPrints, and NASA.

70. **Scott-Levin Marketing Research Audits. Quintiles Transnational: http://www.quintiles.com/products_and_services/informatics/scott_levin/**
A leading syndicated marketing research tool used by the pharmaceutical industry. The audits monitor key areas such as product promotion, patient

visits and associated drug treatment, and market performance in terms of prescriptions and patients.

71. **Search Engine Showdown: the user's guide to Web searching (Greg R. Notess): http://www.searchengineshowdown.com**
    Articles compare and evaluate Internet search engines from the searcher's perspective. Site also includes a search engine features chart, detailed search engine reviews, and a free online newsletter that features statistical analysis and advanced search strategies.

72. **Search Engine Watch: http://www.searchenginewatch.com**
    Web site offers links to search engine reviews, search strategies, and rankings, plus free and fee-based electronic newsletters: *SearchDay* (**www.searchenginewatch.com/searchday**), prepared by Chris Sherman, features Web search news, reviews, tools, and tips and is published daily. *Search Engine Report* (**www.searchenginewatch.com/sereport/index.html**) is published monthly. Free with registration; Search Engine Watch members have access to all issues back to July 1996. *Search Engine Update* is a twice-monthly newsletter available exclusively to those with paid Search Engine Watch memberships. The newsletter features similar content to the *Search Engine Report*, but with longer and more in-depth articles and exclusive features on search engine optimization. US$59 for six-month membership fee; US$89 for a full year.

73. **Securities Exchange Commission (SEC) EDGAR database: http://www.sec.gov/edgar/searchedgar/webusers.htm**
    Free database covering companies publicly traded in the United States. Database also contains reports for private firms and non-U.S. firms that submit data to the SEC. Filings are available from 1993 on, and provide company background information and financial data, executive biographical profiles, and acquisition and merger details.

74. **Semico Research: http://www.semico.com**
    Market research studies and custom consulting for the semiconductor industry. Semico's three areas of emphasis are: semiconductors by product type (e.g., DRAMs), end-use markets (set-top boxes, modems, cell phones, etc.) and manufacturing (foundry supply and demand, wafer demand, etc.).

75. **Semiconductor Industry Association: http://www.semichips.org**
    A major benefit to this Web site is the number of high quality statistics available on the site. Reports such as billings, capacity statistics, and worldwide semiconductor shipments can be viewed or downloaded in portable document format (PDF). Additional detailed information is available only to members.

76. ***Statistical Abstract of the United States* Online (Government Printing Office): http://www.census.gov/prod/2002pubs/01statab/stat-ab01.html**
Individual sections are available in Portable Document Format (PDF) for free on the Web site. From the census.gov product description page: "The government's most important statistical factbook on the social, political, & economic aspects of American life. Includes data on population, births, deaths, life expectancy, marriage and divorce, health and nutrition, education, law enforcement." (See separate listing under Articles, Books for hard copy, and CD-ROM information.)

77. **Stat-USA: http://www.stat-usa.gov**
Online resource developed by the U.S. Department of Commerce that includes country profiles, country commercial guides, international market research, economic and financial statistics from the GLOBUS/NTDB link, and links to Country Background Notes. Single-user subscriptions cost US$17/year; reports can also be purchased individually.

78. **TechEncyclopedia. CMP Media LLC. http://www.techweb.com/encyclopedia**
Online encyclopedia covering 20,000 information technology terms. Many entries also contain graphics.

79. **Technical Insights: http://www.technical-insights.frost.com**
Technical Insights offers market research services and publishes several newsletters focusing on emerging technologies, R&D breakthroughs, new patents, government-sponsored research programs, technology forecasting, technology impact analysis, innovative ideas, contact information for pioneering scientists/engineers, and technology integration strategies. Site offers free access to information with registration.

80. **Teoma: http://www.teoma.com**
A general Web search engine that includes a Refine feature, which suggests topics related to the focus of one's search, and a Resources section, which points to pages that offer collections of links on the subject of the search. Teoma was purchased by Ask Jeeves in September 2001.

81. **Thomson's First Call: http://www.firstcall.com**
Thomson Financial/First Call is a global research network providing real-time equity and fixed income research and data, corporate news, shareholdings data, sell-side workflow tools, and internal research distribution. Subscribers to First Call have access to real-time morning notes and investment house reports. In 2000, Thomson integrated the I/B/E/S (estimation) and Datastream services into First Call.

82. **Timely Data Resources Epidemiology Database: http://www.tdrdata.com**
    Timely Data Resources, Inc. provides primary research services and access to
    three epidemiology databases: The Incidence and Prevalence Database (IPD)
    is for global incidence, prevalence, morbidity, comorbidity, cost data,
    symptoms, and many other health issues for more than 4,700 diseases and
    procedures. The Hospital Inpatient Profile (HIP) database profiles the top six
    related diseases and procedures, payment source, discharge status, and related
    details for more than 7,100 diseases and procedures. The Emergency Room
    Database (ER) contains data on top prescribed drugs, diagnostics provided,
    providers seen, visit characteristics, and payment source for more than 2,600
    diseases and procedures. Searching is free; subscription required for access to
    full information.

83. **Topica: http://www.topica.com**
    This Web site offers links to email newsletters and publication services, and
    discussion groups on diverse topics.

84. **Transnationale.org: http://www.transnationale.org**
    French language site also available in English, Italian, and Spanish. Company
    profiles list brands, selected financials, management team, institutional stock
    holders, and number of employees, as well as layoff announcements, a
    "corruption" section, and image information such as links to video
    advertisements.

85. **Vault—The Insider Career Network: http://www.vault.com**
    Designed for job seekers, this site provides information on job openings,
    company profiles, inside "scoop" for interviewees and links to a message
    board where, for $2.95 up/month one can view messages that mention a target
    company.

86. **Wall Street Analyst Reports (e.g., Lehman Brothers, Goldman Sachs)**
    Selected reports available free on brokerage house Web sites and by
    contacting individual firms, or via databases such as Investext and Multex,
    available direct and through aggregators such as Dialog, Dow Jones, and
    LexisNexis. A standard reference source to locate investment houses and
    company and industry coverage is *Nelson's Directory of Investment Research*.

*   **World Drug Market Manual** *see* **IMS Market Prognosis [45]**

87. **Yahoo! Finance: http://finance.yahoo.com**
    Contains company and industry information such as profiles and recent
    earnings estimates. Searchable by keyword and stock symbol. Provides links
    to download annual reports (free), research reports (fee), financials, stock
    charts, and recent news.

88.   **Yahoo! News: http://news.yahoo.com**
      Offers customized and personalized news pages, as well as news alerts by
      email or Instant Messaging (IM). Registration is free.

ARTICLES, BOOKS, PERIODICALS AND DISCUSSION GROUPS

89.   **"75 Years of Management Ideas & Practice,"** *Harvard Business Review*,
      September-October 1997 Supplement. Reprint 97500. Phone: (800) 988-
      0886 or (617) 783-7500 outside U.S. and Canada; Fax: (617) 783-7555;
      Email: corpcustserv@hbsp.harvard.edu. Mail: Harvard Business School
      Publishing, Customer Service, 60 Harvard Way, Boston, MA 02163 USA.
      Excellent timeline reflecting the evolution of business management in the
      20th century. Starts with 1922, when the *Harvard Business Review* was first
      published, to 1997.

90.   *Against the Gods: The Remarkable Story of Risk*, **by Peter L. Bernstein.**
      John Wiley & Sons, 1998. http://www.wiley.com
      Chronicles the history and evolution of risk and probability starting with
      ancient times. Profiles revolutionary thinkers, including Edward Lloyd of
      Lloyd's of London. $18.95.

91.   *American Metal Market* **(American Metal Market, LLC).**
      http://www.amm.com/index2.htm
      Major daily tabloid for the metals and recycling industries.

92.   *The Art and Science of Business Intelligence Analysis: Intelligence*
      Analysis and Its Applications, **edited by Ben Gilad and Jan P. Herring.**
      Part B, Intelligence Analysis and its Applications. Also known as
      Advances in Applied Business Strategy, **Supplement 2, Part B. Greenwich,**
      CT, JAI Press, Inc., 1996 (out of print).
      Collection of essays on information collection and analysis. "The four
      chapters, written by Bonnie Hohhof, Douglas Bernhardt, Tony Page, and
      Michael Belkine provide the most comprehensive look at the role of analysis
      in information and intelligence collection I have seen to date" (editorial note,
      p. 150).

93.   **Aspen Publishers, Inc. http://www.aspenpublishers.com**
      Publishers of professional periodicals in the financial arena including
      accounting, business, and online legal research.

94.   *Bowman's Accounting Report.* **Hudson Sawyer Professional Services**
      Marketing, Inc, 3445 Peachtree Road NE - Suite 600, Atlanta, GA 30326-
      3240. Phone: (800) 945-6462.

Independent newsletter for reporting and analyzing news, trends, strategies, and politics. US$295/yr

95. *The Business Intelligence System,* **by Benjamin Gilad. New York, AMACOM, 1988. http://www.amanet.org**
Hallmark book for providing a chronology, definition, and approach for business intelligence systems. US$55.

96. *Business Researcher's Handbook* **by Leila K. Kight, Washington Researchers, 1980. http://www.washingtonresearchers.com**
Landmark text on the business research process, from dealing with the information request to reporting research results. Provides model letters and reports (out of print).

97. *Business Week* **(McGraw Hill Companies, Inc.). http://www.businessweek.com**
Major business trade journal. Covers business news, profiles public companies, and publishes several special issues during the year. US$46/year.

98. **BUSLIB-L. http://listserv.boisestate.edu/archives/buslib-l.html**
A business librarians' discussion list relating to the collection, storage, and dissemination of business information within a library setting. Very active list with a wide variety of subscribers. To subscribe, send email to LISTSERV@LISTSERV.BOISESTATE.EDU with the text: SUBSCRIBE BUSLIB-L Your Complete Name.

99. **CAM Promotional Audits. http://www.cam-group.com**
The CAM group audits pharmaceutical indicators and issues in 27 countries. Indicators can be as diverse as promotional spending in five key European countries to urologists in Japan.

100. *CareerJournal* **(companion to *The Wall Street Journal*). Dow Jones & Company, Inc. http://www.careerjournal.com.**
Provides a search tool for available jobs.

101. **"Charting Your Company's Future," by W. Kim and R. Mauborgne.** *Harvard Business Review, June 2002,* **p. 76–83.**
Kim and Mauborgne offer a nontraditional technique for designing the strategic-planning process by drawing a picture: a strategy canvas. This canvas includes the strategic profile of an industry, depicting the various factors that affect competition. It also includes profiles of current and potential competitors as well as the examining company's strategic profile, which considers how it invests in the factors of competition and how it might in the future.

102. **"CI Software Report 2002,"** *Competitive Intelligence Magazine,* **Vol. 5, No. 3, May–June, 2002, p. 15–23.**
     Abridged version of Fuld & Company's *Intelligence Software Report 2002.* Includes updates on software, and on "how well CI software is—or isn't—meeting user needs through the CI cycle." Full version of the report is at www.fuld.com/softwareguide/index.html.

103. *Competencies for Special Librarians of the 21st Century.* **Special Libraries Association.**
     http://www.sla.org/content/SLA/professional/meaning/competency.cfm
     Report outlining the professional and personal competencies necessary to be successful in providing library and information services in the next century.

104. *Competitive Intelligence Magazine.* **Society of Competitive Intelligence Professionals. http://www.scip.org/news/cimagazine.asp**
     This publication is SCIP's bimonthly source for news and "how to" advice for practicing CI. Subscription is free to members; US$89/year (6 issues) for nonmembers. Back issues are US$6 for members; US$7.50 for nonmembers. Special issues carry an additional fee.

105. **"The Competitive Intelligence Opportunity,"** by Norman Oder. *Library Journal,* **Vol. 126, No. 4, March 1, 2001. p. 42–44. (http://www.libraryjournal.com)**
     This article cites specific examples of how librarians have transitioned out of libraries into CI managerial positions. Provides helpful hints on how to make the transition and the benefits of the change.

106. *Competitive Intelligence Review.* **Society of Competitive Intelligence Professionals and John Wiley & Sons Inc.**
     http://www.scip.org/news/cireview.asp, www.interscience.wiley.com
     Quarterly journal of knowledge management and insight. Back issues range in price from US$10–US$35.

107. *Competitive Strategy: Techniques for Analyzing Industries and Competitors,* **by Michael E. Porter. New York, The Free Press, 1980 (reprinted 1998). http://www.simonsays.com/thefreepress**
     Landmark book for analyzing competitors. Provides the four-force model (p. 4) referred to by many CI professionals. Also provides figures, flow charts, and detailed lists for the Wheel of Competitive Strategy (p. xxv), Functions of a Competitor Intelligence System (p. 73), and Sources of Field Data for Industry Analysis (p. 378). US$38.

108. *Consultants News.* **Kennedy Information.**
     http://www.KennedyInfo.com/mc/cn.html
     News, analysis, and industry data for the consulting industry. US$295/year.

109. *Co-opetition*, by Adam M. Brandenburger and Barry J. Nalebuff. New York, Currency Doubleday, 1996.
    Scholars and consultants Brandenburger and Nalebuff present a five-part business strategy using game theory to create win-win situations among competitors, customers, and suppliers. US$18.

110. "Corporate Performance Management: Managing Profitability and Growth in the New Environment," by Juergen Daum, *The New New Economy Analyst Report,* January 26, 2002, p. 3.
    http://www.juergendaum.com/news/01_26_2002.htm
    Traces the need, adaptation, and significance of an information system for management purposes, focusing on the Fugger dynasty in "the era of trade."

111. *Crain's New York Business*. http://www.crainsny.com
    Business journal covering the New York City metropolitan area. Search function is free. Archival access costs US$5/24 hours; US$45/month; US$295/year. Print edition is available to U.S. residents for US$64.95/year. Electronic Edition is US$35/year and includes archives for the past 30 days. Register to receive free email news alerts.

112. *Cyberskeptic's Guide to Internet Research*. Information Today, Inc.
    http://www.infotoday.com
    Published 10 times a year, this newsletter highlights and reviews Web sites of interest to the information research community. "Specialty Scans" review Web sites in the areas of legal/government, technical/medical, news/media, business/finance, the information industry, and international information. US$159/year.

113. *CyberSleuthing*, Job Machine, Inc.
    http://www.jobmachine.net/newsletter.htm
    Offers tips and techniques for finding source experts in a variety of professional disciplines. Designed for executive recruiters. Free with registration.

114. *Defence Systems Daily* & Email Headlines service. Defence Data, Ltd.
    http://www.defense-data.com; email bodecia20@defence-data.com
    Provides daily news on the defense industry worldwide. £200/yr for the newsletter; email headlines are free with registration.

115. "Developing a CI Resume" by Wayne Rosencrans (http://www.scip.org)
    Presented at the SCIP '02 Conference in Cincinnati (www.scip.org/cincinnati/sessions.asp). This reprint is available to conference attendees only, or to those who purchase the US$399 conference CD.

116. "Developing Information Systems for Competitive Intelligence Support" by Bonnie Hohhof. *Library Trends*, Vol. 43, No. 2, Fall 1994.

This entire issue of *Library Trends* is devoted to the library in corporate intelligence activities. Bonnie Hohhof's chapter highlights the various stages where IS systems and services aid in the CI process.

117. **EBN. CMP/United Media. http://www.ebnonline.com**
Delivers news, analysis, and in-depth reporting of business strategies and technology trends in the electronics industry. EBN publishes several newsletters as well as in-depth market reports. Costs range from free to US$3K.

118. *Encyclopedia of Associations*. **Gale Group. http://www.galegroup.com**
A directory of trade and professional associations. US$470.

119. **"European Competitiveness and Business," by Alexis Jacquemin,** *European Commission Forward Studies Unit Work Paper—2000*, **p. 8. http://europa.eu.int/comm/cdp/working-paper/competitiveness_and_business.pdf**
Speaks to the rise of capitalism and the need and drive to seek superior information and intelligence. Also highlights the role of Austrian economist Joseph Schumpeter and his view of competitive forces in the early 1900s.

120. *Evaluate Pharma*. **Evaluate Group. http://www.evaluatepharma.com**
Audited company sales, together with consensus forecasts from leading securities analysts. Quarterly reports are US$2,750 and up.

121. *Fast Company* **magazine. http://www.fastcompany.com**
Editorial focus on how changing companies create and compete, highlighting new business practices, and showcasing those who are "reinventing business." US$29.95/year.

122. *FDC Pink Sheet*. **F-D-C Reports, Inc. http://www.fdcreports.com**
Specialized weekly publication providing coverage of the prescription pharmaceutical industry. Coverage includes regulatory activities of FDA, FTC, and HCFA; Congress, industry, and financial news; new product introductions; executive changes. US$1,300 print and Web; US$1,250 print only.

123. *FedLog*. **Defense Logistics Information Service. http://www.dlis.dla.mil/FedLog**
Catalogs millions of stock and spare part items. Contractor price US$90/year for print copy; US$132 for DVD.

124. *Financial Times*. **Financial Times Limited. http://news.ft.com/home/us**
Major international newspaper with a European perspective. US$149/48 weeks.

125. *Flight International.* **Reed Business Information.**
http://www.flightinternational.com
Provides in-depth technical reporting, geared toward the professional, on world
aerospace news. US$135/year.

126. *Fortune.* **Time Inc. http://www.fortune.com**
Major biweekly business magazine highlighting companies, industries, and
economic trends. US$66.87/year.

127. *FSI State & Local Headline News.* **Federal Sources, Inc.**
http://www.fedsources.com; email editor@fedsources.com.
FSI provides integrated market intelligence solutions to government vendors,
and independent analysis for government executives and the media. Headline
news services are available for federal as well as state and local news. Free
with registration.

128. **"Fugger Family,"** *Encyclopedia Britannica*
(http://search.eb.com/eb/article?eu=36237)
Provides background information on this German mercantile and banking
dynasty during the 15th and 16th centuries. (Direct URL available only to *EB*
subscribers; for subscription information, go to www.eb.com.)

129. **"Fugger Newsletters," by Southland Media,**
http://www.southlandmedia.com/au/smedia1.html
Traces the history, growth, and advancement in printing that enhanced
information delivery during the rise of the Fugger dynasty.

130. **Fuld CI Software Survey: http://www.scip.org/Library/overview.pdf**
See also **CI Software Report**, earlier in this section.

131. *Fulltext Sources Online: For Periodicals, Newspapers, Newswires,*
Newsletters, TV/Radio Transcripts with Internet URLs. **Information Today,**
Inc. http://www.infotoday.com/books/dir/fso.shtml
Published twice yearly, this comprehensive directory of published sources
covers publications for which the complete text is available online. Fields
include science, technology, medicine, law, finance, business, industry, and the
popular press. Each entry provides ISSN, aggregator(s), and database name(s),
dates of coverage, frequency or lag time, and publisher's Web site with archives
when available. Includes subject, geographic, and language indexes, plus a
section listing publications on the Internet. Print edition: US$209.50/year.
Electronic subscription also available.

132. *Harvard Business Review.* **Harvard Business School Publishing.**
http://harvardbusinessonline.hbsp.harvard.edu

Major business magazine including case studies and articles on communication, strategy, and organizational development. US$118/year.

133. **Holden, Jim,** *Power Base Selling.* **John Wiley & Sons. 1999. http://www.wiley.com**
Book offers strategies, cases, and guidelines for defeating the competition by taking advantage of their weaknesses and turning their strengths against them. Shows how to anticipate the competitor's best moves and neutralize them. US$16.95. For his seminar series, see **Holden International** in the Association section.

134. *House of Rothschild: Money's Prophets, 1798–1848,* **by Niall Ferguson. Viking, 1998. Reviewed in "A Power Unto Themselves," by Lance Morrow,** *Time,* **December 7, 1988.**
Morrow reviews this extensive biography of the beginnings and growth of the Rothschild dynasty. He cites the importance and use of a sophisticated communications network that helped their banking houses as well as diplomatic leaders of that time period. Volume I: US$34.95.

135. *ICD-10 (International Classification of Diseases).* **National Center for Health Statistics and World Health Organization. http://www.cdc.gov/nchs/about/major/dvs/icd10des.htm; http://www.who.int/whosis/icd10/index.html**
Systems used to collect, process, classify, and present mortality statistics internationally. Volume 1: US$117, Volume 2: US$36, Volume 3: US$117.

136. *Information Today.* **Information Today, Inc. http://www.infotoday.com/it/itnew.htm**
Monthly trade newspaper targeted to the library and information profession. Includes industry news, feature articles, interviews, and columns. US$62.95/year for eleven issues.

137. *Intellectual Capital: The New Wealth of Organizations,* **by Thomas A. Stewart. Currency/Random House, 1998. http://www.randomhouse.com.**
Book shows how to turn the untapped knowledge of an organization into a competitive weapon. Demonstrates how knowledge has become the most important factor in economic life. Includes practical advice, stories, and case histories. US$16.95.

138. **"Intelligence" and "Intelligence and Counterintelligence,"** *Encyclopedia Britannia, (search.eb.com/eb/article?eu=118859)* **and** *The New Encyclopedia Britannica,* **21, 1998 p. 782–788.**
Provides basic definition and history of intelligence as applied to obtaining information for decision making. (Direct URL available only to *EB* subscribers; for subscription information go to www.eb.com.)

139. *In Vivo: Business & Medicine Report.* **Windhover Information, Inc.**
http://www.windhoverinfo.com
Monthly analytical publication covering the global health marketplace.
Provides insight and analysis into company strategy, marketplace trends, key
industry events, deal making, and management. Covers the pharmaceutical,
biotechnology, medical/surgical, and in vitro diagnostics industries.
US$895/year.

140. **"It's the Analysis, Stupid" by Kenneth Sawka.** *Competitive Intelligence*
Magazine, **Vol. 2, No. 4, October–December, 1999, pp. 43–44.**
Ken Sawka points out that information is not intelligence and shares some
observations about where information has been cast as intelligence when it is not.

141. **Job Machine's** *CyberSleuthing!* **newsletter.**
http://www.jobmachine.net/newsletter.htm
Semi-monthly newsletter provides strategic and tactical methods for finding
and networking with people on the Internet, as well as other tips. Focuses on
how technology can aid in finding source experts in all kinds of professional
disciplines. Free email subscription.

142. *Journal of Competitive Intelligence and Management.* **Society of**
Competitive Intelligence Professionals. http://www.scip.org
This new scholarly journal will publish its first issue in early 2003. Will
include empirical and theoretical studies as well as concise case studies. Free to
SCIP members.

143. **Kennedy Information (Subsidiary of BNA). http://www.kennedypub.com**
A publisher of directory and newsletters for consultants. Titles include
Consultants News, Executive Recruiter News and *e-Services Report.* Prices
range from US$197/year to US$895/year. *Consultants News* is $295/year.

144. *KM News.* **CXO Media, Inc. http://subscribe.cio.com/newsletters.cfm**
"Making the most of intellectual capital." Free with email signup.

145. *KM World.* **http://www.kmworld.com**
Informs subscribers on knowledge management components and processes.
Archive of articles available free at the Web site. Subscriptions free to those
who qualify.

146. *Knowledge Management News.* **Hoyt Consulting. http://www.kmnews.com**
This newsletter focuses on the disciplines of knowledge management, content
management, e-learning, and information management. Free.

147. **"The Library in Corporate Intelligence Activities," edited and with an**
introduction by Thomas D. Walker. *Library Trends,* **Vol. 43, No. 2, Fall**

1994. This thematic issue contains seven articles on corporate library involvement in CI activities.

148. **"Lloyds of London ne Lloyds Coffee House."**
http://www.coffee.com.au/coffee_lloyds.htm
Provides a brief introduction to Lloyd's Coffee House, citing text from *Against the Gods* [90].

149. *Medical Advertising News* **aka** *Med Ad News*. **Engel Publishing Partners.**
http://www.medadnews.com
A leading source of information on the business and marketing activities of the pharmaceutical industry. Published monthly in tabloid format. Considered a standard throughout the pharmaceutical industry for its coverage of news, articles, special features, and annual reports. Free with registration.

150. *Medical Marketing & Media*. **CPS Communications, Inc.**
http://www.cpsnet.com/Pubs/mmm.asp
A monthly business publication distributed to healthcare marketing executives employed by product manufacturers (devices, supplies, Rx, and OTC drugs), ad agencies, media, and service suppliers. Each issue carries a mix of industry news, information on personnel changes, and feature articles by industry experts on a wide variety of topics covering the marketing and promotion of healthcare products. Articles dating from January 1995 may be accessed via the Web site reprints link. Free to those who qualify; US$95/individual/year; US$108/library/year.

151. *Merck Index*. **13th Edition. Merck & Company, Inc.**
http://www.merck.com/pubs/mindex
A one-volume encyclopedia of chemicals, drugs, and biologicals containing more than 10,000 monographs, each one a concise description of a single substance or a small group of closely related compounds. Available in book, CD-ROM, and online versions. US$60 print; US$595 CD-ROM. Online versions available through www.ChemStore.com, US$199–299/year.

152. *Merck Manual of Diagnosis and Therapy*. **Edited by Mark H. Beers, M.D., and Robert Berkow, M.D. 17th Edition (Centennial Edition).**
http://www.merck.com/pubs/mmanual
Widely used and respected general medical text. Includes symptoms, diagnosis, and treatment for thousands of medical conditions. Searchable free online. Print version US$35.

153. *Millennium Intelligence: Understanding and Conducting Competitive Intelligence in the Digital Age,* **by Jerry Miller and the Business Intelligence Braintrust. Medford, NJ, CyberAge Books, 2000.**

http://www.infotoday.com/books/books/MillIntell.shtml
Collection of authors' essays on aspects of intelligence including training,
analytical models, resources, information technology, ethics, and legal
implications. US$29.95.

154. *Most Secret and Confidential: Intelligence in the Age of Nelson,* **by Steve
E. Maffeo. Naval Institute Press, 2062 Generals Highway, Annapolis, MD
2000. 392 pp. http://www.usni.org**
Chronicles how Horatio Nelson, "one of history's greatest commanders,
gathered, analyzed, disseminated, and acted upon intelligence to help gain his
victories." Reviewed by Phillip S. Meilinger,
www.airpower.maxwell.af.mil/airchronicles/apj/apj00/win00/maffeo.htm.
US$32.95.

155. *The New Competitor Intelligence: The Complete Resource for Finding,
Analyzing, and Using Information About Your Competitors,* **by Leonard M.
Fuld. New York, John Wiley & Sons, Inc., 1995. http://www.wiley.com**
Extensive text with practical tips on how to find and analyze business
information for strategic intelligence. Provides examples and case studies.
US$44.95.

156. **Nihowdy. Email: http://webmaster@nihowdy.com**
A weekly alerting service highlighting articles on the open Web about the
personal computer and semiconductor industry.

157. *North American Industry Classification System (NAICS).* **2002 edition.
NAICS Association. http://www.naics.com**
Replaced the Standard Industrial Classification (SIC) system in 1997. This
manual contains the new six-digit code classification for all industries.
NAICS is considered "the" index for statistical reporting of all economic
activities of the U.S., Canada, and Mexico. Order from NTIS (www.ntis.gov)
or from the NAICS Web site. US$35 softcover; US$45 hardcover, US$65
CD-ROM.

158. *ONLINE.* **Information Today, Inc. http://www.infotoday.com/online**
Magazine targeted to professional online researchers. Includes product
reviews, case studies, and informed opinion on selecting, using, and managing
electronic information products available via database systems, CD-ROM,
and the Internet. US$110/year for 6 issues; higher cost outside the U.S.

159. *Oxford English Dictionary (OED).* **Edited by John Simpson and Edmund
Weiner. Second Edition. Oxford University Press 1999.
http://www.oed.com/public/publications**
Revered reference source for origins of most words in the English language.

Provides usage, meaning, and historical context. Cites first uses of words, providing citations of their application in works. Print edition US$995 (20 volumes); Compact edition US$395 (1 volume with magnifying glass); CD-ROM US$295.

160. **"Performance of Information Channels in the Transfer of Technology," by Thomas J. Allen,** *Industrial Management Review,* **Vol. 8, 1966, pp. 87–98.**
Explores sources, "messages," and flow of technical information in institutions. Focuses on information providers and gatekeepers. Considered a major contributor in the history of corporate competitive intelligence.

161. *Pharmaceutical Executive.* **Advanstar Communications, Inc. http://www.advanstar.com/index_allpubs.html**
Considered a key business journal for the pharmaceutical industry. Covers all aspects of pharmaceutical business strategy and marketing, including customer relationship management, promotion, advertising, patient education, public relations, and corporate development strategies. Free to qualified users; US$64 (12 issues/year).

162. *Physician's Desk Reference.* **57th Edition, 2003. Thomson Healthcare. http://www.pdr.net**
Authoritative source of FDA-approved information on prescription drugs. Provides complete data on more than 4,000 FDA-approved drugs, by brand and generic name, including usage information and warnings, drug interactions; includes more than 2,000 photos. US$89.95.

163. **Porter, Michael, "How Competitive Forces Shape Strategy."** *Harvard Business Review,* **March–April, 1979.**
Landmark article introducing the five forces affecting corporate strategy: competitors, new entrants, suppliers, customers, and substitutes. This five-force model is still applied in CI departments today.

164. *Power* **Magazine. (Platt's; McGraw-Hill). www.powermag.com and http://www.platts.com/engineering/index.shtml**
Power focuses on steam and electric-power generation, including electric utilities, manufacturing and process plants, independent power and co-generation plants, waste-to-energy plants, and commercial and institutional plants; plus consulting, design and construction engineering firms, and others allied to the field, including government, that serve them. Free to those in the industry; US$55 for others.

165. **Prescott, John E. and Stephen H. Miller,** *Proven Strategies in Competitive Intelligence.* **Society of Competitive Intelligence Professionals. http://www.scip.org.**

This book is a collection of case studies describing successful CI operations used by market leaders. Studies highlight CI applications in sales and marketing, market research and forecasting, new product development, and teams. It features contributions from CI innovators as well as past and present CEOs. US$40 nonmembers; US$30 members.

166. *Public Accountings Report.* **Aspen Publishers, Inc. http://www.aspenpublishers.com**
This newsletter reports and analyzes news, developments, and trends in the public accounting industry. Topics include breaking news, in-depth firm profiles, mergers and acquisitions, office closings, auditor changes, key personnel moves, legal and regulatory issues, competitive intelligence, niche practices, and product launches. US$297/year (23 issues plus index and special reports).

167. *R&D Focus.* **IMS Health. http://www.ims-global.com/products/lifecycle/r_and_d.htm**
Monitors news on 8,500 drugs in active R&D. Searchable by product, company, phase, mechanism of action, and country. Annual subscription by CD (1–5 licenses): £4,500 monthly, £3,380 quarterly.

168. *The Rational Manager: A Systematic Approach to Problem Solving and Decision Making* **by Charles H. Kepner and Benjamin B. Tregoe. New York, McGraw-Hill, 1965.**
Presents the systematic approach now known as the Kepner-Tregoe method for problem solving and decision making. Approach includes the situation appraisal, problem analysis, decision analysis, and potential problem analysis (out of print). From the same authors: *The New Rational Manager*, Princeton, NJ, Princeton Research Press, 1997; US$13.50 (www.kepner-tregoe.com).

169. *Red Herring.* **Red Herring Communications. http://www.redherring.com**
Magazine providing in-depth analysis and reporting on the forces driving innovation, technology, entrepreneurialism, and the financial markets. US$34.95.

170. *Research Buzz.* **Tara Calishain. http://www.researchbuzz.com**
Weekly newsletter providing news and information on search engines and databases. Archives dating back to April 1998 are searchable on the Web site. Free with online registration.

171. *Scanning the Business Environment* **by Francis Aguilar. Macmillan, 1967.**
Viewed as the first introduction and vision of external forces affecting the competition of companies in the U.S. (out of print).

172. **Schoolnet. http://www.spartacus.schoolnet.co.uk/LONLloyds.htm**
Provides brief history of the birth of Edward Lloyd's Coffee House on Tower
Street and how it grew into an intelligence gathering and publishing
organization.

173. *Scrip Magazine*. **PJB Publications. http://www.pjbpubs.com**
Considered a leading magazine for the pharmaceutical industry. This monthly
publication features commentary, analysis, and insight into the issues at the
top of the pharmaceutical industry's agenda. Scrip Magazine is part of the
subscription to the twice-weekly newsletter, *Scrip World Pharmaceutical
News*, as well as being available under separate subscription. US$555 for the
magazine only.

174. *Searcher*. **Information Today, Inc. http://www.infotoday.com/searcher**
Magazine targeted to professional online researchers. Includes in-depth
articles on search techniques, industry trends, and evaluations of online
resources. US$75.95/year for 10 issues; higher outside the U.S.

175. *Sloan Management Review*. **Massachusetts Institute of Technology (MIT)
Sloan School of Management. http://smr.mit.edu**
A peer-reviewed quarterly business journal aimed at bridging the gap between
management research and practice. Evaluates and reports on new research to
help readers identify and understand significant trends in management. The
journal covers all management disciplines, with emphasis on corporate
strategy, leadership, and management of technology and innovation.
US$89/year for 4 issues.

176. **"Spies Like Us," by Skip Kaltenheuser and Keith Epstein.** *CIO Insight*,
August 1, 2001. www.cioinsight.com/article2/0,3959,44507,00.asp
Article highlights a CI case study involving Wayne Rosenkrans and Bristol-
Myers Squibb.

177. *Standard Rate & Data Service (SRDS) Directory of Business Publications*.
http://www.srds.com
Major resource for media rates and publishing-related information. Business
volume contains profiles of every business publication including advertising
and editorial information. US$733 in the U.S., higher elsewhere.

178. *Statistical Abstract of the United States*. **Government Printing Office.
http://www.census.gov/prod/2002pubs/01statab/stat-ab01.html**
"The government's most important statistical factbook on the social, political, &
economic aspects of American life. Includes data on population, births, deaths,
life expectancy, marriage and divorce, health and nutrition, education, law
enforcement" (from census.gov site). Individual chapters are available in Portable
Document Format (PDF) on the Web site. US$48 hardcover; US$38 softcover.

179. **Strafford Publications, Inc. http://www.straffordpub.com**
A national publisher of newsletters, case law reporters, data services, books, surveys, and special reports serving the accounting, legal, and management consulting professions, and the security and loss prevention industry. Prices range from US$34.50 (books) to US$597 for newsletter yearly subscriptions.

180. *Strategic Management Journal.* **John Wiley & Sons, Inc. http://www.wiley.com**
An academic journal focused on the theory, practice, and advancement of strategic management. Covers topics such as strategic resource allocation, organization structure, leadership, entrepreneurship, and organizational purpose, as well as methods and techniques for evaluating and understanding competitive, technological, social, and political environments; planning processes; and strategic decision processes. An article on the global acquisition, protection, and leveraging of technological capabilities by Sue McEvily, Kathy Eisenhardt, and John Prescott is scheduled for publication in 2003. US$290 for an individual subscription (13 issues).

181. *Super Searchers Do Business: The Online Secrets of Top Business Researchers,* **by Mary Ellen Bates. CyberAge Books, 1999. http://www.infotoday.com/supersearchers**
A collection of interviews with 11 expert business researchers. US$24.95.

182. *The Sword and the Shield: The Mitrokhin Archive and the Secret History of the KGB,* **by Christopher Andrew and Vasili Mitrokhin. Basic Books, 2000. http://www.basicbooks.com**
This story is based on a secret archive of top-level KGB documents smuggled out of the Soviet Union. The archive covers the entire period from the Bolshevik Revolution to the 1980s. Contributes to the understanding of KGB intelligence collection methods, espionage, and covert actions. US$17.50 paperback, higher outside the U.S.

183. *Technical Insights.* **Frost & Sullivan. http://www.frost.com**
Series of newsletters focusing on technology transfer in a variety of fields. Covers engineering, pharmaceuticals, and other technology areas. A popular title in the R&D world is "Inside R&D." *Technical Insights* also offers publications under its Technology Resource Services label for vertical markets such as aerospace and defense, energy, healthcare, and oil and gas. US$2,000–4,000/year for electronic newsletter subscriptions (includes archive); US$1,152–2,160/year for hard copy newsletter subscription; US$14,000–$53,000 for the Technology Resource Services—Vertical Markets.

184. *Technology Review.* **Massachusetts Institute of Technology (MIT). http://www.technologyreview.com**
Considered MIT's magazine of innovation. Promotes the understanding of

emerging technologies and their impact on business and society. Selected issues have annual reviews such as top innovators and top patent issuers. US$30/year (higher outside U.S.), 10 issues.

185. *Theory of Economic Development*, (Theorie de l'evolution economique) by Joseph Schumpeter, Payot, Paris, 1912.
Schumpeter was considered a pioneer in the economics of the capitalist system in Europe. In 1912 he presented his vision of dynamic processes that included a circular flow and the recognition of the competitive forces of new markets, new entrants, and new suppliers. Referenced in "European Competitiveness and Business;" see separate entry in this section.

186. "Toward Strategic Intelligence Systems," by David B. Montgomery and Charles B. Weinberg, *Journal of Marketing*, Vol. 43, Fall 1979, pp. 41–52.
Article cites the dramatic increase in the use of strategic planning tools in the past decade and provides an overview of strategic intelligence systems. The authors share their concern about the lack of focus on the selection, gathering, and analysis of information in the strategic planning process.

187. *Ulrich's Periodicals Directory.* 2003 edition. RR Bowker LLC. http://www.bowker.com
Major reference source for more than 164,000 regularly issued and 3,500 ceased publications. Each serial is profiled, including addresses, phone numbers, email addresses, URLs, and fax numbers for some 80,000 publishers from 200 countries. Ulrich's also covers 27,000 Internet, online, and CD-ROM publications; 6,700 daily and weekly U.S. newspapers in the newspaper volume; and more than 7,000 non-U.S. and topical U.S. papers in the main volumes. US$699 for 5-volume set (annual).

188. *Upside Today*. UMAC, Inc. http://www.upsidetoday.com
Monthly magazine focused on the business of technology. Covers key business issues and trends affecting high-tech companies with an emphasis on financial and management issues surrounding the growth sectors. Free subscription available to qualified professionals in the U.S. only. US$75 for non-U.S.

189. Usenet Newsgroups. http://groups.google.com
Access to dozens of discussion forums on a wide range of topics. Can search by one of 10 subject categories—e.g., biz (business topics), comp (computers)—or through an alphabetical list. Free.

190. *Value Line Investment Survey.* Value Line. http://www.valueline.com
Weekly publication known for its main section "Ratings & Reports," which highlights selected companies in multiple industries. Each selected company receives a full-page profile including historical and recent stock data,

quarterly financial information, news, and performance review. The other sections are "Summary & Index," which provides a key to locating the latest reports on each of the stocks followed, and "Selection & Opinion," providing VL's view of the economy and the stock market, model portfolios, and various economic and stock market statistics. US$598/year.

191. *Veille*. **http://www.veille.com**
In addition to the print publication, *Veille* produces e-publications and hosts discussion lists for the CI professional. All articles and discussions are in French. 151 Euros/yr (10 issues) for addresses in France; higher elsewhere.

192. *VTC Media Availability*. **U.S. Department of Defense. http://www.pentagon.mil/news/subscribe.html, or via email:dladvisories_sender@DTIC.MIL**
Service provides email notices of Video Tele Conference media availability of DoD officials. Related services provide email announcements, news, and speech transcripts. Free with registration.

193. *Wall Street Journal*. **Dow Jones & Company, Inc.: http://online.wsj.com/public/us**
Major business newspaper for the United States. Reports on major company and industry activities. Often profiles companies, industries, and executives. US$189 for 52 weeks.

194. *Working Knowledge: How Organizations Manage What They Know* **by Thomas H. Davenport and Laurence Prusak. 1997 (hardcover) and 2000 (paperback). Harvard Business School Press. http://www.harvardbusinessonline.hbsp.harvard.edu**
Introduces the vocabulary and concepts of knowledge management. Explores how knowledge can be nurtured in organizations and how to create a knowledge-oriented corporate culture. Successful knowledge projects are profiled through case studies. US$29.95 hardcover; US$19.95 softcover

SOFTWARE UTILITIES AND TOOLS

195. **Adobe Acrobat. Adobe Systems Incorporated. http://www.adobe.com**
Desktop software for creating and converting documents to Adobe Portable Document Format (PDF) files, now a worldwide standard. Aids in printing documents in the format and fonts intended and in protecting them from unauthorized access and alterations. Cost for the full Acrobat CD-ROM or download version is US$249. Acrobat Reader, which only reads PDF documents, is available free.

196. **C-4-U Scout. C-4 U Ltd. http://www.c-4-u.com**
A desktop application for monitoring Web page changes at designated URLs.
It runs on all Microsoft *Windows* platforms 95 and up. Available free from the
Web site.

197. **ChangeDetection.com, FreeFind.com.**
http://www.changedetection.com/monitor.html
Service that monitors Web page changes for free. Offers a "wizard" to aid in
setting up the service.

198. **Dialog Alerts. Dialog Corporation.**
http://products.dialog.com/products/dialog/dial_alerts.html
Literature monitoring service for most databases available through Dialog.
Alert frequency varies with the database provider and personal options. Cost
depends upon frequency, print format, and database cost.

* **Docere** *see* **Market Signal Analyzer** [208]

199. **Dow Jones Interactive Custom Clips. Dow Jones & Company.**
http://www.djinteractive.com
The literature monitoring service for newswires, newspapers, magazines, and
newsletters covered in the Dow Jones Interactive Publications Library.
Custom Clips offers several delivery options and updating frequencies. All
Dow Jones Interactive customers will be migrated to Factiva.com by or before
June, 2003. *See also* **Factiva.com Tracks** [200]

200. **Factiva.com Tracks. Factiva. http://www. factiva.com**
Literature monitoring service for newswires, newspapers, magazines, and
newsletters covered in Factiva.com, a joint venture of Dow Jones and Reuters.

201. **Fuld & Company—CI Strategies and Tools:**
http://www.fuld.com/i3/l2.html
Annotated listing of alert and monitoring services particularly relevant to
those performing competitive intelligence.

202. **InfoMinder. iMorph.com. http://www.infominder.com**
A tracking service that notifies subscribers when Web site content changes.
Free trial available. Subscription costs US$24.95/year.

203. **Knowledge Works. Cipher Systems LLC. http://www.cipher-sys.com**
A client-server application designed for use on Lotus *Notes* or Microsoft
Exchange. Provides a workflow component around Key Intelligence Topics
(KIT) and Key Intelligence Questions (KIQs), automated collection of
published information from internal and external sources, the capability to
enter primary information, and advanced search tools for information
retrieval. Contact the vendor for pricing information: +1.800.595.9763.

204. **LexisNexis ECLIPSE Service. LexisNexis. http://www.lexisnexis.com**
A literature search service that tracks publications in the LexisNexis libraries.
Offers various formats, delivery options, and updating frequency. Cost varies
depending upon choice of library, frequency, and delivery option.

205. **Lotus *Domino*. IBM Corporation.**
http://www.lotus.com/products/r5web.nsf/webhome/nr5serverhp-new
The Lotus Domino line of servers facilitates group interactions,
collaborations, and messaging. Enhances group database development. A free
trial is available through Web site download.

206. **Lotus Notes. IBM Corporation. http://www.lotus.com/products**
Groupware that combines enterprise-class messaging and calendaring and
scheduling capabilities with a platform for collaborative applications. A trial
copy can be downloaded for free. Contact 1-888-SHOP-IBM for pricing
inquiries.

207. **L-Soft. http://www.lsoft.com**
Producers of LISTSERV™ list management software. Pricing varies
depending on number of subscribers, delivery speed, etc. Email
sales@lsoft.com for a price quote.

208. **Market Signal Analyzer. Docere Intelligence Inc. http://www.docere.se**
Software that provides a matrix-based framework for collecting and
organizing qualitative information. Aids in identifying and reporting trends
and events that may impact the user's firm (aka early warning). A free trial is
available via the Web site.

209. **Microsoft Excel. Microsoft Corporation.**
http://www.microsoft.com/office/excel/default.asp
Spreadsheet software for data manipulation, charting, and data analysis. Use
of Pivot Tables and Functions aid in financial analysis.

210. **Microsoft Office. Microsoft Corporation.**
http://www.microsoft.com/office/default.asp
Office suite software. The Professional Edition includes Access, Office,
PowerPoint, and Word.

211. **Microsoft PowerPoint. Microsoft Corporation.**
http://www.microsoft.com/office/powerpoint/default.asp
Presentation software.

212. **Microsoft Word. Microsoft Corporation.**
http://www.microsoft.com/office/word/default.asp
Word processing software packaged with many new computers. Also part of

the Microsoft Office family of applications. Special features such as Insert/Index and Table of Contents aid in presenting summarized news items and written research results.

213. **MindIt (Now defunct)**

214. **MyYahoo! http://www.yahoo.com**
Personalized service to set up news and stock alerting services. Available free with registration.

215. **NetMind (Now defunct)**

216. **Office Accelerator. Baseline Data Systems, Inc. http://www.baselineconnect.com**
A powerful address book program that integrates with Windows applications including word processors, email programs, and the Internet. Features document tracking and phone call logging. Standard Edition is US$99.95.

* **PlanBee** *see* **Thoughtscape** [220]

217. **SmartWrap. Selznick Scientific Software, LLC. http://www.selznick.com/products/smartwrap/index.htm**
A software utility that scans text and email, identifies paragraphs and lists, and rewraps the text accordingly. Both Windows and Mac versions are available. This is a shareware product. $15 donation suggested.

218. **Spyonit: http://www.spyonit.com**
On hiatus as of June 2002, but reactivation is expected. The Web-based service keeps looking for the topics specified, and then notifies the requester by email, pager, or other specified delivery device. The service has been free, and the providers expect to keep it free.

219. **Strategy Software. Strategy Software, Inc. http://www.strategy-software.com**
Strategy Software produces four software packages for competitive intelligence activities. Both IntoAction and Strategy! are sold on a per-user basis. Strategy! supports organizing information from several sources. Additional products are InfoAction (for access to internal intranet reports), FastTrack (database aid), and InTouch Hotline (experts). Prices vary; contact provider for pricing information.

220. **Thoughtscape Desktop 3.0. ThoughtShare Communications, Inc. http://www.thoughtshare.com**
Software utility that allows you to create and save copies of Wcb pages. Facilitates collection and distribution of collected Web pages. Free download available for limited usage. Software may be purchased for US$29.95.

221. **TracerLock: http://www.tracerlock.com**
A clipping service that monitors thousands of news sites, online trade journals, and e-zines automatically and emails profile-matching results to subscribers. Individual profiles cost US$4/month and US$19.50/month for five keywords. Tracerlock also offers a newsfeed feature for no additional cost.

222. **TVEyes: http://www.tveyes.com**
TVEyes monitors TV channels and sends email alerts whenever one of up to five sets of keywords is mentioned. Available in three subscription levels: TVEyes Consumer Edition is a free service. TVEyes Gold offers an unlimited keyword list for a low yearly rate. TVEyes Professional Edition features full-text searching of more than 40 stations' content. In addition, TVEyes Political Edition covers the "buzz on the Hill," TVEyes Broadcast Services include the Fastrans Transcription tool and the TVEyes Clip Recorder, as well as a suite of tools for publishing indexed streaming video onto the Web.

223. **Vivisimo: http://www.vivisimo.com**
Document clustering (automatic categorization) software for arranging intranet data into hierarchical folders. Integrates internal and external information on the fly." The Clustering Engine starts at US$25,000. A free version is available at the Web site for general Web searching. Inquiries may be directed to sales@vivisimo.com.

224. **Wincite. Wincite Systems LLC. http://www.wincite.com**
A LAN-based software system designed as a comprehensive CI database tool. Provides analytical frameworks and reporting features. Includes a feature that maps information and intelligence to business processes and areas and related files. The basic system starts at US$15,000.

225. **Wisdom Builder. Wisdom Builder, LLC. http://www.wisdombuilder.com**
A Microsoft Windows-based client-server application to aid in the research process. It is considered unique for its focus on finding hidden relationships among events, people, places, products, and organizations in text such as news articles, press releases, etc. The Wisdom Builder Desktop is two packages combined. Each may be purchased separately: Gold Rush! Single user is US$79.95 and TimeLine Pro Single User is US$249.95.

PROFESSIONAL ASSOCIATIONS, CONFERENCES, CONSULTANTS, COURSES, ETC.

226. **American Management Association (AMA): http://www.amanet.org**
Offers a full range of live, electronic, and printed business education and

management development programs for individuals and organizations in the Americas, Asia, and Europe. Publishes a number of books.

227. **American Marketing Association (AMA): http://www.ama.org**
A professional association of individual marketers. AMA has more than 40,000 members worldwide and serves many levels of marketing practitioners, from executives to students. Publishes several periodicals and books.

228. **American Productivity & Quality Center (APQC): http://www.apqc.org**
An education and research organization whose mission is to improve productivity and quality in organizations around the world through research, education, and advisory services. Offers books and courses in such areas as: benchmarking, best practices, knowledge management, customer-focused systems, organizational effectiveness, and performance measurement.

229. **Association of Independent Information Professionals: http://www.aiip.org**
An international association of approximately 700 people who either own their own information businesses or are interested in the profession. The AIIP membership directory is available at www.aiip.org/directory.asp.

230. **Barndt, Walter**
Walter Barndt, now retired, taught strategic and business intelligence courses for the Hartford Graduate Center, Lally School of Management, Rensselaer Polytechnic Institute from 1983–1996.

231. **Cisek, Robert N., Ph.D.** *See also* **Mercyhurst College** [250]
Dr. Cisek is a professor in the Research Intelligence and Analyst Program, History Department, Mercyhurst College, Erie, PA. He has a background in strategic planning and teaches business intelligence, in addition to other courses in the program.

232. **CI University: http://www.scip.org/education/ciuniversity.edu**
Web site details the courses, certificate, and university programs in place or under development at schools in North America.

233. **Competia: http://www.competia.com**
Canadian-based association and conference vendor for the CI profession.

234. **Conference Board Council on Competitive Analysis: http://www.conference-board.org**
Formed by the Conference Board and the Society of Competitive Intelligence Professionals. Its purpose is to provide a platform for an intensive, off-the-record exchange of ideas and experiences with respect to competitive

intelligence/analysis activities, and to further the professional development of its members.

235. **Dedijer, Stevan. http://www.zapi.hr/dedijer/druga_verzija/Home_2.htm**
Professor Dedijer has been described as the father of business intelligence. He taught courses in the Department of Business Administration, University of Lund, Sweden, from 1974 to 1993. His publications include a regular column in SCIP's *Competitive Intelligence Review*. As of 2000, he was still lecturing at conferences on business intelligence.

236. **Drexel University. College of Information Science and Technology. Competitive Intelligence Certificate Program. 3141 Chestnut Street, Philadelphia, PA 19104. FAX +1.215.895.2494. http://www.cis.drexel.edu**
Credited as being the first university to offer a CI certificate program.

237. **Fahey, Liam, Ph.D. lfahey95@aol.com**
Dr. Fahey is adjunct professor of strategic management at Babson College and teaches strategy in Babson's custom executive education programs. He is the author and editor of six books, including *Learning from the Future: Competitive Foresight Scenarios* and the best-selling *The Portable MBA in Strategy*. Fahey is also an active researcher and consultant to firms in North America and Europe. He previously taught at Northwestern's J.L. Kellogg Graduate School of Management and Boston University's School of Management.

238. **Fleisher, Craig S., Ph.D. fleisher@uwindsor.ca**
Dr. Fleisher is a professor with the Odette School of Business, University of Windsor, Windsor, Ontario. He is also one of the editors of the new SCIP publication, *Strategic Management Journal*, listed separately in the Articles section.

239. **Fuld & Company, Inc. http://www.fuld.com**
Fuld & Company is an international competitive intelligence consulting firm. Founded in 1979 by Leonard M. Fuld, the company performs research and offers seminars and other professional services. Fuld hosts a CI Learning Center, publishes the Internet Intelligence Index, and conducts an annual CI software review. Leonard Fuld is also known for his book, *The New Competitor Intelligence*, listed separately [155].

240. **Fuld War Room. http://www.fuld.com/ciStrategieswarRoom.html**
Interactive multimedia CD for training and reference. Provides training tools and reference materials from CI fundamentals to advanced analytical techniques. Note: Currently out of print but may be republished in the future.

241. **Futures Group. http://www.futuresgroup.com**
A management, marketing, research, and strategic planning organization.

242. **Gilad, Ben, Ph.D. http://www.academyci.com/About/gilad.html**
Dr. Gilad is a former Associate Professor of Strategic Management and a former acting chairman of the International Business Dept. at Rutgers University's School of Management. He created CI courses for Rutgers, New York University, Hebrew University in Jerusalem, and The College of Management in Tel Aviv. He currently serves on the faculty of the Fuld Gilad Herring Academy of Competitive Intelligence.

243. **Herring, Jan P. jpherring@snet.net**
Jan P. Herring, a co-founder and faculty member of the Academy of Competitive Intelligence (ACI), serves as an advisor to business executives and intelligence professionals. Herring is a pioneer and recognized expert in the field of business intelligence. He is a charter member and Fellow of the Society of Competitive Intelligence Professionals (SCIP). Previously he held positions with The Futures Group, a BI consulting firm he founded, was Director of Analytical Research with Motorola, and worked as a professional intelligence officer in the Central Intelligence Agency (CIA). Herring is also known for creating the "Intelligence Cycle," further described in two of his publications, "Building a Business Intelligence System," *Journal of Business Strategy*, May/June, 1988 and "Key Intelligence Topics? A Process to Identify and Define Intelligence Needs," *Competitive Intelligence Review*, Vol. 10, No. 2, 1999.

244. **Hohhof, Bonnie. Intelligent Information. bhohhof@mixedsignal.com**
Bonnie Hohhof is the editor of *Competitive Intelligence Magazine (CIM)*. She started and edited SCIP's first publication, *Competitive Intelligence Review (CIR)* in 1988. Hohhof has written articles and contributed to books on the use of information technology for competitive intelligence activities.

245. **Holden, Jim. Holden International. http://www.holdenintl.com**
Jim Holden is founder and CEO of Holden International. Holden and his team work with companies to gain competitive advantage by applying sales and marketing techniques. In addition to his many seminars, Holden is known for the Strategic Value Selling Methodology and four books, most notably *Power Base Selling*, listed separately in the Articles section.

246. **Innovation Management Seminar, MIT. http://ilp.mit.edu/ilp/events.html**
The MIT Sloan School of Management co-sponsors the Annual Innovations in Management Conference every spring with the MIT Office of Corporate Relations Industrial Liaison Program. Registration is free to members, US$1,450 to nonmembers.

247. **Kassler, Helene**
    Helene Kassler, formerly with Northern Light and Fuld & Company, is known for several of her presentations and published articles on data sources for CI. Articles cited in this book are: "Data in the Corporate Universe: It's a Dangerous World Out There," *Searcher*, March 1, 2001; "Competitive Intelligence on the Web," *Database*, August 1, 1999; and "Wins and Losses: The Latest Developments in Online Competitor Research," *Searcher*, February 1, 1998.

248. **Keim, Daniel A. keim@informatik.uni-konstanz.de; http://www.inf.uni-konstanz.de/~keim**
    Daniel A. Keim is with the Computer Science Institute, University of Konstanz, Germany. His published work includes several articles on visualization techniques, including: "Visualization Techniques for Mining Large Databases: A Comparison" (www.codata.org/meet+reports/Vis-97/s23.htm and citeseer.nj.nec.com/keim96visualization.html).

249. **Kight, Leila**
    Leila Kight, now retired, is a founding member of the Society of Competitive Information Professionals. Her book, *Business Researchers Handbook* (listed separately in the Articles section), published in 1980 by Washington Researchers, is still referred to today for its insight into the entire intelligence process, from understanding the question to delivering a full-blown report.

250. **Mercyhurst College Research/Intelligence Analyst Program: http://www.mercyhurst.edu/academics/riap.htm**
    Grants an undergraduate degree in competitive intelligence. Teaches nuts and bolts of intelligence gathering and analysis. Concentrates on how to do business intelligence, not just how to use the CI department.

251. **Miller, Jerry P., Ph.D. jmiller@simmons.edu**
    Dr. Miller is Director of the Competitive Intelligence Center at Simmons College (see 257). He has taught CI courses in the library school since the early 1990s and has served on the faculty of Simmons since 1989. Jerry has performed research, given presentations, and published several articles on intelligence and competitive intelligence. His book, *Millennium Intelligence,* is listed separately here [153].

252. **National Association of Investors Corporation: http://www.wildcapital.com**
    Professional association for individual investors. Aids/trains members in analyzing companies.

253. **Paap, Jay. California Institute of Technology: www.irc.caltech.edu/ and http://www.jaypaap.com**
    Dr. Paap is President of Paap Associates, Inc. (PAI), a management consulting

firm assisting major corporations in a broad range of business and technology development efforts, and serves on the faculty of the Industrial Relations Center at Caltech. He is a frequent speaker, and participates in seminars for Caltech, MIT, the Strategic Leadership Forum, and other groups.

254. **Prescott, John E., Ph.D. Prescott@katz.pitt.edu**
Dr. Prescott is a professor of Business Administration at the Katz Graduate School of Business. In addition to being one of the first recognized CI professors in the United States, he has written and edited several articles, books, and scholarly journals on competitive intelligence including *Proven Strategies in Competitive Intelligence*, listed separately in the Articles section.

255. **Russo, J. Edward. Cornell University. JER@cornell.edu**
Dr. Russo is Professor of Marketing and Behavior Science, Johnson Graduate School of Management, Cornell University. His research centers on decision making for managers and consumers. His published work deals with confidence and overconfidence issues in decision making. He has explored advertising, behavioral methodologies, consumer-information aids, decision processes strategies, and the distortion of information during a decision. He is the coauthor of *Winning Decisions* (Doubleday 2002).

256. **Shelfer, Katherine. kathy.shelfer@cis.drexel.edu**
Kathy Shelfer is an Assistant Professor in Drexel University's College of Information Science and Technology. She has been instrumental in the CI Certificate program there. See additional information under the separate Drexel University listing [236].

257. **Simmons College, School of Library and Information Science: http://www.simmons.edu/gslis/index.html**
Simmons Competitive Intelligence Center: http://cic.simmons.edu
Simmons was the first known library school to teach competitive intelligence starting in the 1990s. *See also* Miller, Jerry P. [251].

258. **Society of Competitive Intelligence Professionals (SCIP): http://www.scip.org**
An international association of competitive intelligence professionals. Members are primarily involved in corporate competitive intelligence, although some are CI consultants. Web site includes links to members.

259. **Special Libraries Association (SLA): http://www.sla.org**
An international association of librarians primarily in corporations, associations, and government agencies, as distinct from public or school libraries. Primarily U.S. and Canadian membership, with some non-North American regional groups as well. Publishes *Information Outlook*.

260. **Tufte, Edward R: http://www.edwardtufte.com**
Author of several books on visualization including: *The Visual Display of Quantitative Information* (US$40*), Envisioning Information* (US$48), and *Visual Explanations: Images and Quantities, Evidence and Narrative* (US$45). All available from Graphics Press and via Tufte's site.

261. **Washington Researchers: http://www.washingtonresearchers.com**
Produces publications and seminars on research and analysis. Publications may be ordered from the Web site. *See also Business Researchers Handbook,* listed separately in the Articles section [96]

Glossary

Analysis. The process of adding value to the information collected. Example: Financial analysis of a rival's employment levels over time may indicate that the rival is creating a more cost-effective operation, one with lower costs than your own. Value can be added by comparing and contrasting information found, such as through benchmarking or gap analysis or use of the Porter strategy model (*see* Porter Model), as well as other analytical techniques.

Blind Spots Analysis. A technique used to predict a new trend or product arriving in the market that would not be tracked otherwise. Example: a soft drink maker would not just research other soft drink producers; the research scope would be broadened to view any product that quenches a dry throat such as fruit drinks and ice cream. In this case, indicators, such as an increase in consumption of smoothies, would be included in the research process.

Competitor Intelligence. Similar to competitive or business intelligence, this phrase refers to legally and ethically collected information on a rival that has been analyzed to the point where one can make a decision. Example: "Our chief rival, a stock brokerage firm, is reducing its brokerage force by one-third over the next five years in favor of direct Internet electronic sales and transactions. This will reduce their costs, allowing them to cut their transaction fees by one-half, placing us in a high-cost, noncompetitive position."

Conjoint Analysis. A multivariate technique used to quantify the value that people associate with different levels of product/service attributes. Respondents trade product attributes against each other to establish product (brand) preference and the relative importance of attributes. Based on utility theory and consumer rationality. Better for functional than fashionable brands.

Environmental Scanning. A term coined in the mid-1960s by Francis Aguilar, a Harvard Business School professor, to describe the action of watching and collecting information on a company's rivals and on the overall market.

Four-Corners Model. A model proposed by Michael Porter to determine which firms and industries have competitive advantage. The four corners of the diamond include factor conditions, demand conditions, industry strategy/rivalry, and related and supporting industries.

Five-Forces Model. A model proposed by Michael Porter to determine industry attractiveness by performing an analysis of the industry structure. The five forces that typically shape the industry structure are: rivalry among competitors, threat of new entrants, threat of substitutes, bargaining power of buyers, and bargaining power of suppliers.

Intelligence Cycle. A four-step description proposed by Jan Herring to demonstrate how intelligence develops. Step 1: The questions; Step 2: Collection of the information; Step 3: Analysis of the information; Step 4: Delivery of the intelligence to the individual or individuals asking the question in Step 1. At this point, the person asking the question digests the intelligence delivered and may change the questions, starting the intelligence cycle all over again. This question-information-analysis-intelligence cycle may occur a few more times before the person asking the questions is satisfied and makes a decision. At that stage, the cycle stops.

Intelligence Pyramid. A three-step representation of competitive intelligence, proposed by Leonard Fuld, that includes: Level 1: Laying the Foundation; Level 2: Analysis; Level 3: Driving Decisions.

Malcolm Baldrige National Quality Award (MBNQA). An award established by the U.S. Congress in 1987 to raise awareness of quality management and recognize U.S. companies that have implemented successful quality management systems. Two awards may be given annually in each of five categories: manufacturing company, service company, small business, education, and healthcare. The award is named after the late Secretary of Commerce Malcolm Baldrige, a proponent of quality management. The U.S. Commerce Department's National Institute of Standards and Technology manages the award, and the American Society for Quality (ASQ) administers it.

Myers-Briggs Type Indicator (MBTI). A methodology and an instrument for identifying an individual's personality type based on Carl Jung's theory of personality preferences.

Porter Model. The title for the strategy model or framework created by Harvard Business School professor Michael Porter; also described in his book *Competitive Strategy* (Free Press, 1980). A universally applicable model describing how five industry forces affect an industry. One can use the Porter model to focus the analysis on a firm's competitive environment. *See also* Four Corners Model.

Primary Sources (Creative and Basic). People or events that provide information first-hand. For example, an expert who is interviewed is considered a primary source, as is an observation of booth attendance made at a trade show. This is in contrast to *secondary sources* such as newspapers and database material, which are previously recorded, often second-hand accounts or summaries of an event. Most critical, timely intelligence is derived from primary sources, with secondary sources frequently supplying the leads or expert names.

Scenario Planning. An analytical framework used to forecast market conditions and the overall competitive environment by posing hypothetical situations in which alternative sets of conditions are played out.

Scientometric Analysis. *See* Scientometrics.

Scientometrics. The quantitative study of the disciplines of science based on published literature and communications. This could include identifying emerging areas of scientific research, examining the development of research over time, or geographic and organizational distributions of research.

Secondary Sources. *See* Primary Sources.

Strategic Intelligence. Intelligence that has implications for the long term, usually looking one or more years out into the future.

SWOT Analysis. An analytical framework that stands for Strengths-Weaknesses-Opportunities-Threats. A highly useful framework for identifying a rival's weak spots; conversely, a useful tool to examine strategic opportunities. Strength is defined as the company's core competencies. Weaknesses are the company's drawbacks. Opportunities are the characteristics within the larger marketplace that can offer the company a competitive advantage. Threats are conditions in that same market that pose a threat to or block an opportunity for these firms.

Tactical Intelligence. Intelligence that has implications for the short term, usually looking at the current year. Questions on advertising, pricing, or product positioning usually are tactical in nature.

Usenet. A collection of Internet-based electronic discussion groups that can be helpful in identifying experts.

Value-Chain Analysis. A form of analysis that looks at every step a business goes through, from raw materials to the eventual end-user. The goal is to deliver maximum value for the least possible total cost.

War Gaming. A hands-on technique designed to actively demonstrate how a client and competitor match up in the marketplace based on their current capabilities as well as their strengths and weaknesses. The purpose of the game is to develop a strategy to take advantage of strengths and opportunities, and to exploit competitors' weaknesses and vulnerabilities, as well as address the client's own vulnerabilities. War games are conducted at the highest levels of an organization with senior executives involved in key roles.

GLOSSARY SOURCES

Fuld Intelligence Dictionary
www.fuld.com/Dictionary/index.html

"How to Calculate Market Shares" by Estelle Metayer, Competia.com
www.refresher.com/!emmarket.html

Investopedia.com
www.investopedia.com/terms

ISI Glossary
www.isinet.com/isi/search/glossary/index.html

Quality Glossary
American Society for Quality
www.asq.org/info/glossary

Quirk's Marketing Research Review
http://www.quirks.com/resources/glossary.asp

Strategy Glossary
Ampol Partners
www.ampolbiz.com/consulting/resources/strategy_glossary.htm

J. Thomas Consulting Group Inc.
http://www.thomasintelligenceconsulting.com/htmlsite/servi0es.html

About the Author

Margaret Metcalf Carr is principal of Carr Research Group, providing custom research, analysis, and consulting support to business professionals since 1990. Before going out on her own, she was a corporate business information center manager and a technical information specialist in a research and development laboratory. Peggy received a Master of Library Science degree in information retrieval from the School of Information Studies at Syracuse University, and a bachelor's degree in communication and history from Muskingum College. She has used computers to store and retrieve information since the mid-1970s, when punched cards were still in vogue, and has been an online searcher since the late 1970s. During the past 25 years, she has written articles and given several presentations on information issues, including search and business intelligence strategies. She is a Past-President of the Association of Independent Information Professionals and is active in the Mid-Atlantic Planning Association, the Society of Competitive Intelligence Professionals and the Special Libraries Association.

Peggy lives in Baltimore County, MD with her husband David, their four children, and their dog. She strives to balance work with community service and parent taxi duties that encompass church, scouting, music lessons, and sports. She can be contacted at pcarr@carr-research.com or www.carr-research.com.

About the Editor

Reva Basch, executive editor of the Super Searchers series, has written four books of her own: *Researching Online For Dummies* (2nd edition with Mary Ellen Bates), *Secrets of the Super Net Searchers* (Information Today, Inc.), *Secrets of the Super Searchers* (Information Today, Inc.), and *Electronic Information Delivery: Evaluating Quality and Value* (Gower). She has edited and contributed chapters, introductions, and interviews to several books about the Internet and online information retrieval. She was the subject of a profile in *Wired* magazine, which called her "the ultimate intelligent agent."

Prior to starting her own business in 1986, Reva was Vice President and Director of Research at Information on Demand, a pioneering independent research company. She has designed front-end search software for major online services; written and consulted on technical, marketing, and training issues for both online services and database producers; and published extensively in information industry journals. She has keynoted at international conferences in Australia, Scandinavia, Europe and the U.K., as well as North America.

Reva is a Past-President of the Association of Independent Information Professionals. She has a degree in English literature, *summa cum laude*, from the University of Pennsylvania, and a master's degree in library science from the University of California, Berkeley. She began her career as a corporate librarian, ran her own independent research business for ten years, and has been online since the mid-1970s. She lives on the remote northern California coast with her husband, several cats, and satellite access to the Net.

Index

A

academia, 5–6, 55–56, 258–259
Achieving Competitive Excellence
    (ACE) tools, 58
Adis Insight, 126
Adobe Acrobat, 105
advice to new researchers
  Ann Potter, 95
  Anne Henrich, 237–238, 241–242
  Bret Breeding, 187–188
  Clifford Kalb, 136–137
  Cynthia Cheng Correia, 223–224
  Deborah Sawyer, 115
  Dottie Moon, 60–61, 67
  Doug House, 237–238, 241–242
  George Dennis, 82
  John Prescott, 256, 259–260
  John Shumadine, 159–160,
    165–167
  John Wilhelm, 198–199, 202–203
  Ken Sawka, 223–224
  Kim Kelly, 27–28
  Renee Daulong, 39, 46–48
  Roberta Piccoli, 104
  Wayne Rosenkrans, 147–149
aerospace industry, 55
Against the Gods (Bernstein), 3
Aguilar, Francis, 4
Air Transport Intelligence, 55
alert services
  emails, 18, 153, 180, 200
  headlines, 25–26
  newsletters, 54
  resources, 42
Allen, Thomas J., 4
alumni parties, 73, 81
American Management
    Association, 172
American Marketing Association,
    172
American Metal Market, 256
American Productivity and Quality
    Center (APQC), 178
analysis
  benchmarks and, 168

analysis (*cont.*)

by clients, 91

drawing conclusions, 252

framework for, 252

importance of, 29

in-house experts, 235–236

information usage and, 84

multivariant, 257

need for, 47

noise and, 194

post-search, 186

process of, 155

skills needed, 49

techniques, 7, 66

time allocation, 105, 150,
	167–168, 257

annual reports, 195

appendices, 58–59

Archive.org, 238–239

*Art and Science of Business
	Intelligence Analysis, The,* 7

AsiaBizTech, 186

Aspen Publishers, 162

Association of Independent
	Information Professionals
	(AIIP), 36, 46, 88, 106

assumptions, testing, 57

AstraZeneca Pharmaceuticals,
	141–143

authors, 55

automation, 180, 239

AviationNow, 55

B

Barndt, Walter, 5

Baseline Data Systems, 93

BBC, 186

Bell, Warren, 187–188

Bellcore. *See* Telcordia Technologies

benchmarks, 168

Bernstein, 3

biases, 176

bidding, proposal, 15

biographies, 104

Bloomberg, 55, 61, 186

Bowman's Accounting Report, 172

brainstorming, 171

Brandenburger, Adam, 231

Breeding, Bret, 177–190

advice to new researchers,
	187–188

background, 177–178

challenges, 187

coups, 186–187

current function, 178

fee-for-service databases, 183

Internet usage, 183

job satisfaction, 188–189

Power Tips, 190

reports, 184

research strategies, 178–186

software usage, 186

staying current, 187

time allocation, 185–186

toolkit, 181–182

on traits for success, 10

Brint.com, 106

budgets, 40, 45, 46, 68

Business Intelligence and Espionage (Greene), 4
Business Intelligence System, The (Gilad), 4
business reference librarians, 97
business research
    Ann Potter on, 87–88
    Bret Breeding on, 179–180
    Clifford Kalb on, 125–126
    commercial databases and, 176
    Cynthia Cheng Correia on, 210–212
    Deborah Sawyer on, 112
    definitions, 230
    Dottie Moon on, 53–54
    Doug House on, 130
    George Dennis on, 74–75
    John Prescott on, 248–249
    John Shumadine on, 160
    John Wilhelm on, 192–193
    Ken Sawka on, 210–212
    Kim Kelly on, 17–18
    Renee Daulong on, 33
    Roberta Piccoli on, 102
    Wayne Rosenkrans on, 143–144
Business Week, 186
BUSLIB-L, 214

C

C-4-U Scout, 169
CAM Promotional Audits, 127
cameras, 89
candy industry, 253–254
CareerJournal, 106
Census Bureau, U.S., 34

ChangeDetection.com, 219
CIO Magazine, 106
Cipher Systems, 151
Cisek, Bob, 6, 8
clients
    analysis by, 235–236
    expectations, 119–120
    internal, 162
    lines of communication, 198
    understanding needs of, 252
clinical trials, 132
Cnet.com, 39, 186
Co-operation (Brandenburger and Nalebuff), 231
collaboration. *See also* networking
    among CI professionals, 9–10
    on analysis, 235–236
    with client teams, 197–198
    with communications experts, 22
    filling gaps and, 196
    with human resources, 71–74
    as indicator, 55
    internal contacts, 17, 29, 103–104, 125
    with process folks, 215–216
    project planning and, 200
    secondary research and, 148
    with strategic planning, 22
communication
    challenges, 28
    with client teams, 197–198
    in competitive analysis, 201–202
    ethics guidelines, 138
    feedback and, 252
    report writing and, 41, 129–131
    with team members, 165
    teamwork and, 158–160
    terminology, 226

communications experts, 22

companies
   collaborations, 55–56
   portal links, 60
   profiles, 59

Compaq Computer, 177

comparison tables, 232

Compendex, 57

compensation structures, 220

Competia.com, 65, 258

competitive assessment, 229

competitive assurance, 144–145

competitive intelligence
   core work processes, 180–181
   definitions, 1, 193
   history of, 2–6
   legal and ethics policies, 61
   ten key decisions, 250–251

Competitive Intelligence Center, 212

Competitive Intelligence Magazine, 179

"Competitive Intelligence Opportunity," 5

Competitive Intelligence Review, 245, 259

Competitive Strategy: Techniques for Analyzing Industries and Competitors (Porter), 4

competitor intelligence, 249

complaints, value of, 72

Conference Board Council on Competitor Analysis, 135, 139

conferences
   attendee lists, 73
   author names through, 55
   professional exchanges, 222
   recruiting at, 73
   reports from, 60
   staying current and, 46, 153
   vendors at, 106

confidence, need for, 50

Consultant's News, 162, 172

consumer intelligence, 99–109, 249

contact management software, 97

content aggregators, 36

Correia, Cynthia Cheng
   advice to new researchers, 223–224
   background, 207–208
   challenges, 221–222
   coups, 220–221
   current function, 208–210
   fee-for-service databases, 213
   Internet usage, 213
   job satisfaction, 224–225
   Power Tips, 226
   research strategies, 212–220
   software usage, 219–220
   staying current, 222–223
   toolkit, 212–213

cost studies, 242

counterintelligence, 249

Crain's New York Business, 106

Cristina, Suzanne, 53

critical thinking skills, 223

curiosity, value of, 82

currency, maintenance of
   Ann Potter, 93
   Anne Henrich, 240
   Bret Breeding, 187
   Clifford Kalb, 135–136

Conference Board Council on
  Competitor Analysis,
  135–136
Cynthia Cheng Correia, 222–223
Dottie Moon, 64–65
Doug House, 240
George Dennis, 81
John Prescott, 259
John Wilhelm, 202
Ken Sawka, 222–223
Kim Kelly, 27
mentoring and, 255
project focus and, 118
Renee Daulong, 45–46
Roberta Piccoli, 106–107
training and, 240
visiting customers, 187
Wayne Rosenkrans, 153
Current News in Nexis, 55
Custom Clips, 219
customer service departments,
  72–73
*CyberSkeptic's Guide to Internet
  Research, The*, 214
CyberSleuthing, 222

D

data
  collection, 148–149, 155, 183,
    252, 257
  double-checking, 48
databases, home-grown, 62–63. *See
    also* fee-for-service databases
Datamonitor, 127

Daulong, Renee, 31–50
  advice to new researchers, 39
  background, 31
  challenges, 43–45
  current position, 31
  fee-for-service databases, 35
  Internet use, 35
  job satisfaction, 11, 48–49
  Power Tips, 49–50
  report formats, 41
  research strategies, 35–38
  resource selection, 42–43
  staying current, 45–46
  time allocation, 39
  toolkit, 33–34
Davenport, Thomas H., 106
deadlines, impact of, 40
decision making
  CI professionals in, 53–54, 160,
    255
  deliverable formats and, 139
  goals and, 104
  help with, 190
  reference interviews and, 194
  support process, 231–232
  tree formulation, 203
Decision Resources, 127
Dedijer, Stavan, 5
Defense Systems Daily Headlines,
  26
Defense Technical Information
  Center (DTIC), 56
DefenseData, 56
definitions, authority for, 1
deliverables. *See* reports
Dell Corporation, 31–33

Deloitte & Touche, 157–159
Deloitte Consulting, 207
demos, 106
Dennis, George, 69–84
  advice to new researchers, 82
  analysis process, 76–77
  background, 69–74, 71–74
  challenges, 79–81, 83
  collaboration, 73–74
  job satisfaction, 82
  Power Tips, 83–84
  on processes, 7
  staying current, 81
  time allocation, 78
  toolkit, 75–76
  training program, 77–78
Department of Energy sites, 55
"Developing a CI Resume," 153
"Developing Information Systems
    for Competitive Intelligence
    Support" (Hohhof), 9
Dialog, 55, 103, 162, 212
DialogSelect, 18, 20, 25–26
Directory of Business Publications,
    102
discriminators, 24–25, 29
discussion lists, 46, 220
Docere, 219
documentation
  client expectations, 108
  employee-submitted
    information, 60, 63
  sources checked, 37
  staying on track, 199
Dogpile.com, 186
Dow Jones Interactive. *See*
    Factiva.com

downsizing, 64
Drexel College of Information
    Science and Technology, 5, 65
Drexel University, 136
Dun & Bradstreet, 161
duplication, reduction of, 103
Dzerzinksy, Felix, 81

E

EBN, 39
Eclipse service, 200
Eisenhardt, Kathy, 248
EIU, 126
Electric Power Research Institute
    (EPRI), 55
email
  alerts through, 18, 153, 180, 200
  notification via, 93
  personal addresses, 76–77
  response rates, 77
employee-submitted information,
    60, 63, 79–80
employment boards, 220
empowerment, client, 182–183
Encyclopedia Britannica, 1, 2
Encyclopedia of Associations, The,
    34, 88, 102
Espicom Company Profiles, 126
ethics
  CI and, 11
  confidential reports and, 79–80
  corporate policies, 138, 139
  paranoia and, 261–262
  steering committee and, 60

EvaluatePharma, 126

evidence, supporting, 162

Excel

pivot tables, 43

spreadsheets, 25, 38, 42, 91, 93

Web site contents, 75

executive biographies, 104

executive quotes, 56

executive reviews, 37

expectations

communication and, 198

management of, 206

new researchers, 115

unreasonable, 119–120

experience, benefits of, 229

experts

contact lists, 70

external, 19

in-house, 57–58, 72, 125, 235–236

meeting with, 17

at Merck, 128

F

Factiva.com, 162, 186, 212, 219

Fahey, Liam, 5

Fast Company magazine, 106

f*ckedcompany.com, 220

Federal Sources, 18, 26

FedLog, 56

fee-for-service databases

Ann Potter, 89

Anne Henrich, 232–233

Bret Breeding, 183

Cynthia Cheng Correia, 213

Deborah Sawyer, 113

Dottie Moon, 54–56

Doug House, 232–233

John Prescott, 253–254

John Shumadine, 161–163

John Wilhelm, 195

Ken Sawka, 213

Kim Kelly, 19–20

Renee Daulong, 35

Roberta Piccoli, 102—103

Wayne Rosenkrans, 145

feedback

from clients, 180–181, 198

communication and, 252

consistent, 205

research process and, 21

Feron, Frederique, 214, 221

fieldwork challenges, 93–94

6FigureJobs.com, 76

Finance Vision, 186

financial analysts, 59

financial intelligence sites, 126

Financial Times, 55

Five Forces Model, 124–125, 184

Fleisher, Craig, 7

Flight International, 55

forecasting, CI and, 125

Fortune, 240

four-corners models, 198, 231

FreePint, 222

Frost & Sullivan, 186

FSI State and Local Headline News, 18, 26

Fugger, House of, 2–3

Fugger, Jakob, 2–3

"Fugger Family," 2

"Fugger Newsletters," 2–3
Fuld & Company, Inc., 90, 207
Fuld model, 58, 65, 92
Fuld reports, 169
Fuld War Room CD, 61
Fulltext Sources Online, 88
FutureBrand, 100, 101
Futures Group, 211

G

gaps. *See* unknowns
Gartner, 33, 183
Genesis/POV reports, 126
Giga Information Group, 186
Gilad, Ben, 4, 143
goals, understanding of, 104
Goldman Sachs, 126
Google, 220, 238
government resources, 56
Greene, Richard M., 4

H

Harvard Business Review, 153, 172,
   240
Harvard Business School, 124
Haystack, 56
hazardous materials, 56
Headhunter.net, 76
headings, report, 24
headline alert services, 25–26
Henrich, Anne, 227–243
   advice to new researchers,
      237–238, 241–242

background, 227–228
coups, 239
current function, 228–229
fee-for-service databases,
   232–233
Internet usage, 232–233
job satisfaction, 242–243
Power Tips, 243
report customization, 236–237
research strategies, 231–237
software usage, 238–239
staying current, 240
time allocation, 238
toolkit, 231–232
Herring, Jan
   on analysis, 8–9
   on definition of CI, 11
   intelligence cycle, 217
   on IT, 9
   on processes, 7
Hohhof, Bonnie, 9
Holden, Jim, 182
Hoovers, 162, 195
House, Doug, 227–243
   advice to new researchers,
      237–238, 241–242
   background, 227–228
   challenges, 239–240
   coups, 239
   current function, 228–229
   fee-for-service databases,
      232–233
   Internet usage, 232–233
   job satisfaction, 11, 242–243
   Power Tips, 243
   report customization, 236–237

research strategies, 231–237

software usage, 238–239

staying current, 240

time allocation, 238

toolkit, 231–232

House of Rothschild, 3

"How Competitive Forces Shape
    Strategy" (Porter), 4

human resources, 71–74

human source intelligence, 69–84,
    139, 243

hypotheses, planning and, 206

I

IC Insights, 33

*ICD-10 (International Classification
    of Diseases),* 127

IdDB database, 126

IMS Health Market Reports, 127

In Vivo: Business & Medicine Report,
    153

industry publications, 32, 94, 162.
    See also trade journals

Infominder, 93

Information Handling Services, 56

Information Outlook (SLA), 5

Information Plus Group, 111–112

information technology, 9

Information Today, 94, 222

Inspec, 57

*Intellectual Capital: The New Wealth
    of Organizations* (Stewart),
    106–107

intelligence, definition, 1

intelligence cycle, 217, 255–256

Intelligence Data, 33

Intelligence Driven Strategy,
    250–251

Intelliscope, 33

International Data Corporation
    (IDC), 33, 183

Internet resources
    Ann Potter, 89
    Anne Henrich, 232–2323
    Bret Breeding, 183
    Cynthia Cheng Correia, 213
    Deborah Sawyer, 113
    Dottie Moon, 54–56
    Doug House, 232–233
    fee-for-service databases and,
        19–20
    John Prescott, 253–254
    John Shumadine, 161–163
    John Wilhelm, 195
    Ken Sawka, 213
    outsourcing, 84
    reliability, 162
    Renee Daulong, 35
    Roberta Piccoli, 102–103
    staying current and, 240
    training clients, 182–183
    verification, 50
    Wayne Rosenkrans, 145
interviews
    analysis of, 236
    filling gaps with, 103
    human source collection, 84
    in-house, 58
    in monitoring work, 116–117
    post-analysis, 197
    telephone, 75, 108

Intranets, 60, 101, 202
inventors, 55
Investor Relations, 195
IRI Studies, 127
"It's the Analysis, Stupid" (Sawka), 9
ITWorld.com, 186

J

J. Walter Thompson, 99, 100, 101,
    103–104
James J. Hill Business Reference
    Library, 88
jargon, use of, 56–57
Job Machine, 222
Journal of Competitive Intelligence
    and Management, 245, 259
journalism, 86, 95, 260
just-in-time delivery, 51–68

K

Kaiser Associates, 191–192
Kalb, Clifford, 123–139
    advice to new researchers,
        136–137
    background, 123–124
    on business research, 125–126
    challenges, 133–135
    coups, 132–133
    current function, 124
    on filling gaps, 127–128
    job satisfaction, 137–138
    Power Tips, 139
    on processes, 7

project management, 131–132
report presentation, 129–131
research strategies, 126–129,
    132–135
software usage, 132
staying current, 135–136
toolkit, 126–127
on traits for success, 10
Kartoo, 169
Kassler, Helene, 212–213
Kelly, Kim, 13–30
    advice to new researchers, 23,
        27–28
    background, 13–14
    challenges, 26–27, 28
    collaborative activities, 22
    coups, 26
    fee-for-service databases, 19–20
    Internet resources, 19–20
    job satisfaction, 11
    organization of research, 22–23,
        24–25
    Power Tips, 29–30
    research strategy, 15–17, 20–22
    software used, 9, 25–26
    staying current, 27
    time allocation, 25, 29
    toolkit, 18–19
Kennedy Information, 162
Kepner, 4
keyword searching, 36
Kight, Leila, 4–5, 246, 254
King, Don, 189
KIT-KIQ, 148, 149
KMWorld, 106
knowledge gaps, 38. *See also*
    unknowns

Knowledge Management News, 106

Knowledge Management Resource, 106

Knowledge Works, 151, 219

L

labels, 120

language skills, 221

laptops, 75

large studies, 40

lead generation, 162

legal counsel, 60, 61

legal standards, 60

Lehman Brothers, 126

LexisNexis, 20, 162, 195, 200

librarians, research role, 211–212

listening skills, 166, 203

Lloyds, Edward, 3

Lloyds of London, 3

local records, 56

Lockheed Martin, 13–14

Lotus Notes, 257

Lotus Notes/Domino platform, 62–63

M

Management Research Center, 106

manufacturing statistics, 34

maps, 88

market intelligence, 248–249

market research, 74

MarketResearch.com, 36

McCann-Erickson, 101

McEvily, Sue, 248

Medical Advertising News, 126

Medical Marketing & Media, 126

Meilinger, Philip, 2

mentors

advice to new researchers, 237–238

importance of, 255

need for, 61, 68

staying current and, 65

Merck & Co., 123–124

Merck Index, 127

Merck Manual, 127

Mercyhurst College, 5–6

Microsoft Office, 42–43, 50, 91–92, 105, 238. *See also* Excel; Word

milestones, 193, 198

military intelligence, 157

Millenium Intelligence (Miller), 9

Miller, Jerry P., 5, 9

Mindbranch, 36

MindIt, 219

mission statements, 105–106

Monster.com, 76

Montgomery, David, 4

Moon, Mary G. "Dottie," 51–68

advice to new researchers, 60–61, 67

background, 51–52

challenges, 56–57, 63–64, 66–67

collaboration, 59

current function, 52–53

fee-for-service databases, 54–56

Internet resources, 54–56

job satisfaction, 66

Power Tips, 67–68

Moon, Mary G. "Dottie," (*cont.*)
    report structure, 62
    research strategies, 54–59
    standardization, 59
    on state-of-the art techniques, 12
    staying current, 64–65
    time allocation, 62
    toolkit, 54, 62–63
    turnaround times, 59
Most Secret and Confidential
        (Meilinger), 2
motivations, 48
multivariant analysis, 257
My Yahoo! page, 200
Myers-Briggs personality types, 154

N

Nalebuff, Barry, 231
names
    authors, 55
    executives, 56
    inventors, 55
    spelling issues, 221
    from target companies, 75
National Association of Investors
        Corporation, 172
National Security Agency, 143, 154
National Technology Transfer
        Center (NTTC)
negotiation skills, 260
NetMind, 239
networking. *See also* collaboration
    conferences and, 46, 222
    contact management, 97
    decision making and, 190
    industry contacts, 54
    people contacts, 18, 54
    primary research, 127
    Rolodex, 70, 161, 175
    staying current and, 46, 81, 106,
        153, 171, 240
newsletters
    awareness and, 190
    building awareness, 179–180
    industry-specific, 162
    recognition in, 80
    as resource, 54
    staying current and, 222, 240
Nielsen, 127
Nihowdy, 42
North American Industry
        Classification System
        (SAICS), 34

O

Office Accelerator, 93
on-site intelligence gathering,
        85–97
Online, 94
outsourcing
    decisions, 45
    efficiency and, 86
    filling gaps, 233–234
    Net research, 84
Oxford English Dictionary, The
        (OED), 2

P

Paap, Jay, 57
patents, indicators, 55
"Performance of Information
    Channels in the Transfer of
    Technology" (Allen), 4
perseverance, need for, 47
Pharmaceutical Executive, 126
pharmaceutical industry, 124
Pharmaprojects, 126
phone calls
    filling gaps with, 103, 235
    persistence, 120
    scripts, 108
    skill sets, 202–203
    to target companies, 114
    techniques, 96
    use of, 50
Physician's Desk Reference, 126–127
Piccoli, Roberta, 99–109
    advice to new researchers, 10,
        104
    background, 99–101
    challenges, 105–106, 107
    current focus, 100–102
    fee-for-service databases,
        102–103
    Internet usage, 102–103
    Power Tips, 108–109
    report format, 105
    research strategies, 102–105
    software use, 105
    staying current, 106–107
    time allocation, 105
    toolkit, 102
    turnaround times, 101

Pink Sheet, 126
PlanBee, 169
planning
    avoiding gaps and, 234
    efficiency and, 205, 226
    frontloading the process, 199
    libraries, 59
    process of, 7
    time allocation and, 149, 238, 243
Platt's, 55
portals, internal, 60
Porter, Michael, 4, 21–22, 231
Potter, Ann, 85–97
    advice to new researchers, 95
    background, 85–86
    challenges, 93–94, 96
    current function, 86–87
    fee-for-service databases, 89
    Internet use, 89
    job satisfaction, 95–96
    Power Tips, 96–97
    report format, 91–92
    research strategies, 87–94
    staying current, 94
    time allocation, 92
    toolkit, 88–89, 93
    on traits for success, 10
Power, 55
Power Tips
    Ann Potter, 96–97
    Anne Henrich, 243
    Bret Breeding, 190
    Clifford Kalb, 139
    Cynthia Cheng Correia, 226
    Deborah Sawyer, 120–121
    Dottie Moon, 67–68

Power Tips (*cont.*)
  Doug House, 243
  George Dennis, 83–84
  John Prescott, 262
  John Shumadine, 175–176
  John Wilhelm, 205–206
  Ken Sawka, 226
  Kim Kelly, 29–30
  Renee Daulong, 49–50
  Roberta Piccoli, 108–109
  Wayne Rosenkrans, 155–156
PowerPoint presentations
  in reports, 38–39, 41, 42, 91, 93
  Web site contents, 75
*Practical Strategies in Competitive
    Intelligence,* 187
predictions, 155, 180
Prescott, John, 245–262
  advice to new researchers, 256,
    259–260
  background, 245–246
  CI process and, 217
  current functions, 246–248
  fee-for-service databases,
    253–254
  Internet usage, 253–254
  job satisfaction, 260–262
  Power Tips, 262
  *Proven Strategies in Competitive
    Intelligence,* 178
  research strategies, 252–257
  SCIP and, 5
  software usage, 257–258
  staying current, 259
  time allocation, 256–257
  toolkit, 249–252

  on traits for success, 10
presentations
  Clifford Kalb, 129–131
  Deborah Sawyer, 117
  formats, 23, 24–25, 41, 58
  PowerPoint, 38–39
  skill sets needed, 28
  time allocation, 150
Price, Gary, 222
primary research
  Deborah Sawyer on, 114
  description, 16
  internal experts, 57–58
  time allocation, 25, 29, 39, 62, 78,
    105
process metrics, 25
procurement, Dell Corporation,
    31–33
project management
  Clifford Kalb on, 131–132
  coordination skills, 144–145
  limiting scope, 205
  need for skill in, 136–137
  work plans, 193–194
promotional literature, 120
*Proven strategies in Competitive
    Intelligence* (Prescott), 178
proximity searching, 56
Prusak, Laurence, 106
Public Accountings Report, 162, 172

Q

quality improvement, 22–23, 28, 58
questions
  format of, 56–57, 60–61, 68

questions (*cont.*)
    importance of "why," 148, 155,
        243
quotes, 56, 79

R

Rational Manager: A Systematic
    Approach to Problem Solving
    and Decision Making (Kepner
    and Tregoe), 4
R&D Focus, 126
recognition
    importance of, 19
    in newsletters, 80
recruiting, 72, 73, 188, 222
Red Herring, 186
reference interviews, 148, 166, 194,
    214
regulatory intelligence, 249
relaxation, 97
reports
    appendices, 58–59
    client expectations, 108
    comparison tables, 232
    consistency, 23, 24–25
    content, 24–25, 62, 105
    customization, 147, 216, 218,
        236–237
    drawing conclusions, 252
    Excel spreadsheets, 38
    executive reviews, 37
    formats, 8, 41, 58, 78–79, 91–92,
        109
    of implications, 262

    key findings in, 150
    PowerPoint presentations, 38–39
    process flow, 190
    project planning and, 199–200
    summaries, 92–93
    templates, 168
    time allocation, 78, 167–168
    verbatim quotes, 79
research and development, 142
Research Buzz, 222
Research Resources Databases, 202
research strategies
    Ann Potter, 87–94
    Anne Henrich, 231–237
    Bret Breeding, 178–186
    Clifford Kalb, 126–129, 132–135
    Cynthia Cheng Correia, 212–220
    Deborah Sawyer, 113–115
    Doug House, 231–237
    George Dennis, 75–76, 76–77
    John Prescott, 252–257
    John Shumadine, 160–165,
        169–171
    John Wilhelm, 193–200
    Ken Sawka, 212–220
    Kim Kelly, 15–17, 20–22
    reference interviews and, 194
    Renee Daulong, 35–38
    Roberta Piccoli, 102–105
    Wayne Rosenkrans, 144–153
resource selection. *See also Specific*
    interviewees
    experience and, 49
    familiarity with, 83
    management of, 202, 206
    opinions on, 7

"ResourceShelf," 222

resumes, 71–72, 73–74, 76

risk analysis, 31–50

road atlases, 88

Rolodex. *See* networking

Rosenkrans, Wayne, 141–156

    advice to new researchers,
        147–149, 153

    background, 141–142

    challenges, 152–153

    coups, 151

    current function, 142–143

    fee-for-service databases, 145

    Internet usage, 145

    job satisfaction, 153

    Power Tips, 155–156

    on process, 6

    report format, 147, 150

    research strategies, 144–153

    skill sets, 153

    software usage, 150–151

    on state-of-the art techniques, 12

    staying current, 153

    time allocation, 149–150

    toolkit, 144–145

Rothschild, Mayer Amschel, 3–4

Russo, J.E., 253

S

sales personnel, 75

Sandman, Michael, 90

satellite phones, 33, 34, 75

Sawka, Ken, 207–226

    advice to new researchers,
        223–224

    on analysis, 8–9

    background, 207–208

    challenges, 221–222

    coups, 220–221

    current function, 208–210

    fee-for-service databases, 213

    Internet usage, 213

    job satisfaction, 224–225

    Power Tips, 226

    on processes, 7

    research strategies, 212–220

    software usage, 219–220

    staying current, 222–223

    toolkit, 212–213

Sawyer, Deborah, 111–121

    advice to new researchers, 115,
        118–119

    anti-technology bias, 117

    background, 111

    on business research, 112

    coups, 117–118

    current function, 112

    fee-for-service databases, 113

    Internet usage, 113

    job satisfaction, 119–120

    Power Tips, 120–121

    presentations, 117

    professional enjoyment, 119

    report packaging, 115, 116

    research strategies, 113–115

    on software, 9

    software usage, 116–117

    staying current, 118

    time allocation, 116

    toolkit, 112–113

Scanning the Business Environment (Aguilar), 4
scenarios, 74
Schumpeter, Joseph, 4
science and technology intelligence, 249
scientific models, 255–256
scientometric models, 145
Scirus, 213
scope, limits, 205
Scott-Levin Audits, 127
Scrip, 126
Search Engine Showdown, 222
Search Engine Watch, 222
Search Source, 99
SearchDay, 222
Searcher, 94, 222
secondary research
    Deborah Sawyer on, 114
    description, 16
    outsourcing, 148
    starting with, 128–129
    teamwork, 53
    time allocation, 25, 29, 39, 62, 78, 105
Securities and Exchange Commission (SEC), 34, 50, 195
semi-conductor industry, 33
Semico Research, 33
Semiconductor Industry Association (SIA), 34
serendipity, 47, 202
"75 Years of Management Ideas and Practice," 4
Shelfer, Kathy, 6

Shumadine, John, 157–176
    advice to new researchers, 10, 159–160, 165–167
    background, 157–158
    challenges, 170–171
    coups, 169–170
    current function, 158
    fee-for-service databases, 161–163
    filling gaps, 163–164
    Internet usage, 161–163
    job satisfaction, 173–174
    Power Tips, 175–176
    reports, 168
    research strategies, 160–165, 169–170
    software usage, 168–169
    on state-of-the art techniques, 12
    staying current, 171–173
    time allocation, 167–168
    toolkit, 160–161
Simmon's College, 208
simulations, 180, 182
skill sets
    attitude of optimism, 158
    basic, 252
    for CI, 65–66
    communication, 176
    critical thinking, 223
    Deborah Sawyer on, 118–119
    George Dennis on, 82
    journalist skills, 260
    Kim Kelly on, 27–28
    languages, 221
    listening, 166, 176
    Myers-Briggs personality types, 154

skill sets (*cont.*)
negotiation, 260
organization, 226
questioning, 166
Renee Daulong on, 46–48
Wayne Rosenkrans on, 153
Sloan Management Review, 172
SmartWrap, 220
Society of Competitive Intelligence
Professionals (SCIP)
foundation of, 4–5, 245, 258
staying current and, 65, 106, 172,
223
Web site, 153
software usage
Anne Henrich, 238–239
Bret Breeding, 186
contact management, 97
Cynthia Cheng Correia, 219–220
Deborah Sawyer, 116–117
Doug House, 238–239
John Prescott, 257–258
John Shumadine, 168–169
John Wilhelm, 200
Ken Sawka, 219–220
review of, 219
Roberta Piccoli, 105
selection of, 25–26, 132
Wayne Rosenkrans, 150–151
Sognnaes, Hana, 53
Special Libraries Association (SLA)
Information Outlook, 5
networking through, 36
skill sets and, 65–66
staying current and, 46, 65, 106,
223

spies, history of, 2–6
Spyonit, 219
*Standard Rate & Data Service
(SRDS)*, 102
standardization
customization and, 91–92
at J. Walter Thompson, 104
process improvement and, 22–23
reports, 184
templates and, 59–60
Stat-USA, 126
*Statistical Abstract of the United
States*, 102
statistics, 252
steering committees, 61
Stewart, Thomas A., 107
Strafford Publications, 162
strategic early warning, 147
Strategic Management Journal, 248
strategic modeling, 198
strategic planning, 22, 64–65
"Strategic Value Selling
Methodology (Holden), 182
Strategy Software, 219
Strength-Weaknesses-
Opportunities-Threats
(SWOT) analyses, 145, 155
stresses, 96, 97
subcontracting. *See* outsourcing
summaries
executive, 59, 104
format of, 84
in reports, 59, 62, 92–93
Super Searchers Do Business, 213
supply chain risks, 32
surveys, 74, 253
Sword and the Shield, The, 81

T

Taxol project, 151–152
teamwork
  with clients, 197–198
  communications and, 165
  creativity and, 171
  cross-functional structure, 125
  feedback loops and, 21
  filling gaps, 163–164
  internal experts and, 17
  at Merck & Co., 124, 128–129
  research based on, 157–176
  secondary research and, 53
  separation of functions, 158–159
  specialization and, 146–147
  staying current and, 65
TechEncyclopedia, 35
technical analysts, 59
Technical Insights, 54
Technology Review, 153
Telcordia Technologies, 69
telephone headsets, 89
templates, archiving, 59
10K Wizard, 34, 50
Teoma, 213
Texas Instruments, 249, 252
Theory of Economic Development
  (Schumpeter), 4
Thompson's First Call, 183
time allocation
  10 step process, 131–132
  Ann Potter, 92
  Anne Henrich, 238
  budgets and, 214–215
  customization, 217–218

Deborah Sawyer, 116
Dottie Moon, 62
Doug House, 238
fee-for-service databases, 54–55
framework, 199
Fuld model, 92
George Dennis, 78
Internet resources, 54–55
John Prescott, 256–257
John Shumadine, 167–168
Kim Kelly, 25, 29
project management, 176
Renee Daulong, 39
Roberta Piccoli, 105
workflow, 121, 185–186
Timely Data Resources
  Epidemiology Database, 127
toolkits
  Ann Potter, 88–89, 93
  Anne Henrich, 231–232
  Bret Breeding, 181–182
  Clifford Kalb, 126–127
  Cynthia Cheng Correia, 212–213
  Deborah Sawyer, 112–113
  Dottie Moon, 54, 62–63
  Doug House, 231–232
  George Dennis, 75–76
  John Prescott on, 249–252
  John Shumadine, 160–161
  John Wilhelm, 193–194
  Ken Sawka, 212–213
  Kim Kelly, 18–19
  Renee Daulong, 33–34
  Roberta Piccoli, 102
  Wayne Rosenkrans, 144–145

"Toward Strategic Intelligence
  Systems" (Montgomery and
  Weinberg), 4
TracerLock, 220
trade journals, 94, 256–257. *See also*
  industry journals
trade shows, 46, 72–73, 75, 81, 109
training
  clients, 182–183
  George Dennis on, 77–78
  road map, 185
  staying current and, 240, 255, 259
Transnationale.org, 222
travel, 60, 187, 225
travel departments, 73–74
Tregoe, 4
trends analysis, 28, 30, 74, 94, 172
Tufte, Edward R., 257
turnaround times, 101
TVeyes, 220

U

Ulrich's Periodicals Directory, 88
United Technologies Corporation,
  51–53
unknowns
  benefits of collaboration, 196
  Clifford Kalb on, 127–128
  filling gaps, 90–91, 163–164, 214
  identifying gaps, 108
  outsourcing, 233–234
  recognizing, 77–78
  strategy for handling, 103
  testing, 57

Upside Today, 186
Usenet newsgroups, 76–77

V

value-added opportunities, 87
Value Net, 231
ValueLine, 162
Vault, 220
Veille, 222
vendors, 106
verification of data, 47–48
visualization software, 63, 92, 257
Vivisimo, 213
VTC Media Availability, 26

W

Wall Street analysts, 35, 50
Wall Street Journal, 106, 186, 240
Wall Street Journal Online, 55
war gaming software, 63
Washington Researchers, 65,
  227–229, 246
Web sites
  development of, 262
  monitoring, 219–220
  target company's, 75
  tracking changes, 93
WebLog, 222
Weinberg, Charles, 4
Wendell, Florence, 53
white boards, 88–89
white papers, 59

Wilhelm, John, 191–206
    advice to new researchers,
        198–199, 202–203
    background, 191–192
    challenges, 201–202
    coups, 200–201
    current function, 192–193
    fee-for-service databases, 195
    Internet usage, 195
    job satisfaction, 203–204
    Power Tips, 205–206
    reports, 199–200
    research strategies, 193–200
    software usage, 200
    staying current, 202
    time allocation, 199
    toolkit, 193–194
Wincite, 219
Wisdom Builder, 219
WISE (Worldwide Information
    Sharing Enterprise), 126
Word, 42, 75, 91, 93

workflow
    core CI processes, 180–181
    planning, 193
    process steps, 6–8
    schedules and, 121
Working Knowledge: How
    Organizations Manage What
    They Know (Davenport and
    Prusak), 106
world atlas, 88
World Drug Market Manual, 126

Y

Yahoo!, 186
Yahoo! News, 195

Z

Zeneca, Astra, 12

More Great Books from Information Today, Inc.

Assessing Competitive Intelligence Software
A Guide to Evaluating CI Technology

By France Bouthillier and Kathleen Shearer
Foreword by Chun Wei Choo

As commercial software products for Competitive Intelligence (CI) emerge and gain acceptance, potential users find themselves overly dependent on information supplied by the software makers. This book is the first to propose a systematic method firms can use to evaluate CI software independently, allowing them to compare features, identify strengths and weaknesses, and invest in products that meet their unique needs. Authors Bouthillier and Shearer demonstrate their 32-step methodology through an evaluation of four popular CI software packages. In addition, they identify important sources of information about CI software, map information needs to intelligence outcomes, and describe key analytical techniques.

2003/hardbound/ISBN 1-57387-173-7 • $39.50

Millennium Intelligence
Understanding and Conducting
Competitive Intelligence in the Digital Age

By Jerry P. Miller and the
Business Intelligence Braintrust

With contributions from the world's leading business intelligence practitioners, *Millennium Intelligence* offers a tremendously informative and practical look at the CI process, how it is changing, and how it can be managed effectively in the Digital Age. Loaded with case studies, tips, and techniques, chapters include: What Is Intelligence?; The Skills Needed to Execute Intelligence Effectively; Information Sources Used for Intelligence; The Legal and Ethical Aspects of Intelligence; Small Business Intelligence; Corporate Security and Intelligence; ... and much more!

2000/276 pp/softbound/ISBN 0-910965-28-5 • $29.95

The Skeptical Business Searcher
The Information Advisor's Guide to Evaluating Web Data, Sites, and Sources

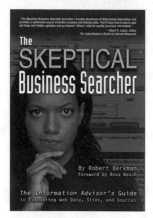

By Robert Berkman • Foreword by Reva Basch

This is the experts' guide to finding high-quality company and industry data on the free Web. Information guru Robert Berkman offers business Internet users effective strategies for identifying and evaluating no-cost online information sources, emphasizing easy-to-use techniques for recognizing bias and misinformation. You'll learn where to go for company backgrounders, sales and earnings data, SEC filings and stockholder reports, public records, market research, competitive intelligence, staff directories, executive biographies, survey/poll data, news stories, and hard-to-find information about small businesses and niche markets. The author's unique table of "Internet Information Credibility Indicators" allows readers to systematically evaluate Web site reliability. Supported by a Web page.

2003/softbound/ISBN 0-910965-66-8 • $29.95

Building and Running a Successful Research Business
A Guide for the Independent Information Professional

By Mary Ellen Bates • Edited by Reva Basch

This is *the* handbook every aspiring independent information professional needs to launch, manage, and build a research business. Organized into four sections, "Getting Started," "Running the Business," "Marketing," and "Researching," the book walks you through every step of the process. Author and long-time independent researcher Mary Ellen Bates covers everything from "is this right for you?" to closing the sale, managing clients, promoting your business, and tapping into powerful information sources.

2003/360 pp/softbound/ISBN 0-910965-62-5 • $29.95

Business Statistics on the Web
Find Them Fast—At Little or No Cost

By Paula Berinstein

Statistics are a critical component of business and marketing plans, press releases, surveys, economic analyses, presentations, proposals, and more—yet good statistics are notoriously hard to find. This practical book by statistics guru Paula Berinstein shows readers how to use the Internet to find statistics about companies, markets, and industries, how to organize and present statistics, and how to evaluate them for reliability. Organized by topic, both general and specific, and by country/region, this helpful reference features easy-to-use tips and techniques for finding and using statistics when the pressure is on. In addition, dozens of extended and short case studies demonstrate the ins and outs of searching for specific numbers and maneuvering around obstacles to find the data you need.

2003/336pp/softbound/ISBN: 0-910965-65-X • $29.95

The Web Library
Building a World Class Personal Library with Free Web Resources

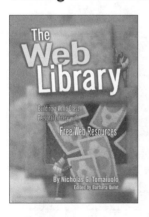

By Nicholas G. Tomaiuolo
Edited by Barbara Quint

With this remarkable, eye-opening book and its companion Web site, Nicholas G. (Nick) Tomaiuolo shows how anyone can create a comprehensive personal library using no-cost Web resources. If you were to calculate the expense of purchasing the hundreds of print and fee-based electronic publications that are available for free with "The Web Library," you'd quickly recognize the potential of this book to save you thousands, if not millions, of dollars (fortunately, Nick does the calculating for you!). This is an easy-to-use guide, with chapters organized into sections corresponding to departments in a physical library. *The Web Library* provides a wealth of URLs and examples of free material you can start using right away, but, best of all, it offers techniques for finding and collecting new content as the Web evolves. Start building your personal Web library today!

2003/softbound/ISBN 0-910965-67-6 • $29.95

Web of Deception
Misinformation on the Internet

Edited by Anne P. Mintz
Foreword by Steve Forbes

Intentionally misleading or erroneous information on the Web can wreak havoc on your health, privacy, investments, business decisions, online purchases, legal affairs, and more. Until now, the breadth and significance of this growing problem for Internet users had yet to be fully explored. In *Web of Deception*, Anne P. Mintz (Director of Knowledge Management at Forbes, Inc.) brings together 10 information industry gurus to illuminate the issues and help you recognize and deal with the flood of deception and misinformation in a range of critical subject areas. A must-read for any Internet searcher who needs to evaluate online information sources and avoid Web traps.

2002/278 pp/softbound/ISBN 0-910965-60-9 • $24.95

Net Crimes & Misdemeanors
Outmaneuvering the Spammers, Swindlers, and Stalkers Who Are Targeting You Online

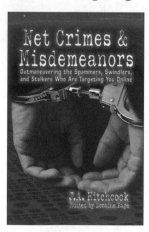

By J. A. Hitchcock
Edited by Loraine Page

Cyber crime expert J.A. Hitchcock helps individuals and business users of the Web protect themselves, their children, and their employees against online cheats and predators. Hitchcock details a broad range of abusive practices, shares victims' stories, and offers advice on how to handle junk e-mail, "flaming," privacy invasion, financial scams, cyberstalking, and indentity theft. She provides tips and techniques that can be put to immediate use and points to the laws, organizations, and Web resources that can aid victims and help them fight back. Supported by a Web site.

2002/384 pp/softbound/ISBN 0-910965-57-9 • $24.95

Smart Services
Competitive Information Strategies, Solutions, and Success Stories for Service Businesses

By Deborah C. Sawyer

"Finally, a book that nails what every service business needs to know about competition and competitive intelligence. Smart Services *offers competitive information strategies that firms can put to immediate use."* —Andrew Garvin, CEO, FIND.SVP

Here is the first book to focus specifically on the competitive information needs of service-oriented firms. Author, entrepreneur, and business consultant Deborah C. Sawyer illuminates the many forms of competition in service businesses, identifies the most effective information resources for competitive intelligence (CI), and provides a practical framework for identifying and studying competitors in order to gain a competitive advantage. *Smart Services* is a roadmap for every service company owner, manager, or executive who expects to compete effectively in the Information Age.

2002/256 pp/softbound/ISBN 0-910965-56-0 • $29.95

Naked in Cyberspace, 2nd Edition
How to Find Personal Information Online

By Carole A. Lane
Foreword by Beth Givens

In this fully revised and updated second edition of her bestselling guide, author Carole A. Lane surveys the types of personal records that are available on the Internet and online services. Lane explains how researchers find and use personal data, identifies the most useful sources of information about people, and offers advice for readers with privacy concerns. You'll learn how to use online tools and databases to gain competitive intelligence, locate and investigate people, access public records, identify experts, find new customers, recruit employees, search for assets, uncover criminal records, conduct genealogical research, and much more.

2002/586 pp/softbound/ISBN 0-910965-50-1 • $29.95

Super Searchers Go to the Source
The Interviewing and Hands-On Information Strategies of Top Primary Researchers—Online, on the Phone, and in Person

By Risa Sacks • Edited by Reva Basch

For the most focused, current, in-depth information on any subject, nothing beats going directly to the source—to the experts. This is "Primary Research," and it's the focus of the seventh title in the Super Searchers series. From the boardrooms of America's top corporations, to the halls of academia, to the pressroom of the *New York Times*, Risa Sacks interviews 12 of the best primary researchers in the business. These research pros reveal their strategies for integrating online and "off-line" resources, identifying experts, and getting past gatekeepers to obtain information that exists only in someone's head.

2001/420 pp/softbound/ISBN 0-910965-53-6 • $24.95

Super Searchers Cover the World
The Online Secrets of International Business Researchers

By Mary Ellen Bates • Edited by Reva Basch

Through 15 interviews with leading online searchers, Mary Ellen Bates explores the challenges of reaching outside a researcher's geographic area to do effective international business research. Experts from around the world—librarians and researchers from government organizations, multinational companies, universities, and small businesses—discuss such issues as nonnative language sources, cultural biases, and the reliability of information.

2001/250 pp/softbound/ISBN 0-910965-54-4 • $24.95